D0983418

The Weak King Dilemma
in the
Shakespearean History Play

The Weak King Dilemma
in the
Shakespearean History Play

MICHAEL MANHEIM

 Syracuse University Press / 1973

Library of Congress Cataloging in Publication Data

Manheim, Michael.
  The weak king dilemma in the Shakespearean
history play.

  Bibliography: p.
  1. Shakespeare, William, 1564-1616—Characters—
Kings and rulers. I. Title.
PR2992.K5M3   822.3'3   72-9921
ISBN 0-8156-0090-9

Manufactured in the United States of America

To my family
AND TO THE MEMORY OF

Hereward T. Price
AND

Oscar James Cambbell

MICHAEL MANHEIM is professor of English and former chairman of the Department of English at the University of Toledo, Toledo, Ohio. His articles and reviews have been published in such journals as *Renaissance Drama, Shakespeare Studies, Renaissance News, Studies in English Literature,* and *The American Benedictine Review.* Manheim received the B.A., M.A., and Ph.D. from Columbia University.

Contents

Acknowledgments

Having tried to cut back as far as possible on footnotes, both for the sake of the reader's patience and the publisher's budget, I have reserved discussion of much of the scholarship on which this book is based for a brief section at the end called "Bibliographical Remarks." In this section, I have begun with comment on such matters as twentieth-century interpretation of the history plays, especially the work of E. M. W. Tillyard, Lily Bess Campbell, and some of their many followers; recent post-Tillyardian interpretations of those plays, most notably in studies by David Bevington and Wilbur Sanders; and the nature of Machiavellianism in sixteenth-century England. Following that, I comment on some of the writing which has directly influenced my understanding of the individual plays I look at: for example, A. P. Rossiter on *Woodstock*, Clifford Leech on Marlowe's *Edward II*, John F. Danby on the relation between Shakespeare's Henry VI–Richard III tetralogy and *King John,* and Una M. Ellis-Fermor on *Henry V.*

Although they are mentioned infrequently or not at all in my text, Alfred Harbage, Oscar James Campbell, Hereward T. Price, John Arthos, and S. F. Johnson—many of whose works I have of course read, but with all of whom I have either studied Shakespeare or talked about the plays—helped most to shape my critical views over the past twenty years. Recently, Norman Rabkin's *Shakespeare and the Common Understanding* (New York: The Free Press, 1967); R. A. Foakes's *Shakespeare: The Dark Comedies to the Last Plays* (Charlottesville, Va.: The University Press of Virginia, 1971); and Michael Goldman's *Shakespeare and the Energies of Drama* (Princeton, N.J.: Princeton University Press, 1972)—though only occasionally focused on the plays discussed here—have helped redirect my thinking about Shakespeare. I am also grateful to Samuel Schoenbaum for his general encouragement and for having published my pilot study, "The Weak King History Play of the Early 1590s," in *Renaissance Drama*.

The editions of the plays used in this book are as follows: For *Woodstock* and *The Troublesome Reign: Six Early Plays Related to the Shakespeare Canon*, edited by E. B. Everitt, *Anglistica*, XIV (Copenhagen: Rosenkilde and Bagger, 1965), 253–307 and 145–93. For *Edward II: The Complete Works of Christopher Marlowe*, edited by Irving Ribner (New York: The Odyssey Press, 1963), pp. 283–353. For *Richard II*, the three parts of *Henry VI*, *Richard III*, *King John*, the two parts of *Henry IV*, and *Henry V: The Complete Works of William Shakespeare*, edited by G. B. Harrison (New York: Harcourt-Brace and Co., 1952).

Briefly, I should also like to thank The University of Toledo for providing the sabbatical leave during which this book was first drafted and its College of Arts and Sciences for the two research grants which made possible the typing of all drafts and revisions; the staffs of The University of Toledo Library and Baker Memorial Library at Dartmouth College for their assistance; and Mrs. Jean Quigley, who was patient and indefatigable in typing the numerous drafts of this work along the route from tape recorder to final copy. Finally, I wish to thank David Bevington for reading and commenting on the manuscript; W. Eugene Hollon for his scholarly example and advice; and my wife Martha Manheim for love and support equaled only by her editorial wisdom and deep scholarship.

Toledo, Ohio   MICHAEL MANHEIM
Autumn 1972

*The Weak King Dilemma
in the
Shakespearean History Play*

I   *Of Strong Kings and Weak*

One of the ideas we are beginning to question quite seriously as we approach the last quarter of the twentieth century is the time-honored assumption that a man must be a "politician," with all the seamier connotations that word possesses, if he is to be a successful leader in government. Throughout the history of our own country, and over the past two to three hundred years in England, politically astute men, while paying lip service to the Christian virtues as necessary qualities of a successful governor, have paid far deeper homage to the art of creating and maintaining a popular image and the ability to coerce others gracefully and subtly. Generally, of course, these qualities have been viewed as political necessities—necessities based on the belief that men must be fooled and frightened if they are to be led. Political maturation in the West has come to mean acceptance of the political "truth" that a leader must always give the appearance of being strong, secure, and wise, while never being overly scrupulous about how his actions might personally affect others. Political maturation has in short come to mean acceptance of something approaching a Machiavellian perspective in the assessment of leadership.

Why the young in particular are beginning to question such a view of political sophistication is obvious. The idea that even a benevolent leader must deceive and coerce his constituents in order to "get things done" simply has not worked. Somehow in the midst of his image-making and his authority, he invariably finds himself unable to keep in touch with the moral and social objectives which first made him seek power. He finds that his means and his ends cannot be separated, that not what he hopes to achieve by his actions but those actions themselves determine the nature of his leadership.

In the last quarter of our century we may well enter a period in

1

which our whole view of leadership will change, in which we will insist, as men once insisted, that before all else a leader must be what he seems—despite the inevitable cluster of human foibles, fears, and indecisions such an image will include. Men and women may be coming to understand deeply that only by genuine acknowledgment of any leader's human limitations and by admission that image-making is an evil which must result in greater evil can mankind make significant headway in improving the lot of the many and not just the lot of the few. It may be that political sophistication may mean rejection of a Machiavellian view in favor of one which insists upon uncalculating and perhaps rather homely leadership. The lion, the fox, and the pelican might all give way to that infinitely more talented, but also infinitely more complex and uncertain animal, the human—his strengths and his weaknesses all fully exposed.

In the last quarter of the sixteenth century, men seem to have been going through a similar change, only with the process reversed. And the image of leadership they were rejecting may bear some resemblance to the one we may be on the verge of creating. Certainly the image they were accepting is familiar to us. The success of the Tudors was a triumph in the application of a Machiavellian view of leadership, whether they would acknowledge it under that name or not—and there is ample evidence of the approving familiarity men in Tudor English public life had with Machiavelli, despite their official opposition to his name and ideas.

But I am less concerned with the governing class of that age than with the public, whose acceptance of political realities naturally followed that of their superiors. The chief political reality in question was the inadequacy of a medieval view of kingship to assure a stable monarchy. That view was, of course, the simplest possible. The king, as God's sole deputy in the earthly kingdom, inherently possessed all the Christian virtues; using those virtues in his decisions and actions, he governed his people as the good shepherd watched over his flock. Assured of his invulnerable position in the earthly hierarchy, the king need only live a humble, devout life as ruler to be assured the unity and stability of his kingdom.

A look at what happened to the English crown during the

turbulent fifteenth century was as convincing evidence that such a view was inadequate as anyone needed. The Wars of the Roses mangled the country for several decades; and the only king who held his crown long in that century, though virtuous enough, seemed a helpless pawn in a monumental power struggle. The kings who knew brief and qualified success were those who, by Tudor tradition at least, put deceit and ruthlessness well before their Christianity. The political truth the playgoing public of Elizabethan England was coming to accept was the same truth which has been dominant in political thinking since: that a successful king (or leader) had to be devious and ruthless. But if the plays they viewed are any indication, that truth appears to have been a hard pill to swallow. What we find in Shakespeare's history plays seen as a whole is a pattern of rather bitter political maturation—a pattern which has become an archetype of political maturation in Western nations since his time.

The ideas underlying this book began taking shape as I read the history plays some years ago for perhaps the twentieth time, trying, like many others unsuccessfully, to apply the then-fashionable attitudes concerning these plays as reflections of political orthodoxy. As "mirrors" of Elizabethan policy, they seemed inconsistent and contradictory. Yet a massive response of some kind to a political question of the age did seem to underlie them, and that response seemed unquestionably related to the image of the monarch. Clearly, ambiguities in the figure of the king are central to these plays. The dominant characterization of the royal figure in most plays of the 1590s is a composite of Shakespeare's Henry VI, Richard II, and John—kings who are inconsistent and generally disappointing. They try without success to benefit their country, and though at times Richard and John may ineffectively attempt to deceive people, they all believe themselves sincere. None of the three is knowingly evil. Rather, all seem painfully familiar and extremely human.

The rapid succession of plays in the decade (by Shakespeare and others) which deal with this homely image of the monarch made me begin to suspect that Shakespeare and his audience might be in despair about any monarch's actually succeeding unless he used means which by Christian standards were anathema. No number of good intentions, and certainly no special relationship with God, could prevent him from making critical human errors. The only alternative seemed a skillful and subtle craft in deceiving others about one's true intentions and a willingness to use violence or the threat of violence. That is to say, the only alternative was accommodation to the view of leadership propounded by that devil-philosopher whose very name was to the Elizabethan synonymous with all that lay outside the realm of Christian ethics: Machiavellianism.

But what made these plays particularly interesting from a late twentieth-century perspective is the change that obviously came over Shakespeare, and quite probably his audience, between the writing of *Henry VI* at the beginning of the decade and *Henry V* at the end. In the former, there is no question of the king's failure to rule successfully. Yet unlike John and Richard II, Henry VI sincerely tries to govern well, using all the precepts his Christian training and background have provided him. He fails because his normal human weaknesses and inconsistencies make him no match for the treacherous and brutal tactics of those around him, yet he himself has neither the ability nor the inclination to employ those tactics. He loves and trusts his fellow man, and in return he is deceived, abused, deposed, murdered. In *Henry V*, on the other hand, the tactics of Henry VI's enemies are employed by the king, only in far more attractive garb. Henry V could not be called treacherous, but he clearly succeeds in deceiving others about his true intentions and definitely possesses the ability to threaten violence, or even use it when he deems necessary. He carefully constructs an image for himself which will assure his being popular and feared. In keeping such a monarch attractive to his audience despite what they might know or suspect about his methods, Shakespeare was creating a model for most Western political leaders to follow—be they kings, prime ministers, or presidents.

The change that came over late sixteenth-century Europe and England, reflected in the popular appetite which prompted the writing of the Shakespearean history plays, was the change from horror at Machiavellian tactics to acceptance of them, in somewhat tamed form, as the only means by which men could successfully be governed. That is the compromise implicit in these plays, and it is the compromise we all make in becoming politically sophisticated (or cynical). But lurking behind the magnificently masked Machiavellian nature of Henry V is the figure of the open, honest, and humane Henry VI, the painfully human king who sought to "learn to govern better" but was never given the chance. And in the growing impatience finally of our age with the Henry V-type leader, the Henry VI image begins to seem once more attractive. But the question remains: Will we give him the chance? Many of our young people seem ready to try.

If what I have been saying suggests that I am primarily interested in contemporary history and politics in writing this book, such is not the case. My primary end is to illuminate a group of significant works of art dealing with a central political problem of the Renaissance. In so doing I am influenced, obviously, by my understanding of Tudor England, where my curiosity has been mainly focused on the theatre-going public of the 1590s. I have read extensively in history and political theory related to the period and in works considering public attitudes on a wide variety of problems. But the deeper political concerns of that public have not been sufficiently stressed by historians, and this is true in part because there are few records of those concerns. As they affect the Elizabethan public theatre audience, the records are treated as exhaustively as it is possible to treat them in Alfred Harbage's *Shakespeare's Audience* (New York: Columbia University Press, 1941). Little outside the plays themselves can tell us much about the unspoken aspirations, desires, and uncertainties which reside beneath the surface of an Elizabethan audience and which a sensitive dramatist instinctively recognized and appealed to. The plays, then, are the chief documents revealing the deeper fears and concerns of one segment at least of the Elizabethan public, and through what we learn from the plays as documents their illumination as works of art becomes possible. The plays I shall look at indicate that unspoken fears and dilemmas about monarchy were present in a great many Englishmen of the 1590s. The manipulation of these fears and dilemmas in dramatic form constitutes the art of these plays.

But if some intimations about the nature of today's crises should result from this study, then the wisdom of great art has been assured—if it needed to be. Like any searching layman contemplating the political crises of his age, I tend to see those crises as reenactments or variations of past crises. Throughout this study, even where I make no explicit statements on the matter, I am interested in the ways these plays articulate a twentieth-century concern with the problems of leadership as well as a sixteenth-century concern. While there are obvious differences between our ages, and these differences should be identified as precisely as possible to help prevent misinterpretations, I believe our mutual responses to lines and actions which invite sympathy or antipathy only occasionally differ. We are a good deal more like Shakespeare's audience responding to his kings than we are different. Antipathy to arrogance, deceit, and stupidity—sympathy with kindness, justice, and intelligence—these tend to be universal responses. It is for this reason that I occasionally refer to both the Elizabethan audience and the modern one by the universal pronoun *we*, though where it seems necessary to distinguish the two, I usually do so. My underlying concern throughout is the catharsis these plays may achieve of deep feelings regarding the universal dilemma that a leader to be truly successful must be human, yet the human qualities of a leader seem inevitably to be his downfall.

My preceding remarks have constituted a sort of preamble to this work as a whole—a statement of what led me to write it and a suggestion of its larger objectives. I have hardly touched on my critical approach to the works or on their intellectual background. What follows is a more systematic introduction to the salient qualities of the plays in question and a brief discussion of the complex response a late sixteenth-century popular audience might have to Machiavellianism, the chief cultural force affecting political life and attitudes of the age.

Except for *Henry V*, none of Shakespeare's histories has at its center the image of a strong, virtuous monarch, and even in the case of Henry, there is much disagreement as to the true scope of his virtue. For a dramatic genre which for years was interpreted

as the articulation of a nation's nationalistic fervor over its establishment as a world power through victory in a great sea battle,
the symbol of that nation—the king—is surely unexpected. The
image of the English monarch in *Henry VI, King John,* and
Richard II is hardly one which may effectively serve as a rallying
point in an appeal for national unity. These kings seem to reflect
a spirit more of national confusion and uncertainty than of national purpose and determination.

When English kings appear in most non-Shakespearean plays
in the 1590s, plays which are hardly known to modern readers,
the usual image is one of strong, flawless leadership. The strong-
king image in such plays varies a good deal. His personal troubles
or escapades may provide the plot-interest of the play, as in the
anonymous *Fair Em* and *Look About You* and Thomas Heywood's
1 Edward IV; or he may exist solely as a shadowy protector who
appears to right the wrongs done by unworthy subjects, as in
Greene's *Friar Bacon* and *George-a-Greene.* He may of course
also be the national warrior-hero of the anonymous *Famous
Victories* and Peele's *Edward III.* But in all cases he is in his
leadership a figure of strength, courage, and Christian virtue.
Though he may reveal nearly scandalous personal flaws along the
way, there is never any link between those flaws and the quality
of his reign. The perfection of that reign is never questioned.

But monarchs are not perfect, as Elizabethan playgoers well
knew—even those living monarchs who carefully constructed
myths about their personalities. And that deep-seated audience
awareness of any monarch's imperfections seems clearly to underlie a group of plays which are much better known than those
which deal with kings whose leadership is never questioned. Lily
Bess Campbell pointed out some years ago that when one talks
about Shakespeare's history plays, one is talking not about plays
dealing with strong kings, but with weak kings.[1] That small but
fairly well-known group of plays, plus a few non-Shakespearean
history plays of the period, seem the outgrowth of genuine uncertainty whether an inadequate monarch ought to be deposed
(and all monarchs at one time or another seem inadequate to

1. *Shakespeare's Histories: Mirrors of Elizabethan Policy* (San Marino, Calif.:
The Huntington Library, 1968), p. 11.

their subjects). Specifically, the plays that concern me are the anonymous *Woodstock*, Marlowe's *Edward II*, Shakespeare's *Richard II* and *Henry VI*, the anonymous *Troublesome Reign of King John*, Shakespeare's *King John*, and perhaps surprisingly Shakespeare's *Henry V*. *Richard III* and *Henry IV* are also in this group, but from my point of view they are by-products: the former being the terrible effect of a weak king's reign and the latter the prelude to the reign of, by tradition at any rate, a strong one. Except for *Henry V*, the royal image in these plays is one of human limitations so great as to provoke ambivalent feelings about the king in his subjects—those in the play and those in the audience—and except in *Henry V* these limitations cause the king's personal and political downfall. The limitations are also present in *Henry V*, but they are successfully masked and bring about no downfall.

The writers of these plays have employed a common device, both to elicit inherent audience ambivalence toward the monarchic figure and also perhaps to avoid the threat of official censorship. With greater or lesser dramaturgical skill, each has invited us to shift our feelings about the king sharply in different situations; yet in all these plays the king is intended to be a consistent figure in human terms. In *Woodstock*, *Edward II*, and *Richard II*, pleasure-loving kings earn our displeasure, even contempt, early in the plays, only to become nearly saintly, martyred figures at the plays' conclusions. In the Henry VI and King John plays, where the kings seem more immature and inexperienced in their weaker moments, our attitudes toward them vacillate, sometimes chaotically; though in these, too, there is a kind of martyrdom at the end. But even martyred, these kings never leave us assured in retrospect exactly how to feel about them. The image of their abuses early in the plays makes so strong an impression that the tragic or pathetic conclusions only temporarily overshadow it. By means of those conclusions, our negative responses are strongly suppressed but not erased. In thinking about the play after the fact, we may well question the king's actions, just as we did earlier. The subordination of our negative feelings achieved by the play's ending never quite overcomes the sense that the king is really unfit to govern.

At the same time, the playwrights have made use of the official political mythology of the age. The guilt-provoking nature of their endings suggests that the lessons concerning Divine Providence and retribution are an important part of the audience response invited toward these plays. The audience reaction sought is undoubtedly one divided between exasperation with tired, incompetent monarchy—exasperation frequently reflected in that of the rebellious figures of the play—and subservience to the opposing force of the myths, which becomes particularly strong when a king in a play becomes vulnerable. Fear of divine punishment for those who would depose a lawful king was obviously still great in the 1590s. This fear, coupled with an awe for the crown better understood perhaps by a twentieth-century Japanese than by his Anglo-American counterpart, might well provoke the kind of horror and guilt at deposition aroused by the conclusions of Marlowe's *Edward II* or Shakespeare's *Richard II*. The impact of the endings of all these plays is most important. If the phrase "God's deputy" did not have a very precise meaning, it nevertheless had powerful mystical connotations. In this respect, the responses of an Elizabethan audience might well differ from ours, as Tillyard has suggested; and the effect of Tudor propaganda, though it is hardly a guide to the nature of political reality in these plays, is certainly one of the raw materials the playwrights employ.

Ernst Kantorowicz[2] has discussed in admirable detail the theory of the medieval king's "two bodies," one human and one divine, and has applied that theory to Shakespeare's *Richard II*, certainly illuminating that play as a work of art by suggesting that its tragic conclusion may result from the fact that the two bodies prove incompatible. My interest is complementary to that of Kantorowicz. I am concerned with the artistic means by which responses are invited of an audience which would have little or no knowledge of the religious and legal documents underlying a theory of kingship, but would be quite affected by superstition and by their appetites in reacting to a kingly image: an audience which would fear God's punishment for the deposing of a king, yet would know

2. *The King's Two Bodies: A Study in Medieval Political Theology* (Princeton, N.J.: Princeton University Press, 1957), pp. 24–41.

that if the king were a weak man, they would probably not have enough to eat and perhaps be in personal danger. Divinity of the crown or no, deposing a king might be the only hope to fill an empty stomach or to assure easy rest at night.

This conflict between dissatisfaction with a monarch and guilt over his possible deposition—explicitly reiterated so relentlessly in a group of plays performed over a period of no more than eleven years and possibly as few as eight[3]—reveals the universal contradiction about monarchy beginning to run deep in Elizabethans of the 1590s. As our age seems vitally uncertain and frightened over whether civil disobedience is necessary to achieve social change, the Elizabethan age seems similarly uncertain and frightened over whether deep loyalty to the crown might have to give way to something else, a concern which we now regard as a foreshadowing of democratic attitudes. This fear is seen in drama through the image of the weak king, the depth of the fear quite possibly accounting for the strength of the dramatic conflict in these plays and their appeal to later audiences. It is the nature of that strong conflict as it is expressed in artistic terms which will be the chief concern in this book.

But the dilemma of the weak king is not left altogether unresolved in these plays. Of equal force in them is that radical challenge to the medieval "world picture" known today as Machiavellianism, and the relationship between Machiavellianism and the weak king is great. With the realization that kings are human and therefore innately weak, some means of at least obscuring that weakness was sought; and Machiavellianism, first rejected in these plays, comes to be tolerated in them as a means of countering the sense of despair the weak king inevitably engenders.

I shall not now attempt to describe the nature of Machiavellianism in these plays in specific terms. But it is necessary to point out that when I speak of Machiavellianism affecting society's

3. The Harbage-Schoenbaum *Annals of English Drama* (Philadelphia, Pa.: University of Pennsylvania Press, 1961), which I find little reason not to follow, dates the plays as follows: *Woodstock*, 1591–95; *Edward II*, 1591–93; *Richard II*, 1594–95; *1 Henry VI*, 1592; *2 Henry VI*, c. 1590–92; *3 Henry VI*, c. 1590–92; *The Troublesome Reign*, c. 1587–91; *King John*, 1591–98; and *Henry V*, 1599.

reactions in the sixteenth century, and through society the reactions of English dramatists of the final decade, I am speaking in terms comparable to the popular conceptions of Freudianism or Marxism in our own century. I am not talking about a fully conceived philosophy adhered to by followers who think they know what they are adhering to. Such a Machiavellianism may have existed, as such a Freudianism or Marxism exists today, but it had little to do with what appeared in English popular drama of the 1590s. I am not speaking of a formalized political philosophy at all but of a rather vague set of attitudes and modes of behavior associated with a name: Machiavel! Or a title: *Il Principe.* And those attitudes and modes of behavior at times have little directly to do with what the man wrote, ambiguous as even that can be.

Machiavelli himself cannot, of course, be ignored in talking about late sixteenth-century Machiavellianism, but his direct influence is comparatively small in considering the effects of the "ism" in popular drama of a different country appearing some eighty years after he wrote. What he wrote and quite probably its style gave impetus to the radical change in political thinking and popular response associated with his name; but once the impetus was given, Machiavellianism developed on its own and in ways that varied a good deal in late sixteenth-century England. To the young Cambridge intellectuals Gabriel Harvey describes in the late 1570s happily putting aside their Latin authors in their rage to read pirated translations of *The Prince,* it provided a refreshing change from hypocritical adherence to worn-out Augustinian concepts of good government. To the "practical" politicians of the Elizabethan regime, it raised questions about the true nature of political morality, undoubtedly allowing some to commit atrocities in the name of political necessity. And to the playgoing public of the 1580s and 90s it provided the "stage Machiavel," the arch-villain who somehow became more strangely appealing the craftier and bloodier he got. All these varieties of Machiavellianism play an important part in the drama here.

Felix Raab describes the effect of the name *Machiavelli* in late sixteenth-century England in these terms:

> He horrified them, instructed them, entertained them—in fact he affected them over the whole attraction/repulsion spectrum

through which basically new concepts are often seen in times of rapid social change. The period of Tudor rule was such a period, a period when events themselves were shaking the ideological structure in terms of which men saw the world. Thus Machiavelli, himself a product of an earlier phase of the same process of change, caused some Englishmen to nod or shake their heads very vigorously, according to their temperaments and the degree to which they were prepared to accept the new world. Others closed their eyes, but very few shrugged their shoulders. Particularly was this so near the end of the century, when the storms of his ideas raged more fiercely as the wider implications of his doctrine came to be more clearly understood.[4]

Subsumed in this statement are the three types of Machiavellian appeal I refer to, and more. Raab makes quite clear how imbued were Elizabethans with the new political ethos, even those who might most vociferously condemn the Machiavel. But he also makes clear that they were uncertain. And that uncertainty, like their uncertainty about the weak king, underlies the plays we shall be looking at.

What we see through these plays is a public disturbed over whether the craft, the violence, and the image of invulnerability might indeed be requirements for effective political leadership and a public concerned over the rather sudden acceptability of such means as the way of political life. Attitudes which might appall a youthful dramatist like Shakespeare in the late 1580s were coming to be so much the accepted code of political behavior that within ten years even that same still youthful dramatist might find it necessary to articulate his audience's grudging acknowledgment of the inevitable and perhaps necessary permanence of those attitudes. That acknowledgment is closely tied to the parallel acknowledgment that the monarch would always possess unavoidable inadequacies. Only by energetically employing Machiavellian methods could a king succeed, yet energetic employment of those methods could by Christian standards only be deeply and shamelessly immoral. The result is the attempt at some sort of compromise between Christian and Machiavellian

4. *The English Face of Machiavelli* (Toronto: University of Toronto Press, 1964), p. 67.

leadership. It is a compromise the governors of Elizabethan England undoubtedly felt they were making; it is one Shakespeare, or his audience for him, seems reluctantly forced to make in the history plays which closed the decade.

The following chapters, then, examine a group of plays which are representations of the ambivalence of subject toward monarch, be that monarch wanton or meek (two of the predominant historical images of medieval kingship). The plays discussed in Chapters II and III do not dramatize any kind of resolution to that ambivalence. The weak kings in Chapter II—those in *Woodstock, Edward II,* and *Richard II*—cannot be different from what they are, and what they are is completely intolerable until the point at which they become genuinely vulnerable. Then what had seemed intolerable is obscured for a time by our sense of their human tragedy. Under the threat of deposition, the king makes us staunch defenders of the crown, as earlier we had been attackers. Although the image of Henry VI (Chapter III) is quite different, he is nevertheless as weak as the kings discussed in Chapter II. He has the attributes, if any man can have them, suitable by Christian standards for moral, just, God-fearing government; but in the whirl of a court now dominated openly by sixteenth-century Machiavellian standards, those older Christian virtues seem useless. Like every human being, Henry has defects—if not those of the wastrel, then those of the humble and meek. He is craven and he is henpecked. The Henry VI plays in no way extenuate these qualities. Thus, we are finally moved to condemn him almost as much as we condemn the wastrel kings.

In Chapters IV and V, on the other hand, the plays discussed represent in dramatic terms the acceptance of Machiavellian behavior as a means of resolving the dilemma of the weak king— an acceptance which is very much the political mood of the 1590s. In these plays, the king, weak though he is, must give the appearance of being strong. The old divinity of the king is changed into one form of royal window-dressing. He must appear to be divine, with no thought on his part that he actually is. And this guise involves acceptance of deception, intrigue, and even violence as legitimate instruments of political behavior. It is an acceptance on the part of the commoner who makes up the majority of the audience. Any knowledge of the Elizabethan court must tell us that acceptance by the governing class had taken place already.

To see how fears and dilemmas concerning the monarch are realized in dramatic terms, I shall in the chapters that follow review each play in detail. Deducing attitudes from the work itself, as well as from other works and from my knowledge of history, I shall concentrate on scenes which play directly on audience sympathies toward the king and shall trace the probable movement of audience sympathies from scene to scene. In general, I shall follow the chronological progression of events both because the pattern of audience response is best observed that way and because I feel criticism which ignores or distorts the chronology of events can frequently be misleading. I shall also try to visualize the stage as a whole in discussing a scene, not neglecting characters who in their silence may strongly influence the direction of audience sympathies. I shall attempt to work from the various ways an audience may feel about a king toward a sense of the impact these plays make in revealing any king's inescapable shortcomings and the bitter but apparently unavoidable consequences of those shortcomings.

This book largely concerns the manipulation of audience sympathies toward the monarch in the plays discussed. What has given several of the plays the reputation for being episodic, ill-constructed works of art may be the playwright's attempt to represent in drama the audience's incessant vacillation and uncertainty toward the royal figure. These shifting sympathies do not cease, but they do abate as the king, or someone else for him, learns how to create and maintain an illusion of royal perfection. I shall examine the ways in which these plays reflect through their art a critical turning point in public attitudes toward the monarchic principle. And underlying my discussion is the constant awareness that William Shakespeare's astonishingly deep knowledge of man has resulted in several works of art which have as much impact upon our own feelings about political problems and events as they did upon the feelings of audiences in their own time.

II *The Wanton King*

Richard the Second was a *deposed king*. Considering the Elizabethan fascination with oxymoron, this was not too different from thinking of a woman as an *honest* (i.e., chaste) *whore*. That no English king disturbed Elizabethan thinking about the political system more than did this unfortunate Richard is revealed by the several plays in the early 1590s which centered on him and on his still more unfortunate great-grandfather, Edward II. A *deposed king*. As Shakespeare's Richard rolls this concept about in his mind in the deposition scene of *Richard II*, thinking Englishmen of the 1590s were doing the same:

> Nay, if I turn mine eyes upon myself,
> I find myself a traitor with the rest;
> For I have given here my soul's consent
> T'undeck the pompous body of a king. . . .
> [*Richard II* IV.1.247–50]

All that Tudor chroniclers and propagandists had been teaching for nearly a century about submission to the crown regardless of who happened to be wearing it was deeply questioned by the story of this monarch—true Plantagenet and unchallenged successor to the throne—and of his similarly pleasure-loving ancestor. That the growing plausibility of deposition was getting through to the authorities themselves is suggested by the fate of at least one late chronicler,[1] by a statement, possibly apocryphal, attributed

---

1. Sir John Hayward was sent to prison for dwelling too lengthily on the weaknesses of Richard II in his *History of Henry IV*, even though he argued against deposition under any circumstances. See David Bevington, *Tudor Drama and Politics* (Cambridge, Mass.: Harvard University Press, 1969), pp. 11 and 318, n. 37.

to the queen herself,[2] and by the arrest of the company which produced Shakespeare's play on the eve of the Essex rebellion (1601). And a large part of what we get from the plays is the conflict surrounding the idea of deposition in the public mind.

The point which needs to be stressed about *Woodstock*, Marlowe's *Edward II*, and Shakespeare's *Richard II*, even more than it has been by A. P. Rossiter,[3] is that these are very similar plays, so similar as to suggest strongly that they grew out of a common response to some specific set of circumstances in late Tudor England. In all three, court favorites are corrupt, youthful comelatelies whose political abuses are paralleled by varying degrees and forms of personal corruption. Arrayed against them are the leading nobles of the land, a chorus of uncles, both figuratively and literally, who are dismayed at the decline in moral standards which has accompanied the rise of the favorites and who fret long and sometimes violently over the state of the nation. Missing from *Woodstock* but all-important to the Marlowe and Shakespeare plays is the youthful protégé of the uncles, their version of what a king should be, who in Shakespeare of course ultimately makes it to the throne. Equally important—in *Woodstock* the most important—is the uncle who is caught between his clear vision of the king's excesses and his deep-seated loyalty to the crown—the ambivalent uncle who stands between the avuncular group and the favorites. Kent in *Edward II* and York in *Richard II* have the same barometric function as "plain" Thomas of Woodstock, though they are less dominant in their respective plays.

The conditions under which events take place are also similar. In all three plays one climax has already been reached just before the opening, and events gather momentum from there. The attempt to poison the uncles in *Woodstock* is paralleled by the king's calling back of the once-banished Gaveston in *Edward II* and by the recent murder of Woodstock in *Richard II*. Each of the plays is thus concerned with a conflict which has reached, or even exceeded, a critical point.

The plays are also linked by the clear shifts in appeal to au-

2. "I am Richard II. Know ye not that?" Quoted by Bevington, p. 11, and M. M. Reese, *The Cease of Majesty* (New York: St. Martin's Press, 1961), p. 160.
3. *Preface to Woodstock: A Moral History* (London: Chatto and Windus, 1946).

dience sympathy toward leading characters. The favorites are contemptible to begin with but noble in death. The uncles' cause at first seems just, but they appear ruthless in their hounding of a defeated king. The king, more consistent than the other characters in all three plays, elicits rebellious anger at the start which gives way to intense pity at his downfall—pity which obscures our recollection of his earlier abuses. In all three plays, too, the figure of the queen has a catalytic effect on our shifting sympathies toward the king. Most important of all in understanding these plays as works of art is that in none of them is any attempt made to resolve their central dilemma. Whether or not deposition is justified remains uncertain. Politically sensitive viewers of the 1590s must have been at a point where they could no longer abide the king's enormous inadequacies but at the same time could not go against their deep, quasi-religious commitment to the crown. The contending forces in the plays are the contending forces in the viewer. One of the forces temporarily may get the upper hand, but not sufficiently to outweigh the other permanently. Through the experience of the play, intense feelings about the problem may be drained, but nothing has happened or is suggested to prevent the pressure of those feelings from building once more in intensity. The wound cannot be healed.

Nevertheless, these plays are hardly carbon copies of one another but are distinct dramatic entities as different from each other in personality as are their respective authors. To see how each author treats the weak king and the dilemma to which he is central, the plays must be discussed individually. If the anonymous author of *Woodstock* has provided little artistic competition for Marlowe and Shakespeare, he has nevertheless created in somewhat homely terms a potent expression of the temptation to rebel countered in equally homely terms by those feelings which act against rebellion. Marlowe sees the conflict primarily in terms of activity which transgresses moral limits. And Shakespeare, by relentlessly exploring the impact of the experience in human terms, moves it toward the genuine tragedy it potentially is. Despite similarities in theme and dramatic construction, each of the plays examined on the pages that follow is treated as a distinct work of Elizabethan popular art.

WOODSTOCK

In its time, *Woodstock* must have been a shocking play, not because it contains anything of a particularly lurid nature—the lurid was so common in English Renaissance drama as to be hardly shocking at all—but because with considerable economy of language and action, it poses the question whether a king clearly unfit to govern should be allowed to reign. The harsh, pressing insistence of the problem is evident partly because the author has succeeded in keeping the issues free of the traditional accouterments of popular Elizabethan drama: sideshows of terror and the macabre on the one hand and of empty farce on the other. The force of the play—and Rossiter has quite rightly defended the vision and artistic competence of its unknown author—lies in how it probes its central dilemma. The two twentieth-century critics who have given the play most critical attention, A. P. Rossiter and Irving Ribner, admire it. But perhaps since both find it "unorthodox" in terms of the order-oriented approach they take to the history plays, it has received little other discussion since Tillyard's *Shakespeare's History Plays* led most discussions to concentrate on evidences of political orthodoxy in these works.

If the play does precede Marlowe's *Edward II* and Shakespeare's *Richard II*, as Rossiter suggests,[4] then never before in drama had the extravagances and foibles of a post-Norman English king been seen in quite the light they are here. Obviously, moral excesses are related to the king's ability to govern, as they were not in previous images of English kings. But at the same time, this Richard has not "hacked" his way to the throne with "a bloody axe." His claim upon it is entirely legitimate, and thus, if we are to follow Tillyard, his authority ought to go unchallenged. As Rossiter observes, "from the orthodox viewpoint of degree and due submission, etc., the chronicle material could equally have been used for a play with Woodstock as something near enough to a *villain*."[5] But Woodstock is not a villain and the king is not a martyr. Quite the contrary. This play shows loyal English subjects upholding the belief that the legitimate, reigning

4. *Ibid.,* p. 17.
5. *Ibid.,* p. 25, n. 1.

king of England is unfit to rule. His personal foibles and idio-
syncrasies are not simply the vagaries of youth but legitimate
causes for deposition. Always lurking in the background is the
knowledge that Richard would one day be deposed. The impact
of this play would have been great upon an audience just beginning to see a clash between kingly behavior and Tudor assumptions about absolute monarchy, just beginning to articulate the
questions Malcolm asks of Macduff in *Macbeth* IV.3.[6]

Is *Woodstock*, then, a play implicitly advocating the overthrow
of incompetent kings? That would, of course, be tantamount to
sedition under the Tudors. John Hayward was imprisoned in
1599 for writing a history accused of such intent; and in any
popular play which advocated it such sentiments would either
have to exist between the lines or in passages which are explicitly
negated by other passages. Two seemingly unrelated passages do
suggest the existence of such covert intent in *Woodstock*. In IV.2,
"plain Thomas," spokesman for wisdom and sound judgment in
the play, finds himself strongly tempted by rebellious inclinations.
Informed of Richard's "Blank Charters," Woodstock rages:

> Blank charters call ye them? If any age
> Keep but a record of this policy—
> I phrase it too too well—"flat villany,"
> Let me be chronicled Apostata,
> Rebellious to my God and country both.
> [III.2.1369–74]

He says he "cannot blame" the rebels now rising up in Kent, and
asks whether they should indeed be called "rebels" at all. Then,
without warning, Woodstock suddenly returns to his orthodoxy:
"I speak but what I fear: not what I wish" (III.2.1381).
There may be in this turnabout a suggestion equivalent to that
of Lear's fool covering his tracks. "If I speak like myself in this,
let him be whipped that first finds it so" (*King Lear* I.4.178–80).
In the following scene in *Woodstock*, a clownish schoolmaster

6. As Malcolm questions whether a prospective king, ostensibly himself, who is
unscrupulous and perhaps lecherous is fit to govern, so too do the plays in this
chapter. Macduff ultimately agrees that there must be limits, and Malcolm admits
that he has only been testing Macduff. The chief issue of the plays discussed here
is precisely focused in their dialogue.

assures the audience that his seditious verses will never get him into trouble since he has ended each stanza with the refrain: "God bless my Lord Tresilian." This seems a comic parallel to Woodstock's earlier disclaimer. Ominously, perhaps, the schoolmaster is swept into the execution cart more swiftly even than the other unhappy commoners in the scene who have grumbled at their fate.

But whatever the hidden intent of its author, *Woodstock* is not a seditious play. It does not directly advocate the deposing of tyrant kings. Rather, with considerable impact it poses the problem such kings create, not what should be done about that problem. It gives dramatic life to the dilemma, and it does so in part through its shifts in appeal to our sympathies. Because *Woodstock* may be less familiar than the other plays to some readers, I shall summarize the action which produces that shifting appeal before going on to more detailed discussion of its critical scenes.

The central figures of the play are on one side the libertine young King Richard II; his sycophantic favorites Bushy, Bagot, and Green; his ruthless upstart counselor Tresilian; and Tresilian's comic assistant the Vice (clown) Nimble. On the other side are Richard's uncles Woodstock (the king's legal protector), Lancaster, and York. Though Lancaster is, of course, historically the same person as Shakespeare's John of Gaunt in *Richard II*, it is old Thomas of Woodstock rather than his defiant brothers Lancaster and York who most resembles Shakespeare's famous elder statesman in virtue and wisdom.

The first act states the opposition between king and uncles emphatically. There is no sense of emerging dissatisfaction on the part of the older nobles. The first impression made on us in I.1 is by the discovery that the king of England has conspired with his friends to poison all the leading lords of the realm, and in I.2 by the rage of the king and his favorites at the plot's failure. At the start we are strongly pulled toward Lancaster's outspoken desire to resist violently, though the temperate urgings of Woodstock that the uncles be patient with the young king give us pause early in the play. But even old Woodstock, in spite of himself, is enraged a scene later when the king promotes the favorites in a manner obviously calculated to exacerbate the uncles. The second act then repeats the movement of the first. The king and his favorites conclude (from "chronicles" of their own choosing) that Richard has reached his majority. In a bitter confrontation before parliament, Richard tells Woodstock he is no longer protector, dismisses the uncles from his council, and replaces the uncles with the favorites. The break between nephew and uncles is complete, and only the sympathetic queen is left with hopes of healing the rift (II.3).

At the opening of the third act, however, even the queen's hopes are dashed by the king's unshakable hostility toward his uncles. We are introduced by the scheming Tresilian to the first of two intolerable royal policies: that all citizens who appear to be of means must sign "Blank Charters" which will enable the king to tax them at any time and rate he pleases. This policy nearly prompts Woodstock himself to rebellion (III.2), though he does not in fact rebel; and its effect on the audience intensifies as the charters are presented and reluctant citizens are arrested (III.3). Mistakenly anticipating that Woodstock will really rebel, Tresilian and his favorites persuade Richard to kidnap the old man and transport him to Calais (IV.1). Richard readily enough agrees to this; and though he unexpectedly balks at Tresilian's second proposal, that England shall be "farmed" (rented) to the four favorites, he finally agrees to this, too. In the following scene (IV.2) the unwary Woodstock is abducted from his castle by the royal faction in disguise as Masquers. Except for the fleeting moment in IV.1 when he becomes inexplicably penitent, the image of base weakness in Richard continues, while that of perfidy and gross corruption in Tresilian and the favorites steadily increases.

With the report of the queen's death (IV.3), a penitent Richard suddenly vows to reform, and sends orders to Calais that Woodstock's secret execution be revoked, thus inviting a more sympathetic response toward him on our part. But in Calais, no message is received, and Woodstock is murdered (V.1). The king, if no longer base, now seems utterly ineffective, and Woodstock's murder sets off the long-expected rebellion. Tresilian, sensing defeat, plans to run away with his money (V.2). Richard and his uncle Lancaster confront each other with threats and oaths (V.3), but the battle is never in doubt. Lancaster wins. The rebels triumphant, Richard once more is penitent, distraught both at Green's death in battle and at the murder of Woodstock (V.4). Our feelings about him are strongly divided. Tresilian's escape is frustrated by his turncoat servant Nimble (V.5); and as Lancaster is proclaiming victory, Nimble brings in his prisoner (V.6). There the text is abruptly cut off, the remainder of the manuscript lost.

Though the action of greatest importance thematically centers about Woodstock, most of the scenes in the play show one or another of the excesses and abuses of Richard and his favorites. Our first impression of that group, that created by the poisoning conspiracy, while shocking, does not really set the tone to be employed later. The playwright has a hard time making them look as base as this conspiracy implies they are. Except for Tresilian, they are not arch-villains, but rather selfish, petulant adolescents. Richard seems more the child who resents avuncular authority, and his chief favorite Green a pouting schoolboy who refuses to participate unless he can have his way. They take childish pleasure in referring to the uncles as "old doting graybeards" and to the citizens as "hogsface" and "codshead." Tresilian, at whom we shall look more closely later, seems the only adult in the company, though as a true "Machiavel," which he is frequently called, even he falls short.

But distasteful as Richard is, not hatred but uncertainty concerning the young king is the chief attitude invited. We may dislike him and the group with which he has surrounded himself, but the question is whether or not his abuses are sufficient grounds for deposing him. This question is focused in the reactions of Woodstock, the barometer by whom one may tell whether the play is tending toward rebellion or submission. At all key points he is unsure, and so are we. Throughout, Woodstock cannot decide whether Richard is truly vicious or merely a callow youth misled by corrupt, ambitious upstarts. Taking his cue early in the play from that ideal image of traditional English squirehood Sir Thomas Cheyney, he holds strongly for the first alternative and despite critical lapses never really forsakes that position:

> King Richard's wounded with a wanton humor,
> Lulled and secured by flattering sycophants,
> But 'tis not deadly yet; it may be cured. . . .
> [I.1.153–55]

Plain Thomas at first seeks to cure the wound the only way he knows, by cauterizing it. He will confront the king with the defects of his frivolous followers, and the force and truth of his assertions will bring the youth to his senses. Woodstock, as we shall see, is himself the one most shocked and dismayed by his failure.

The depth of feeling the dilemma evokes in the play is achieved not only by what plain Thomas says but by what plain Thomas is and represents. He has been compared in the past both with Shakespeare's good Duke Humphrey in *Henry VI* and John of Gaunt in *Richard II*, and he does indeed resemble them in his strength and patriotism. But looking at him from the perspective of Thomas Dekker's laudable father figures rather than Shakespeare's, we get an image less elevated and cerebral.[7] When plain Thomas lapses into prose for his droll exchange with the "spruce Courtier" in III.2, we hardly have any sense of change from the verse of his earlier passages. He is like Dekker's voluble shoemaker Simon Eyre speaking the plain prose of the English citizenry throughout, utterly free of the affectations associated with courtly speech and dress. Yet his nobility of spirit is as sure as that of his birth. He embodies all the native English virtues, those of castle as well as those of common. Throughout he is "plain Thomas still," to use his own catch-phrase. His most characteristic quality is the homespun, almost crotchety, sense of humor that first called Dekker to mind. And that it is this earthy paragon who has doubts about his loyalty to the crown suggests that the public attitudes reflected are indeed changing ones.

Woodstock's sole confrontation with the favorites (I.3) deserves more critical attention than it has received. As he does else-

---

7. Thomas Dekker's well-known popular comedies *The Shoemakers' Holiday* and *The Honest Whore* were written several years after *Woodstock*, but there is so much in the language of plain Thomas (and others) that calls the exuberant Dekker to mind that it is hard to believe he did not have a share in writing the anonymous *Woodstock*. Multiple authorship was, of course, the rule in the writing of anonymous plays in the age.

where, the author evokes levity which shifts suddenly to outrage to intensify the effect he is after. Despite Woodstock's anger, and at the urging of his brothers, he sheds his "frieze" and dons courtly robes to help celebrate the king's marriage to "fair Anne a Beam," thereby eliciting jovial comments from those around him. But the break in the tense relations between uncles and nephew his appearance provides is short-lived. Woodstock himself is the cause of suddenly renewed hostility. His speech of welcome to Queen Anne employs quite uncourtly diction in warning the young queen of Richard's foibles:

> Sweet queen, y'ave found a young and wanton choice,
> A wildhead, yet a kingly gentleman,
> A youth unsettled, yet he's princely bred, . . .
> [I.3.377–79]

Woodstock no doubt feels he is sufficiently magnanimous by attributing Richard's follies to youth; but Richard decides to take offense, and his jests, while airy enough, are in fact calculated to provoke the loss of the old man's known short temper:

> How comes this golden metamorphosis
> From home-spun huswifery? Speak, good uncle;
> I never saw you hatched and gilded thus.
> [I.3.429–31]

It is in part the king's courtly diction and persiflage itself that irritate plain Thomas, who feels out of sorts anyway because of his "gaudy" attire.

The confrontation between Woodstock and Richard is inevitable, of course, just as is that between Shakespeare's Gaunt and Richard in *Richard II*. And in the end it serves more the interests of the king and his favorites than those of the uncles. In the course of the exchange, the cooler king systematically adds fuel to the old man's fire; when the outburst comes, the volatile old protector does not disappoint his audience (neither the courtly nor the actual one). He attacks the favorites, saying he does not need his "other hose" to be "plain":

> Ay, ay, mock on. My t'other hose, say ye?
> There's honest plain-dealing in my t'other hose.

. . . .
They tax the poor and I am scandaled for it
That by my fault those late oppressions rise
To set the commons in a mutiny,
That even London itself was sacked by them;
And who did all these rank commotions point at?
Even at these two, Bagot here, and Green,
With false Tresilian, whom your grace, we hear
Hath made chief justice.
                         [I.3.456–57, 477–84]

He is an easy mark for Richard because he finds it impossible
not to be himself. At no time during his outburst is there any
rebellious intent. Woodstock speaks as the Dutch uncle, nothing
more. Had he any idea that he was being genuinely insubordinate,
he would be the first to condemn his own tone. If he becomes
aware of anything as the result of this exchange, it is not that he
is a rebel but that he no longer fits in at court. As its fashions
have changed, so have its ways of doing business. No longer is
there a place for the plainspoken man in the affairs of state. His
later refusal of Richard's invitation to return to court, which
Richard takes as a direct sign of rebellious intent, is actually made
on these grounds alone. So, too, may be Woodstock's quiet rather
than wrathful resignation of his protectorship two scenes later.
Woodstock is tempted by genuinely rebellious impulses in the
play, but neither at the time nor with the result that Richard
suspects.

Actual rebellion is introduced from the outside. What cuts the
argument off in I.3. is news of insurrection from the countryside.
Although Woodstock has had no thoughts of revolt, it is now in
the air. And it is the assumption of Richard and the favorites—
almost their hope—that Woodstock will become party to it that
makes the young men so unattractive. Our knowledge (acquired
in II.1) that Woodstock and his brothers are not immediately cut
down only because the king fears the popular reaction does more
to debase Richard himself than even the Blank Charters and the
farming of England, where he may more easily be viewed as the
victim of corrupting influences. The murder of Woodstock is thus
hinted at early in the play, and were the king's personality to

follow its initial course an outright call for deposition would seem justified (and possibly have made this a seditious play in the eyes of Elizabethan authorities). But it does not follow its early course—quite.

The center of the play thematically (III.2) is at Plashey, Wood-stock's ancestral home, away from court intrigue and court affectation, where plain Thomas endures his one brief but nearly overpowering impulse to support insurrection. Less important here than the Blank Charters is the impact of that response itself. In Shakespeare's *Richard II*, old John of Gaunt never has such an impulse. He is loyal to the crown throughout, pointedly rejecting the duchess of Gloucester's appeal that he rebel. The fact that Woodstock, if anything even more an image of conservatism and stability than Shakespeare's Gaunt, should be so strongly tempted to join in civil dissension is what makes this play surprising. What is important is not that Woodstock overcomes the impulse, but that he has it at all. The central dilemma of the play is focused on this point. Woodstock's view of the ancient verities of rule is shaken. Significantly, his vision of himself at this point is represented in religious terms. "Let me be chronicled Apostata," he cries (III.2.1371), thus posing very deep questions about the idea the Tudors, through their propaganda and power, had worked hard to make axiomatic: that an English king, hereditary successor and duly crowned before God and man, must be submitted to regardless of the distaste one might have for a particular action or policy, and that this was God's will. Woodstock's response here is as shattering to that doctrine as any other single rebellious impulse in the weak-king plays.

Then comes his disclaimer: "I speak but what I fear, not what I wish." Such a statement is hard to accept in this situation, but easier in the over-all context of the play. For in the next act comes our first sight of a penitent Richard, and that would have made more difference in the 1590s than it may to us.

Following almost immediately in this scene is the episode of plain Thomas and the "spruce Courtier on horseback," who mistakes the Duke for a stableman. If the play in general has not received its due (except from Rossiter), this brief episode certainly has not. It is the confrontation of soldier and courtier, of

plainspoken gentleman and "dandified gallant"—the confrontation
of Kent and Oswald or Hamlet and Osric. And its purpose is the
same: to satirize the affected courtier, or in this scene the "new"
courtier. The gruff, proverb-filled, almost coarse diction of the
blunt Woodstock is the more apt here. Shakespeare captures the
silken language of the likes of Bushy, Bagot, and Green as the
author of *Woodstock* never does, despite his best attempts; but
that unknown author is quite effective with plain Thomas. The
courtier, having offered Woodstock a "tester" to walk his horse,
goes in to seek "the Duke," and the old man is left to converse
with no less a personage than the famished horse himself. One
hears again the tones of Dekker—of his Orlando Friscobaldo in
2 The Honest Whore—in Woodstock's remarks:

> Oh, strange metamorphoses. Is't possible that this
> fellow that's all made of fashions should be an
> Englishman? . . . [To horse.] Come on, sir; you have
> sweat hard about this haste; yet I think you know little
> of the business. Why so I say, you're a very indifferent
> beast. You'll follow any man that will lead you. Now
> truly, sir, you look but leanly an't. You feed not
> in Westminster Hall a'days, where so many sheep and
> oxen are devoured. I'm afraid they'll eat you shortly,
> if you tarry amongst them. You're pricked more with
> the spur than the provender, I see that.
>
> [III.2.1443–60]

The issue which links this comic sequence to the earlier portion
of the scene is again the vital decline in virility, good will, and
honesty in court affairs, and the question of whether this decline
is so threatening as to justify deposition. The tendency of this
author, as he does here, to use comedy to engage his audience
with the chief issues of the play has already been demonstrated
in I.3 and will be again in the scene following this one (III.3).
    Woodstock's suggestion of religio-political apostasy earlier in
III.2 must have sent shock waves through a popular audience of
the 1590s. That the affected courtier can take plain Thomas for
a stableman and that the old lord can relate to the horse in the
homely-wise terms he does also identifies him with that audience.
Thus, it is reasonable to conclude that unspoken rebellious feel-

ings in the audience are being appealed to in these scenes. In
personality and cultural attitudes, as now in their dilemma concerning the sanctity of the crown, plain Thomas and the people of
England (in the play and in the audience) are one. This scene
has focused on the old lord and his responses. The next will focus
on the people and their responses.

But before examining the following scene, we should return to
the favorites and their activities which prepare us for it. If the
uncles stand for those virtues traditionally associated with experience, industry, and compassion, the favorites, by their petulance,
rashness, and indolence, should stand for those associated (at
least by the greybeards of an age) with inexperience. Such qualities certainly fit the hedonist Green, the most libertine of the
group. But his is not the dominant image of the favorites. We
have thus far neglected Tresilian, whom Rossiter finds second in
importance only to Woodstock in the play. Through Tresilian, the
"new man," we may best see how the image of royal favorite
might have been understood by a popular audience of the 1590s.
And it is against Tresilian that the play's rebellious animus is
directed. While Green dies and Richard sees the error of his ways,
Tresilian must be driven from the kingdom near the end of the
play before peace may be restored.

The "new man" recently and suddenly elevated to political
power was a distasteful figure as early as Henry Medwall's *Fulgens
and Lucrece* (1497), as Bevington shows,[8] and continued to appear in plays throughout the century. His role is important here
because of his immediate and direct involvement with the English
crown, with royal decision-making, and with the execution of
policy. The author of *Woodstock* seems through Tresilian to be
evoking the fear and hostility of an audience responding to a new
governing class it did not like but could do very little about. That
many in this class were originally commoners only made them
more frightening to Elizabethans of the 1590s. The royal favorite
as seen through Tresilian is a petty tyrant whose chief interest
seems the quick profit to be made through a period of power and
influence which he seems to realize may be short-lived. He is as

8. Bevington, *Tudor Drama and Politics,* pp. 42–53.

contemptuous really of the whimsical young lords (including Richard) as he is of the uncles, and quite as willing to cheat them. He also panics easily. He is ready to run at the first news of Lancaster's revolt. Only at one point does something like humanity shine through, and then it is a paltry image indeed. He will not join his youthful allies in their most rash gesture of contempt for age and authority: he will not shave his beard. Too long has he struggled, it would appear, for the place he has achieved to do away with that outward sign of wealth and power. In the end he is trapped, Volpone-like, by his own man. And this is fitting since, like Volpone, his chief lust throughout has been for gold.

That Rossiter finds Tresilian "underdeveloped for his place" in the play is not surprising. Although hardly neglected, Tresilian's personality is less important than the effects of his "reign." The author touches the most exposed nerve of his audience in III.3, the episode at Dunstable, which contains atrocities Tresilian clearly has instigated. Rossiter asks whether "the dread of an indignation at injustice" implicit in this scene does not lead one to "wonder if the author was among those Elizabethans who were aware of the Tudor hysteria hidden behind the word 'treason.' "[9] We are now far enough away from Tillyard and the "world picture" to loudly answer yes. Represented in the scene is life in a police state, in which the signing of blank checks is enforced, and in which honest citizens are arrested for "grumbling," "whispering," and even "whistling." While Tresilian never appears in the scene, the intimidation that we witness is clearly his means of imposing his will on the community. It is a scene in which audience indignation at the abuses of ruling authority and compassion for its victims are aroused.

But again, the author drives home the rather strong feelings prompted by the scene with comic, even farcical, action. And the agents of that comedy are stock figures, the Vice Nimble and the foolish law officer the Bayley Ignorant. And while the utterly unsophisticated quality of their humor lessens the indignation the scene might otherwise invite, the political import of seemingly

---

9. *Preface to Woodstock*, p. 36.

light material is shown by Bevington in many popular comedies of the sixteenth century. Members of the audience were quick to recognize their own situations in such action. The alliance of the ruthless Tresilian with the utterly foolish law officer makes its relevance to the overall meaning of the play unmistakable. Following the Bayley's discussion of his ancient and honorable lineage (all "Ignorants"), we meet three citizens—a farmer, a butcher, and a grazier—who are quite agitated over a rumor. The farmer asks if a bear has broken loose, but the butcher knows better. He reports that Lord Tresilian has "sent down into every county of England a sort of *Black Chapters*" (III.3.1585, italics added), echoing Woodstock's earlier observation that the *Blank Charters* are a black chapter indeed in English history. The Grazier knows what the charters are and what they will be used for, but even he does not yet realize that they have all signed their death warrants by even discussing them. When Nimble presents the charters to the citizens, each seals his fate by showing his displeasure at signing. They are, we soon learn, to be "sent up th' court for privy whisperers." More ominous still, when they acknowledge fear of hanging, Nimble assures them "that's the least on't." Then follows a series of minor atrocities—still treated humorously. After the citizens are carted off, we meet our friend the schoolmaster whose frustrated attempt to escape punishment may embody a warning to the educated that the new, late-Elizabethan governing group is not to be outwitted so easily as its predecessors. It may have been possible to get around the "Ignorants" of the past, but the Tresilians and their Nimbles are another story. The schoolmaster is followed by one who enters "a-whistling" for his lost cattle. He is thrown in for good measure, though he has been guilty of nothing in particular. Such satiric thrusts at political repression undoubtedly struck home with the popular audience of the 1590s.

The Dunstable scene (III.3) effectively stresses the theme of governmental abuse in commonplace and immediate terms. The author's characteristically spare treatment of the episode results in a coherent, if not fully realized, political satire—satire directed at the methods of petty Elizabethan authorities or, for that matter, of any police state. As such, this scene and the one preceding it showing Woodstock's struggle with his own rebellious impulses constitute the thematic as well as physical center of the play. In both, anti-royal feeling is given emphasis not equaled in any play about a historical English king in this period, and through both, one senses feelings of audience hostility toward contemporary political abuses. Although *Woodstock* is no more a propaganda play than the other weak-king plays, it does represent the very powerful appeal of rebellion against ruthless, irresponsible leadership. But it also represents the powerful awe inspired by the crown. As in the other plays considered here, there is a clear shift in appeal to audience sympathy toward this king, if not toward his favorites.

One of the artistic differences between this play and Shakespeare's—and even Marlowe's—is the awkward way this shift is first indicated in IV.1, surprisingly awkward in view of the comparative facility of the Woodstock-Courtier and Dunstable sequences. Without warning, the author abruptly tries to shake our earlier response to Richard. The king suddenly and without apparent motivation feels intense shame at having sunk so low as to rent his kingdom:

> We shall be censured strangely when they tell
> How our great father toiled his royal person,
> Spending his blood to purchase towns in France
> And we his son, to ease our wanton youth,
> Become a landlord to this warlike realm, . . .
>   [IV.1.1883–87]

Rossiter finds this unexpected attack of guilt consistent with Richard's character throughout: "uncertain, unreliable, excessive."[10] But these lines are not of the same texture as any of Richard's earlier utterances. He may be inconsistent, but here he is not frivolous. Richard has not had similar misgivings about the Blank Charters, though he would have had as much reason. To be sure, this outburst of conscience is directly followed by dialogue so unrelated to it that the guilt seems as ill-motivated as it is short-lived. Rossiter suggests that the speech may belong somewhere else in the play or have been interpolated. Under any circumstances, the point holds; the author seems suddenly to be

10. *Ibid.*, p. 45.

inviting a sympathetic response to the king. However awkward and ill-motivated, even the suggestion of guilt would go a long way to redeeming Richard in the eyes of an ambivalent Woodstock—or an ambivalent audience. The awe in which the royal figure is held is such that the impact of Richard's doubts in this scene must not be underestimated.

But what follows severely reverses these initial feelings of sympathy for the king; and our sympathies are rudely thrust about from this point on, much as they are in the Henry VI and King John plays. Having quite suppressed his guilt, Richard eagerly leases his kingdom to his favorites, saving the largest segment for his darling Green. He then proposes that they carry out their plan to kidnap Woodstock. The opening of IV.2 shows Woodstock deluded by the same false confidence which precedes the downfall of many powerful noblemen in Shakespeare. Having sent his duchess to the side of the ailing queen, he is defenseless before his enemies, Richard included, who arrive in the guise of masquers and listen as he describes the sorry condition of the kingdom and the irresponsible behavior of the king. Even when warned that his castle is surrounded by armed men, Woodstock assumes they are rebels seeking his help for their cause. Ironically, though, he continues to affirm his unswerving loyalty to the crown—even when he has been surprised and is being led off stunned to his captivity. The pitch of rebellious feeling prompted by all we have seen is constantly offset by the old divinity that hedges the golden crown.

In IV.3 there is another obvious attempt by the author, this one well-motivated, to reverse the direction of audience feelings. And as in Shakespeare, the figure who acts as catalyst in the king's transformation and thus in shifting audience sympathies is the queen, though in *Woodstock* she performs this function in death as she could not in life. Tresilian, having effectively suppressed the few sheriffs who dare to resist carrying out their terrorist orders, is on the threshold of total success when he receives word of Richard's grief at Queen Anne's death and his determination to redeem himself by reprieving his kidnapped uncle, now condemned to death at Calais. The king who enters is distraught and painfully aware through his wife's death of his own sins. The mere sight of him is an effective counterweight to the rebellious impulses we have been feeling:

> Then let sad sorrow kill King Richard too,
> For all my earthly joys with her must die,
> And I am killed with cares eternally,
> For Anne a'Boehme is dead, forever gone.
> She was too virtuous to remain with me,
> And heaven hath given her higher dignity.
> Oh God, I fear, even here begins our woe.
> Her death's but chorus to some tragic scene
> That shortly will confound our state and realm.
> Such sad events black mischief still attend,
> And bloody acts I fear must crown the end.
> [IV.3.2344-54]

Again, it is easy to acknowledge the significance of this scene without taking full cognizance of its impact in a play written in the early 1590s. The whole thrust of Tudor propaganda was to win adherence to the monarch, even in the face of his mistakes or inadequacies. An arrogantly debauched king, the pawn of corrupt, self-seeking favorites, challenged that propaganda outright. But not so a repentant king. Now the homily on obedience once more might do its work.

Were the play to end with the image in IV.3. of Richard beating his breast in grief and demanding Woodstock's reprieve, the king would have won full possession of our sympathies—despite all we have seen and responded to at Plashey and Dunstable. Perhaps a scene of similar impact ended the play; we do not know. What we do know is that with the opening of the last act our sympathies again shift violently. The brutal murder of Thomas of Woodstock is comparable to Shakespeare's political murders in its controlled, dignified image of suffering nobility. Lapoole, who is both royal hatchet man and moral commentator in one, makes the issue explicit:

> The king commands his uncle here must die,
> And my sad conscience bids the contrary,
> And tells me that his innocent blood thus spilt
> Heaven will revenge. Murder's a heinous guilt,

> A seven times crying sin. Accursed man,
> The further that I wade in this foul act
> My troubled senses are the more distract,
> Confounded and tormented past my reason;
> But there's no lingering. Either he must die
> Or great King Richard vows my tragedy.
>   [V.1.2420–29]

Great King Richard, of course, has just vowed Lapoole's tragedy if Woodstock does die—and this irony may remove some of the blame from the king himself. But Woodstock's death again throws the weight of our sympathies firmly on the side of rebellion.

The use of conventions of Senecan revenge tragedy at this point seems inappropriate. The somewhat verbose ghosts of Edward III and the Black Prince who warn Woodstock of his danger lessen the intensity of the scene, though their rebellious sentiments clearly increase the pull on our sympathies toward rebellion. But ghosts do not take over the scene. The dominant images are those, first, of Woodstock, "plain Thomas still," declining Lapoole's suggestion that he entreat Richard for mercy in favor of a letter admonishing Richard "that he forsake his foolish ways in time," and, second, of Woodstock savagely strangled. Significantly, the second murderer acknowledges that he has laid hands on England's "truest subject." *Woodstock* is thus a play about the murder of England's "truest subject" by England's lawful king, and the problem implicit in such a situation seems quite unresolvable. Is deposing a lawful king ever justified?

The final scenes feel anticlimactic. Lancaster's successful revolt seems perfunctory, and Richard in his last extant appearance, before battle, wears alternately his defiant, then, with the death of Green, his penitent, masks. (Green's death apparently stirs his guilt anew.) With Woodstock gone, the attitudes Richard's speeches generate in us are clearly divided. In opposing Lancaster, he is, after all, the true king putting down insurrection in his kingdom; he has a right to his arrogance here. Lancaster has not evoked our sympathies as Woodstock has. On the other hand, the image of Woodstock's murder is fresh in our minds; the pull toward deposition is still quite strong. Both feelings and thus our

ambivalence are intensified by Richard's last speech which re-
freshes our memory of the murder and also reinforces the image
of the repentant king:

> Oh, my dear friends, the fearful wrath of heaven
> Sits heavy on our heads for Woodstock's death.
> Blood cries for blood, and that almighty hand
> Permits not murder unrevenged to stand. Come, come,
> We yet may hide ourselves from worldly strength,
> But heaven will find us out, and strike at length.
>   [V.4.2899–904]

We do not know how the play ends. The last extant scene is
of Nimble turning state's evidence against Tresilian. But we know
that a reconciliation of some kind takes place between Richard
and his remaining uncles, and we also know that Richard will one
day be deposed. Kingly penitence and reconciliation with the
uncles suggest that the system could be endured, as Tudor propagandists would have it. Deposition suggests that perhaps it could
not, as Tudor authorities were perhaps beginning to fear. Neither
the author nor, implicitly, the audience seems ready to decide.
But the impact of the problem is represented with great clarity
by the author of *Woodstock*—as great really as that achieved by
Marlowe and Shakespeare, despite the superiority of their plays.

Edward II and *Richard II* add few other issues to the presenta-
tion of the problem in *Woodstock*. The central dilemma remains
the same. Marlowe, as Clifford Leech and Douglas Cole show,
adds the quality of true suffering in a weak king, Shakespeare the
great range of sensibilities that may underlie the personality of
a weak king. Both, too, handle the shift in appeal to audience
sympathies more deftly. But both deemphasize the Woodstock
figure, who engenders and echoes the bifurcated feelings of the
audience. Marlowe's Kent and Shakespeare's York are secondary.
Plain Thomas is the central character in *Woodstock* and the chief
reason for this play's effectiveness. For it is plain Thomas who
from beginning to end gives the play the force it has. The opening
scene is an unexpected, chaotic affair until he appears and, calling
attention to the favorites, throws the question of the king's perfidy
into balance. And it is his personality that dominates the confron-

tation at the royal wedding, the scene at Plashey, the kidnapping episode, and of course the murder itself. The scenes in which he does not appear are lesser scenes, the importance of favorites to the underlying theme notwithstanding. Only the Dunstable episode is an exception, and its fresh, homely flavor makes it of a piece artistically with the Woodstock scenes. Throughout, it is Woodstock who gives dramatic weight to the play; it is not surprising that the early editors should have used his name as its title. Through Woodstock alone, the problem is articulated. Can a system which tolerates major crimes on the part of God's supposed deputy be God's system? Thomas the true subject has grappled with the problem. Now members of the audience as true subjects must do so as well.

EDWARD II

Christopher Marlowe's *Edward II*, long disregarded in studies of the Elizabethan history plays, is similar to *Woodstock* in that it represents the reign of a king dominated by favorites, in fierce conflict with the most powerful lords of his realm. In this case, the king's interest in his favorite, the upstart Gaveston (like Tresilian, of humble origins), is unmistakably homosexual in nature, but the political problem remains the same. Because of his attempts to protect Gaveston from his lordly enemies, the king fails to fulfill even the basic obligations of his reign. Edward's queen (Isabel), somewhat like Richard's queen in *Woodstock*, tries early in the play to make the king more attentive to her and to his kingly responsibilities. The king's chief adversary, Young Mortimer, is a lord whose outrage at the king's behavior seems just early in the play, but turns into an ambitious conspirator later in the play. Following the murder of Gaveston midway through the play, Young Mortimer becomes an outright villain; and the formerly hapless queen unexpectedly becomes his mistress and evil accomplice. The play ends with the imprisoned king horribly murdered following a period of humiliation in a castle sewer.

W. D. Briggs, the first critic to seriously examine *Edward II* in this century, saw in clear and simple terms how its political ambiguity is reflected through the basic shift in sympathy which takes place toward the king during the play:

> The strife of Edward with his nobles falls naturally into two stages: the struggle of Young Mortimer and his fellows, together with Isabel, against Gaveston who is supported by the king, and the rebellion of Isabel and Young Mortimer after the death of Gaveston. In the first the king is the culprit—in the second, the martyr; in the first the nobles are just judges—in the second, unjust and cruel executioners. In the first, again, our sympathy goes out to the injured queen and the insulted barons. In the second, however, it is quite as clearly cast with the suffering king.[11]

Briggs does not link this play quite so closely with the others discussed here, nor does he envision the inner struggle of an audience undecided between rebellion or obedience in the face of outrageous monarchy; but his observations are nevertheless the first of their kind. Most critics since have either had to support and elaborate his view or take issue with it and thereby find a form in the play carefully distinguished from his.

Clearly I share Brigg's view of the shift in appeal to our sympathies in *Edward II*, but it is not possible to overlook the apparent confusions in the play which obscure or deny the presence of any kind of coherent pattern. Some see the play as nothing more than a texture of the suffering woven out of Edward's misfortunes. Others, unable to find even that much purpose, have thrown up their hands. Wilbur Sanders searches in vain for any kind of morality (political or otherwise) underlying the play: "It is as if the concerns which, in the first place, directed his [Marlowe's] attention to this reign—the weak homosexual king, the sensational violence of his death, the Machiavellian ambition of a Mortimer—take charge of his pen; and when their momentum is spent, he is obliged to trace meaningless patterns on the paper till the imaginative fit seizes him again."[12] And David Bevington, who at one point links the play to *Richard II* in its shift in sympathies toward the image of the king, comes to feel that "one

11. *Marlowe's Edward II* (London: David Nutt, 1914), p. cvii.
12. Wilbur Sanders, *The Dramatist and the Received Idea* (Cambridge: At the University Press, 1968), p. 125.

cannot postulate a straight-forward, edifying pattern of transferred sympathies, as in *Richard II*, by which the barons are
largely in the right until they reach the point of open defiance."[13]
Bevington feels, as it is hard not to feel after extensive study of
the first acts, that there is no particular attitude or set of attitudes
which one is clearly supposed to support or oppose. The chief
issues early in the play—attitudes toward Machiavellianism implicit in Gaveston's opening speech and actions, attitudes toward
political responsibility in foreign affairs (notably in the wars
against France), attitudes toward papal authority—all seem in a
state of chaos. As a result, there appears little to back the clear
assertion that the rebel side is intended to be sympathetic and
that the king should arouse our antipathy. And there seems little
to justify this jumble in our sympathies. Our responses to the
opening act, while quite intense at times, apparently lead nowhere. By contrast, the last acts of the play are quite clear.

But Briggs and his many followers are right about the play. In
the first part, the king is "the culprit" and the lords "just judges."
The problem is that Marlowe had more trouble making his king
unappealing in debauchery than did the author of *Woodstock* and
Shakespeare. The latter two deplore the irresponsibility implicit
in the king's frivolous attitudes toward his favorites, while Marlowe finds it difficult to create a similarly distasteful impression
of that irresponsibility. In fact, most of the imagery of Gaveston's
speeches, the intensity of the king's feelings, and even the responses of other characters suggest that the author not only shares
the king's interest in his tempting pastimes, but comes close to
feeling that they transcend affairs of state in importance. Many
look at the Marlowe of *Tamburlaine* and *Doctor Faustus* as one
who exults in the forbidden, whose heroes indulge their fantasies
in a wide variety of ways before succumbing to the higher force
that must inevitably strike them down; yet rarely is this view
transferred to *Edward II*—notably because its hero is weaker than
those of *Tamburlaine* and *Faustus* and seemingly concerned with
objects of lesser magnitude. The subject Marlowe here chose to
work with denied him a Herculean hero, but the nature of the

---

13. *Tudor Drama and Politics*, p. 218.

king's irresponsibility could nevertheless have appealed to Marlowe for its involvement with the forbidden, just as do the farther-
reaching activities of Tamburlaine and Faustus. The king's lust
for Gaveston, in short, is of the same order if not the same magnitude as Tamburlaine's for empire and Faustus' for knowledge.

In seeking words and images to suggest Edward's political
shortcomings, Marlowe uses a world with which he is quite
familiar and which he undoubtedly loves, and the attractions
nearly outweigh their intended reprehensibility. When Young
Mortimer attacks the king for going to battle once with soldiers
who "marched like players,/With garish rogues, not armour," and
himself "Bedaubed with gold" (II.1.183–85), it is not difficult to
sense the presence of the acting company in the author's mind.
There is an immediacy comparable to that in the player scenes
in *Hamlet*. So, too, when Gaveston plans his special entertain-
ments for the king, his (and Marlowe's) mind first turns to the
world of the arts and court drama, which blends significantly into
those images suggesting sexual proclivity toward males:

> I must have wanton poets, pleasant wits,
> Musicians, that with touching of a string
> May draw the pliant king which way I please.
> Music and poetry is his delight;
> Therefore I'll have Italian masks by night,
> Sweet speeches, comedies, and pleasing shows;
> And in the day, when he shall walk abroad,
> Like sylvan nymphs my pages shall be clad.
> My men, like satyrs grazing on the lawns,
> Shall with their goat-feet dance an antic hay.
> Sometime a lovely boy in Dian's shape,
> With hair that gilds the water as it glides,
> Crownets of pearl about his naked arms,
> And in his sportful hands an olive tree,
> To hide those parts which men delight to see,
> Shall bathe him in a spring; and there, hard by,
> One like Actaeon peeping through the grove,
> Shall by the angry goddess be transformed,
> And running in the likeness of an hart,

> By yelping hounds pulled down, and seem to die—
> Such things as these best please his majesty.
>   [I.1.51–71]

The life of kingly irresponsibility seen through this speech feels close to Marlowe's own, and he cannot represent it in terms other than attractive, certainly by Renaissance standards. Homosexuality was morally forbidden then as now, but allusion to it was common and perhaps more familiar to a popular audience than it would be today. It should be borne in mind, too, that the love of Gaveston and Edward tends to be light and frivolous. Only when they are forcefully separated does it take on serious overtones. The quoted speech suggests that the sexuality itself is not treated too deeply or seriously, even if it does defy moral standards. The sense of deep psychological disturbance which prompts its ironic association by William Empson and others with the means of Edward's horrible death seems inappropriate. I doubt that Marlowe, who undoubtedly found the images of Gaveston's speech appealing, would have made such an association—consciously— and it is conscious irony I assume the critics are referring to. The sins of the Edward-Gaveston relationship are those of excessive frivolity, not of gross sexual perversion.

Just as Edward's preoccupation with Gaveston suggests the author's ambivalence, so Edward's and Gaveston's attack on the bishop of Coventry is an instance of ambivalence on Marlowe's part. The language they use employs the standard diction of antipapal abuse in drama of the age:

> *King Edward.* Throw off his golden mitre, rend his stole,
>   And in the channel christen him anew.
> *Kent.*   Ah, brother, lay not violent hands on him,
>   For he'll complain unto the see of Rome.
> *Gaveston.*   Let him complain unto the see of hell; . . .
>   [I.1.187–91]

Although Edward later attacks Rome in more dignified terms, the purpose of this exchange is unquestionably to debase Gaveston and, in turn, the king; yet the outlook represented toward Rome is one which Marlowe and the audience share. It comes ready-made out of their most mundane prejudices. The result is the same chaos in appeal to audience sympathies which results from Gaveston's proposed sensuous theatrics. That which is used to elicit contempt and anger at the king may instead, because of language or theme, elicit sympathy, interest, or agreement. Nevertheless, the intent if not the effect seems clear enough. It is as if Marlowe, trying to write a play like *Woodstock*, keeps allowing his personal predilections creep in, and these predilections play upon the covert sympathies of the audience.

The character who, like plain Thomas in *Woodstock*, has long been identified as the one whose shifting responses trace the probable course of audience sympathies toward the king is of course the earl of Kent. But as most discussions correctly find greater clarity in the closing acts of the play than in opening acts, Kent's later conversion back to Edward is usually stressed at the expense of his far more complex responses early in the play. Yet it is Kent in the first act whose responses and actions suggest the degree of license a king may be permitted. And it is significant that Kent is at first on Edward's side. To him is left the job of telling the barons that they are exceeding their limits as subjects, and he warns them pointedly that their words would have cost them their heads during the reign of Edward I. At the same time Kent is himself shocked by the titles Edward showers on Gaveston and takes exception to the rude treatment by Edward and Gaveston of the offending bishop. An early warning by Edward ("Cease, brother, for I cannot brook these words" I.1.160) renders Kent silent on the subject of kingly excess; his silence makes him so trusted an ally that Gaveston actually confides in him, and the nobles have him imprisoned along with the royal favorite. But his defection in II.2 makes clear that he has been responding deeply to the king's behavior all along:

> *Kent.*   My Lord, I see your love to Gaveston
> Will be the ruin of the realm and you,
> For now the wrathful nobles threaten wars,
> And therefore, brother, banish him for ever.
> *King Edward.* Art thou an enemy to my Gaveston?
> *Kent.*   Ay, and it grieves me that I favored him.
>   [II.2.206–11]

Kent's outburst resolves the implicit debate about kingly responsibility that has been going on in him and presumably in the audience. What Kent finds is that Edward's desire for his lover is not of itself enough to warrant the kind of attack which the nobles make. Kent's rationale, if stated, might not be dissimilar from that of Mortimer Senior in a moment of unexplained tolerance: "Let him without controlment have his will. / The mightiest kings have had their minions" (I.4.389–90).

Even the appeals and lamentations of the queen, which do so much to make Edward unsympathetic early in the play, do not affect Kent. But when it becomes clear that the kingdom itself suffers because of the king's misguided affections and that real injustice is done the nobility of the land by the useless elevation of a social climber, then Kent turns on his brother and joins forces with the nobles—becomes, in short, the severe uncle we met in *Woodstock* and will see again. France is lost, the Danes threaten to command "the Narrow seas," foreign princes indicate their contempt for England, rebellion runs rampant in the land, the Irish are up in arms, the Scots have made greater headway than ever before, and Edward refuses to ransom a leader who has been taken prisoner fighting for the crown. Kent allows Edward any excesses he wishes so long as they do not affect England's security and her standing among the nations. But when it is clear that Gaveston means potential disaster for the realm, then Kent shifts—and in all likelihood the audience then, too, makes its terrible decision: this king may have to be deposed.

But the play's construction in the first two acts is, unfortunately, close to the hotchpotch Sanders finds throughout. Before the point at which Kent decides the king's weakness can no longer be tolerated, at which the nobles have finally made their cause seem just, and at which the realm seems doomed to a state of chronic instability so long as Edward rules—our sympathies have in fact already begun to shift. Kent's first conversion takes place unaccountably late in the proceedings. Just as *he* decides to turn against the king, *we* are beginning to see the king as sympathetic. The cause of this shift is not so much the king himself as those around him. Throughout Act I, the nobles, particularly Young Mortimer, are attractive figures; the one set of feelings with which we can identify swiftly and easily is their outrage, so long as it is mere outrage and nothing more. We know the indignation that must accompany royal incompetence. But at the first sign of direction to that outrage, which can only be toward deposition, Elizabethan viewers must quickly retreat into their more orthodox selves.

Actually, that first sign precedes Kent's outburst. It is in I.4, a long scene chronicling the first coercion of Edward by the nobles, followed by their first truce. Deposition is suggested in I.4 by Young Mortimer, and the figure who backs him up represents Rome. The bishop of Canterbury here functions quite differently from the bishop of Coventry in the earlier scene. There the focus was on the rude treatment of a churchman by Edward and Gaveston; here it is on the rude treatment of Edward by his rebellious nobles in unholy alliance with that arch-enemy the pope.

As Sanders suggests, the line between confusion and subtlety on Marlowe's part is frequently hard to draw, and such is the situation again in I.4. The intent is to jolt an audience leaning strongly toward sympathy for the nobles and antipathy for the king, and that jolt is achieved with that single word: *Depose!* But perhaps to intensify the jolt, there is the dubiously logical insertion of Rome, that eternal red herring in these plays. Thus our first invitation to political sympathy with the king is chiefly in mutual opposition to the pope. Edward's powerful speech ending the episode (I.4.94–105) appeals to passions seething mightily in a 1590s audience and thereby draws its sympathy to him; but the issue actually has little to do with the play. Whether intended by Marlowe or not, the papal red herring in I.4 takes our attention away from the theme of deposition, since a king may be deposed only by his own subjects, not by a foreign prince. The episode is confused, but again the direction is evident. As the nobles begin speaking of the deposition of a monarch, rather than just sputtering angrily, we begin to become defenders of the crown.

Our sympathies in *Edward II* are thus kept off balance throughout the first third of the play. The attractions of Edward's excesses almost outweigh the antagonism they are intended to evoke, and the barons almost go too far in their just function as watchdogs of the kingdom, as Kent points out. The extent to which Marlowe is in control of these reactions, too, is dubious, but the chief signs make the intent clear. A Gaveston who rejects the petitions of suffering men from his own class in order to woo a lover-king to his own great advantage, a king who takes part in baiting a defenseless churchman, a gentle Queen despised—all indicate that, however uncertainly, we are intended to resent Edward's behavior early in the play. His offense is not so much the nature of his behavior—which the Elizabethans would find abnormal, though not taboo—as his failure to fulfill his God-given obligations to his subjects.

Of the various "structures" suggested for *Edward II*, J. B. Steane's tripartite division seems the most accurate. He notes that despite the impression that there are two parts to the play—the first concentrating on "the homo-sexual King and his favourite" and the second on the fall of Edward—there are actually three. The construction, says Steane, "includes an important middle section marked out from the rest by the fact that in it the king is for a short time strong, determined, and victorious."[14] This middle section constitutes a sort of brief romance of the king's vengeance for the murder of his lover. And the nature of that love, once Gaveston is defeated by his enemies, no longer seems corrupt. Threatened, the "filthie" (according to Holinshed) Gaveston suddenly becomes a version of the faithful shepherd who protests his loyalty in a fashion which reinforces our new admiration for the king and resentment at his attackers. Before Gaveston dies in III.1, we meet his replacement Young Spencer; but only in his first appearance (II.1) does Spencer closely resemble the earlier image of his predecessor. Following Gaveston's death Spencer is represented only as the faithful squire who yields his life rather than betray his master. The total change in perspective toward the king and his favorites and toward the rebellious lords, a change which characterizes the midsection of the play, is reflected in the assault upon Spencer by the lords. Immediately following the treacherous murder of Gaveston, the king receives word from the lords that the price of peace is now the swift removal of Spencer, though they can hardly know so quickly that Spencer is Edward's new favorite. The whole Gaveston affair is

14. J. B. Steane, *Marlowe* (Cambridge: At the University Press, 1970), p. 205.

thus to begin anew with Spencer, only this time the king is in the right. The lords are militantly attempting to restrict the monarch's God-given freedom, and this time the king is temporarily the victor.

Following Edward's unlikely military success over the lords (III.3), rendered no less miraculous by its accurate adherence to Holinshed, the heroic interlude, Steane's "middle section," is suddenly concluded. The puzzle is, why is it there at all? There is much that seems meaningless throughout *Edward II*, as has been suggested, and in seeking the underlying shape of the work, I hardly wish to force significance on details which seem inescapably the result of artistic indifference on Marlowe's part. There is, for example, no reason in the play why Marlowe should spare Mortimer while sending Warwick and Lancaster to the block. In Holinshed, Mortimer is a slight figure in this revolt, and thus his more lenient treatment there is more plausible. Marlowe, on the other hand, has made him chief leader of the rebels from the start. His gentle treatment here simply does not make sense.

But the whole of the middle section cannot be dismissed as bad dramaturgy. Marlowe, who omitted many other events and campaigns, stresses Edward's "brief authority." The middle section includes practically everything in the play from II.2 until IV.5. Rather than resulting solely from Marlowe's incompetence as a dramatist, the mid-portion of the play seems to be representing a monarch as he ought to be. Marlowe in these scenes may be looking for an ideal against which we may contrast the image of the weak king.

But what he comes up with is typically contradictory. At one point, in welcoming the scholar Baldock to his service, Edward sounds like Shakespeare's holy Henry VI:

> Baldock.   My name is Baldock, and my gentry
>   I fetched from Oxford, not from heraldry.
> King Edward. The fitter art thou, Baldock, for my turn.
>   Wait on me, and I'll see thou shalt not want.
>   [II.2.241–44]

At another, he sounds like Tamburlaine swearing vengeance upon his enemies:

> If I be England's king, in lakes of gore
> Your headless trunks, your bodies will I trail,
> That you may drink your fill, and quaff in blood,
> And stain my royal standard with the same,
> That so my bloody colors may suggest
> Remembrance of revenge immortally
> On your accursed traitorous progeny,
> You villains that have slain my Gaveston!
>   [III.2.135–42]

Undoubtedly, Marlowe might conceive of each image as one of Harry Levin's *libidos* driving his hero's action,[15] but the confusion renders this play's mid-section almost as unintelligible as its opening. Both come close to tracing the "meaningless patterns" Sanders describes. Yet again the intent is there, if characteristically garbled. It is a brief, superficial, and contradictory wish-fulfillment—a blurred vision of what an English king should be.

The final segment of the play is quite separate both in construction and feeling from what has gone before. Almost always willing to sacrifice plausibility and depth for outlandish statement and intensity of audience response, Marlowe up to this point keeps the action moving at an extremely rapid pace. Events incomplete in their emotional effect on the characters involved—events hastily and explosively explored—dash into each other. The final episodes are more controlled artistically, and their effect, it would seem, more genuinely what the author sought. Marlowe's problem, of course, was easier in the final acts. There were many images and ambiguities to contend with in Act I, but only one theme to be concerned with in Act V: the misery of the king's downfall.

The final episodes present three very different variations of that theme. In the following paragraphs, I shall examine those episodes in detail, bearing in mind that all of them are intended to elicit feelings of guilt in an audience for rebellious impulses which had been aroused by earlier portions of the play. The first and last of these episodes (IV.6 and V.3) stimulate immediate and intense reaction in the audience, but they reveal little—

15. See Harry Levin, *The Overreacher* (Cambridge, Mass.: Harvard University Press, 1952), pp. 176–78, *passim*.

certainly nothing subtle—about the depths of response in the central character. The second episode (V.1), on the other hand, is so deeply and, for Marlowe, uncharacteristically concerned with the subtler human feelings involved that Shakespeare seems to have borrowed much from it for his own image of the deposed monarch.

The first (IV.6) takes place at Neath Abbey, where the king, Spencer, and Baldock have taken refuge before Mortimer's victorious army. Because it uses the convention of the careworn king seeking escape from the trials of this world, the scene has been compared with Henry VI's observations on the molehill (3 *Henry VI* III.2); Henry's speech, however, has a quite different meaning and even effect from Edward's lines here. Henry's pastoral idyll describes an ordered way of life which is desperately needed in Henry's England. Edward's attitudes suggest aimless alienation, desire for withdrawal which has no such political or moral overtones. He wishes to study philosophy in a monastic setting, not in search of ways to "rule better," but merely so that he may be consoled. Of the study of Plato and Aristotle Edward says, "this life contemplative is heaven" (IV.6.20). His image of Baldock, who "suckedst" his learning from the philosophers, is that of the baby taking sustenance from the mother, an image reinforced by Edward's reclining his "head laden with mickle care" upon the lap of the abbot. All the final episodes are intended to evoke compassion for the king, but the image here can only evoke a compassion which wants Edward released from his misery. He is infantile, and far from lamenting the loss of his birthright, here he seeks to be free of it. Here, as in his passion for Gaveston, he is apolitical. He wishes no part of the responsibilities of his office. This is a scene depicting personal downfall, and were there no scene to follow, one might say, with some critics, that the play had gone from political concern to something approaching exclusively personal concern. But there are two episodes to follow—one of which makes the issue as political in nature as it was at the start.

The scene in question (V.1) takes place at Killingworth Castle where Edward is later to die under very different circumstances, and it clearly constitutes the chief respect, dramatically speaking, in which *Edward II* and *Richard II* are very similar plays. Shakespeare, who was accused by Robert Greene of borrowing others' feathers, normally discarded the language and insights of others because he no doubt felt he could do better on his own. But when he found an emotion deeply felt and suitably expressed, as he did here, he made few changes. The feelings and some of the language in the deposition scene in Shakespeare's *Richard II*, are quite close to this scene. There are two superficial differences. One is that Edward is not deposed in full court, and while this is not exactly a private scene, it is not, too, the public scene that Shakespeare's deposition scene is. The other is that Edward is given a far more persuasive, if no more sincere, reason for abdicating than is Richard. Leicester tells him explicitly that should he not now immediately resign the crown, it might well go to someone other than his son (obviously Mortimer), and that his only hope at least to keep the crown in the family is to abdicate. But these differences are insignificant, compared to what the scenes have in common.

It is necessary to stress in *Edward II*, as in *Richard II*, particularly in view of the contention made by some today that Richard voluntarily yields his crown, that severe if indirect coercion is involved in both. It is difficult to imagine that anyone who has lived in an age of brainwashing and forced confessions could feel that there is anything really voluntary about the kings' abdications in these plays. The instrument used by both Machiavels—the stage Machiavel Mortimer and the far deeper Machiavel Bolingbroke—is the character of the man they are dealing with. When we say these kings depose themselves, we should mean that both are brought by a not-too-subtle psychological campaign to the point where they are willing to depose themselves. In both cases the scenes in question are a response to popular demand that the abdications be voluntary. Such ends can be achieved by torture, but that is hardly necessary, as Mortimer and Bolingbroke know. All that is needed is a stern questioner: "Will you resign or no?" And the king, being more sensitive than anyone around him and thus more deeply aware of his failures, is overcome by the deep irony of his failure, by the real myth of his "divinity," by his inescapable vulnerability. Confrontation by a cold, insensitive interrogator is enough—even if he uses as few words as the bishop of Winchester in *Edward II*. The kings put themselves through torture as painful as anything the rack could provide.

Shakespeare seems to have used Act V, scene 1 of *Edward II* as a sketch for his deposition scene in *Richard II* and employed elements of it in other situations as well. Marlowe has Edward allude vaguely to "strange despairing thoughts,/Which thoughts are martyred with endless torments" (V.1.79–80). Shakespeare identifies far more of the thoughts than Marlowe, both here and in Richard's death-scene, but it is these tones and inflections of Edward's that he uses throughout:

> But when I call to mind I am a King. . . .
> [V.1.23]
>
> But tell me, must I now resign my Crown?
> [V.1.36]
>
> Here, take my Crown; the life of Edward too;
> Two kings in England can not reign at once.
> [V.1.57–58]
>
> See, monsters, see, I'll wear my crown again.
> What, fear you not the fury of your king?
> [V.1.74–75]
>
> And therefore let me wear it yet awhile.
> [V.1.83]

Marlowe's effect of self-pitying irony in this scene is practically identical to Shakespeare's throughout *Richard II*. F. P. Wilson, in *Marlowe and the Early Shakespeare* (Oxford: At the University Press, 1953), finds that this effect derives from the total lack of any kind of psychological armor in these kings. They speak their sorrow unrestrainedly, in often embarrassing but invariably eloquent, original, and genuine human terms. They are hypersensitive but forthright, articulate, and extremely alert. They use words not to hide feeling but to make it as vivid as possible. Yet both are frustrated that all they say can be but the shadow of the massive agony beneath, which can never be expressed. In *Edward II*, V.1, the weak kings of Marlowe and Shakespeare fuse into an image which is probably the dominant image of the weak king in the drama of the 1590s. In him, in the essence of the weak-king figure, the political and the personal are indistinguishable.

The impact of these deposition scenes is that they engage audience doubts and uncertainties regarding not only the king but ultimately themselves.

> Here receive my crown.
> Receive it? No, these innocent hands of mine
> Shall not be guilty of so foul a crime.
> He of you all that most desires my blood
> And will be called the murderer of a king,
> Take it. What, are you moved? Pity you me?
> Then send for unrelenting Mortimer
> And Isabel, whose eyes, being turned to steel,
> Will sooner sparkle fire than shed a tear.
> Yet stay, for rather than I will look on them,
> Here, here! [*He gives the crown.*]
> Now, sweet God of heaven,
> Make me depise this transitory pomp
> And sit for aye enthronized in heaven.
> Come, death and with thy fingers close my eyes,
> Or if I live, let me forget myself.
>   [*Edward II* V.1.97–111]

Edward's and Richard's brilliantly penetrating suffering arouses feelings in the audience best expressed by these lines and by Richard's deepest fear: "I am myself a traitor with the rest." The king's suffering is the audience's suffering at having in their hearts deposed a king, their suffering at being unworthy subjects, their suffering at being sinful man.

> And must I ravel out
> My weaved-up folly? Gentle Northumberland,
> If thy offenses were upon record,
> Would it not shame thee in so fair a troop
> To read a lecture of them?
>   [*Richard II* IV.1.228–32]

The king's suffering is implicitly linked with the knowledge that such is man's lot. As kings fall, men fall. As deposition is inevitable, so is human failure. Underlying these primarily political scenes are far-reaching intimations of the tragic. Not only are humanity and kingship incompatible, so too are humanity and almost any kind of completely successful human endeavor. These two scenes achieve an identification of viewer and central figure beyond anything in the history plays.

A good deal has been written about Edward's terrible demise (V.5), to which not much will be added here. While his death is one of the most horrible in a dramatic tradition noted for its simulation of gruesome events, some recent critics have tended to make it even worse than it is. Marlowe's language actually leaves the means of Edward's death vague—it could be by suffocation—but the red-hot poker intended to be anally inserted into the king and by tradition to be the means of his murder is referred to in V.5.30. One idea now current finds this means of Edward's death condign punishment, given the nature of his sin. But the symbolic association of the homosexual act with Edward's murder is one I doubt Marlowe or any Elizabethan would have made, obvious as it may seem to some today. Marlowe, the chroniclers, perhaps even Edward's murderers themselves reveal a fascination with the means selected for Edward's murder which may suggest unresolved psychological problems. But the symbolism is out-of-place. The homosexuality suggested in the first act is morally forbidden but not darkly disturbed. Its punishment would, I suspect, take no different form than that for any type of sexual excess. No separate circle of Hell need be reserved for it.

I also feel we may betray our own fears when we allow the final scene to blind us to the rest of the play. For years, nothing in *King Lear* could get through to me because of the terror I felt at Gloucester's blinding, the horror of which action clearly has its function in the play but is hardly intended to overshadow all other events. I think my over-reaction to Gloucester may be similar to some present-day reaction to *Edward II*. Edward's death is the awful demise of the weak king, whose excesses and frivolity have helped bring about a downfall, deserved we all once felt, but now a shocking, guilt-provoking image of martyred royalty. It is in keeping with other scenes of torture in Elizabethan drama. Marlowe even obscures rather than intensifies the specifics presented in the chronicles—where the final torment and death are stressed far more than they are in the play. He has not in any sense transcended or departed from the dramatic or historical traditions with which he worked.

Act V, scene 4 of *Edward II*, the death of Edward, needs to be seen in proper proportion to the rest of the play and particularly to the other concluding episodes, in each of which our sympathy for the king is aroused. Each in a different way evokes compassion for Edward and anger at his enemies. The final episode uses physical torture, but the one previous to it uses a psychological suffering which is in retrospect far more terrifying because it is something all may know from everyday experience. In V.1 Edward as man and king had come face to face with the realities of his being. It is as subtle a scene, as unexpectedly knowledgeable about human reactions in a time of trial as there is in Marlowe (and I include here the final scene of *Doctor Faustus*). If we have become more affected by the far less subtle, bludgeoning action of V.4, the fault may be Marlowe's; but he went beyond himself in psychological understanding in V.1, and Shakespeare at least seems to have realized it.

Marlowe's *Edward II* has not one guilt-provoking final scene, but three, all with the same intent as far as audience sympathies are concerned, but each quite different in texture and dramatic subtlety. From the sentimentalism of Edward's self-pity at the Abbey, Marlowe goes to the true psychological complexity of the abdication scene and finally to the gross horror of the king's demise. At least in this final segment, the playwright's purposes are clear, which cannot be said for the earlier portions of this unquestionably confusing work of art.

After several decades of praising Marlowe, we seem again to find ourselves disappointed by the promise of incredible achievement never fulfilled. Nowhere is this better illustrated than in *Edward II*, where obviously there is less attempt at poetic brilliance than anywhere else in Marlowe, yet more attempt—which could at times best be called Shakespearean—to provide some vision of the well-springs of human emotion and the unseen forms that emotion takes. Yet, perhaps because of the attempt, the results are the more disappointing. With one-tenth of the poetic or dramatic talent, the unknown author of *Woodstock* was more certain about what he wanted to do. *Edward II* presents fragmentary, contradictory emotions in moving but confusing passages amid a numbing deluge of often repetitious events. In Act I, Marlowe seems caught in a struggle between his personal delight with Gaveston's world and his knowledge of the disastrous political effects of Gaveston's influence on Edward. In the middle portion of the play, he seems to want to represent how Edward should have reigned, but he is uncertain whether his ideal king should be a Henry VI or a Tamburlaine. In the final acts, at his best in evoking our sympathy for the hounded, victimized King, Marlowe sacrifices the deep passion of Edward's deposition for the *grand guignol* effect of Edward's death. Perhaps a popular Elizabethan audience demanded as much, but they settled for a lot less horror from Shakespeare and the author of *Woodstock*. Marlowe may have missed his finest opportunity as a dramatist in not having used the insight he reveals in V.1 throughout the play. His play would have then been more successful political drama and far better tragedy. But as in *Woodstock* and *Richard II*, the central purpose of the play, however successfully reflected, is to articulate the dilemma involving an inadequate monarch and the divinity of the crown.

RICHARD II

In discussing *Richard II* along with the other plays in this chapter, I may seem to be suggesting that it is best understood apart from what has been called the "second tetralogy." But since Shakespeare wrote no real trilogies or tetralogies—even his two- and three-part plays indicate only a chronological continuation of events—I am hardly doing more than rearranging for convenience' sake groupings which other interpreters have created for convenience' sake. Obviously, much separates *Richard II* and *Henry IV*. Although they are linked in one sense by the character and reign of Bolingbroke, of greater importance to Shakespeare when he wrote *Richard II* was the agony surrounding the question of rebellion or obedience toward a monarch who was unwilling or unable to fulfill the minimum requirements of his office. The role of Bolingbroke in *Richard II* is both perplexing and important; but it is in the image of the weak king that the greater force of this play resides, and this means it is Richard's play. In this sense it is a member of the different sort of trilogy discussed here—one in which three very different playwrights respond in comparable terms to the same basic national or political dilemma. *Woodstock, Edward II,* and *Richard II* could almost have been written for an ancient Greek dramatic contest.

Recent interpretations of *Richard II* have pointed the way I follow. As indicated in the introductory chapter, Ernst Kantorowicz, basing his approach to *Richard II* on medieval religio-legal theory, explores the play as a manifestation in art of the irreconcilable nature of the king's human and divine "bodies." And L. S. Friedman suggests that our divided sympathies toward Richard reflect the political dissatisfaction weak monarchs inevitably inspire.[16] Both Wilbur Sanders and John R. Elliott see the play as an implicit "critique" of established Tudor policy—not one which promulgates rebellion certainly, but one which does strongly question blind submission to corrupt or flaccid rule.[17] The struggle is seen, Elliott suggests, in almost every one of the play's many conflicts. Obviously, it is there at the start. The memory of the recently murdered Woodstock in the opening scene recalls the excesses of royal prerogative felt deeply at Woodstock's murder late in the anonymous play. I do not, like some, consider Shakespeare's play the sequel to the earlier one (J. D. Wilson feels it might be based on a lost sequel), but its opening scene does follow hard upon the conclusion of that play, both in action and appeal to audience sympathies. In both, the image of Thomas of Woodstock, duke of Gloucester bears little resemblance to the shrewd manipulator in the chronicles. Shakespeare clearly followed the anonymous playwright in suggesting the kind of man Woodstock was and thus, it may be assumed, in his basic conception of the personality of the king as well. Both authors seem fundamentally concerned with the insoluble problems which en-

16. "Kingship and Politics in Shakespeare's *Richard II*," unpublished dissertation, University of Iowa, 1966, pp. 100–101.
17. John R. Elliott, "History and Tragedy in *Richard II*," *SEL*, VIII (1968), pp. 253–71.

sue when a youthful, pleasure-loving monarch is unwilling to do his job.

Elliott sees the basic dilemma of the play reflected in the second scene, for some time considered in Tillyardian terms the focal point of the play's Tudor establishment outlook. Recent interpretations like Elliott's still see it as crucial, but in other than straight Tillyardian terms. The duchess of Gloucester here enunciates the spirit of rebellion in her desire that Gaunt revenge Woodstock's death; and her lines, Elliott feels, are, by virtue of their passion and duration, more forceful than tired, old Gaunt's appeals to divine sanction. While Gaunt speaks of "God's quarrel," the duchess speaks of blood relationships, injustices, and outrages which she insists can only be answered on an earthly level, that is, with direct force of arms. Richard's later dismay at the absence of any avenging angels tends to bear out her argument. Elliott links this scene to one much later in the play, V.2, in which a duke and duchess once again argue over loyalty to the crown opposed to loyalty to a blood relation, this time a son. I refer of course to the reactions of the duke and duchess of York to Aumerle's participation in a seditious conspiracy against Bolingbroke (now King Henry IV). Even under so different a monarch, the dilemma must begin anew. What the nation gains through Bolingbroke's more kingly personality, it loses through his faulty title. He is still the weak king, and the conflict between rebellion and obedience goes on. Purgation of audience feelings associated with the dilemma abounds—but, as in *Woodstock* and *Edward II*, solution to it is practically nil.

Many recent interpretations give new importance to Bolingbroke, but despite the fascinating ambiguity of the usurper, which is discussed later in this chapter, it is the shift in sympathy toward Richard which constitutes the basic movement of this play. Even more than the king figure in the other plays, Richard excites antagonism in the early acts, and this antagonism is maintained until the first sign that he is vulnerable. Then he becomes sympathetic. The shift is unexpected, but his personality does not change in the process; and far less than in *Edward II* do the personalities of his attackers change.

The elements which go into the unsympathetic portrait of

Richard in the first two acts have been examined before. Toward the conclusion of the play's opening scene, Richard sternly insists: "We were not born to sue but to command"; but his ability to command in any effective fashion is persistently belied by his frivolous, whimsical attitudes and actions. The snickering, schoolboy contempt which openly dominates his conversation with Aumerle about Bolingbroke's departure in I.4 is also evident beneath the veneer of verbal propriety and regal bearing in the scenes at court (I.1) and Coventry (I.3) which precede it. His suggestion that "Our doctors say this is no month to bleed" is a frivolous, indecorous, insulting response to both Mowbray and Bolingbroke; and whimsical to the point of utter irresponsibility is his handling, at the frustrated tournament, of the sacred rituals of combat. Having allowed the combatants to be roused to fever pitch—colors flying, chargers pawing the ground, and the whole event as alive with excitement and expectation as it could be— Richard throws his "warder down," stopping the festival at its point of chivalric fulfillment. He could not have antagonized his subjects more. He deeply offends not only the combatants but also the elders, to whom the trial by combat is richly satisfying.

Richard has his reasons, of course—reasons which accord with the slovenly Machiavellianism which governs many decisions in Shakespeare's political drama—but they are abysmally applied. He knows that if "Right Be Done," Bolingbroke will defeat Mowbray, who is certainly guilty of complicity at least in Woodstock's murder. He is afraid of the Lancastrian faction—enough to banish its youthful scion before his popularity becomes a real challenge to the crown, but enough also, because of Gaunt and York, to make that banishment a light one. Richard's "policy" is almost haphazard—based on considerations which pop into his head. This is not "the breath of Kings" but the breath of weak kings—kings who resolve their problems superficially, on the spur of the moment, without bothering to give even the appearance of wisdom and considered judgment.

Early in the play, Shakespeare's Richard is the most unsympathetic of the weak kings in this chapter because he is the most sensitive and intelligent—the same reasons he is later the most sympathetic of the three. Failing to use his fine qualities of mind as he could, his abuse of his authority is the most comtemptible of all. In *Woodstock*, Richard first appears as simply immature, and the very ambivalent first image of Edward petulantly defending Gaveston is that of a compulsive neurotic. Shakespeare's Richard is mature enough and psychologically normal. But he is lazy and so self-centered as to be quite oblivious to the needs of his kingdom and its people. No favorites like Tresilian or Gaveston hold sway over this king. He has his drinking and jesting companions, but he dominates them rather than they him. His crimes cannot really be blamed on others, despite Bolingbroke's accusations in III.1. This king's own ego is at fault throughout, and there is no vacillation on this point by the author, as there seems to be in the other plays. The incompatibility between man and job appears most clearly and emphatically in *Richard II*.

Richard's treatment of Gaunt's illness and death in I.4 and II.1 is the high point of his abominations. Frivolous, whimsical, and lazy, he also reveals a coldness as numbing as anything like it in Shakespeare. The Northumberland who later acts as official state prosecutor (IV.1) and who cuts short Richard's farewell to his queen (V.1) is no more icily impenetrable than the Richard who can listen with such insufferable indifference to Gaunt's famed and ringing patriotism and York's appeals on behalf of the time-honored conventions of inheritance. At the first news of Gaunt's illness, Richard's earlier frivolity gives way to a more virulent strain:

> Now put it, God, in the physician's mind
> To help him to his grave immediately!
> The lining of his coffers shall make coats
> To deck our soldiers for these Irish wars.
> Come, gentlemen, let's all go visit him.
> Pray God we may make haste, and come too late!
> [I.4.59–64]

His attention to the dying Gaunt is upon the nature of the old man's language rather than upon its substance—"Can sick men play so nicely with their names?"—and his outrage at Gaunt's attack focuses entirely on the insubordination, not at all on what Gaunt has accused him of. It is clear that he is not listening to the

accusations. To Richard, Gaunt has "the sullens." The king is deaf
to the larger issues of royal responsibility and the welfare of the
nation. Both flippant and angry, he betrays a nearly autistic concern with his own being. Gaunt could be preaching to the wind.
And there is no break in his tone with Gaunt's death. Richard's
unbelievable "sentence" about the "ripest fruit" (II.1.153–54) is
followed by seizure of Gaunt's lands and by his same flippant
treatment of York. He speaks with the impatient brevity of the
executive who has more important things on his mind: "Why,
uncle, what's the matter?" The king can not be reached, the conclusion seems clear. Nothing short of what is to come can break
his will to be irresponsible.

Shakespeare prepares us for the shift in sympathy toward the
king less than do the other playwrights, yet that shift is far more
plausible. When the author of *Woodstock* awkwardly introduces
the theme of Richard's guilt with the death of his queen, it seems
clear that he is ineffectively working for something like a transition in our response to the king. And Marlowe provides the interim
mid-portion of *Edward II* in which our sympathies are pulled
toward the king by the duplicity and irresponsibility of the lords
as well as by the new (though contradictory) tone of Edward's
speeches. In *Richard II,* the shift in our sympathies is brought
about with the least damage to the king's essential character, an
achievement in some measure attributable to Shakespeare's treatment of the queen. As in the other plays, the queen acts as a catalyst whereby our sympathies toward Richard change, only here
she does so alive and part of the action until the last act. Since
she does play an important part in changing our feelings toward
the king, I should like to digress briefly to consider the scenes in
which she appears to see how her attitudes affect our responses.

The scene in which our sympathies are first worked on through
the queen's statements and feelings is II.2, immediately following
Richard's departure for Ireland. The very same Richard who has
demonstrated such absence of feeling and whose ear has been
deaf to anything that does not feed his own ego is suddenly
presented as someone who can be missed, whose well-being can
be feared for, and who is capable of a relationship involving
loyalty, truth, honor, and good faith. Unwittingly we must begin

to feel differently about him. These qualities, it should be noted, are not really incompatible with what we know. If Richard has been frivolous in important scenes of state, it is because that is how he has wanted to be, and if he has not listened to Gaunt, it is because he has not wanted to listen to Gaunt. This scene simply makes us consider him from the viewpoint of someone who honestly loves and needs him. Childless, the queen has only Richard, and his absence can breed only sadness, not children. But the scene also makes clear, as if to counter Marlowe, that relations between the queen and the favorites are good and that homosexuality is not one of Richard's defects. There seems such readiness to associate this particular vice with the abuses of kingship that Bolingbroke makes the assumption himself (or craftily uses it because it is a popular assumption) in reciting to Bushy and Green the crimes for which they must be executed:

> You have in manner with your sinful hours
> Made a divorce betwixt his Queen and him,
> Broke the possession of a royal bed
> And stained the beauty of a fair Queen's cheeks
> With tears drawn from her eyes by your foul wrongs.
> [III.1.11–15]

The Bushy thus attacked we have seen drying the tears of that queen in II.2 and giving her counsel which, if quite inaccurate, suggests a more genuinely compassionate nature than seen among royal favorites, the mutable Spencer and Gaveston included.

It would be easy to say that this scene and the two other scenes involving the queen—the garden scene (III.4) and the farewell scene with Richard (V.1)—are purely personal, that they tell us Richard and his wife have been loving and loyal to one another but that this lies outside the political meaning of the play. But there is, I believe, no distinction between the personal and political in these plays. The personal is the means by which audience emotion attached to the political experience is evoked. If the queen acts as catalyst in transforming our sympathies in Richard's favor, it is the king of England, who never is anything but a person, to whom these sympathies are newly directed.

Mildred Hartsock[18] sees the dilemma of the weak king explicitly stated in the garden scene (III.4). Using a conception introduced by Wilhelm Creizenach and H. T. Price, she calls that scene a *stillstand*, a quiet scene usually lying outside the action, which reflects the underlying issues of a play or which helps the audience change the direction of its sympathies. I agree with Ribner, who suggests in *Patterns in Shakespearean Tragedy* (London: Methuen, 1960), p. 47, that the queen's attitudes actually begin our "change in empathy" toward Richard as early as II.2. But the garden scene, as Miss Hartsock suggests, does set the two images of Richard—both political—in sober contrast to each other: one the political misfit described by the gardener, the other England's true and lawful king. The figure who prompts the queen's anxiety and for whom the gardener will finally plant a "bank of rue" is both misfit and "deputy anointed by the lord." From the garden scene, our conflicting sympathies may confront each other on neutral ground as it were, free from the stress and histrionics of the surrounding action.

But the scene which does the most to draw our sympathies toward Richard is the farewell scene (V.1). That scene at first seems free of political connotations, and indeed would be if only Richard and his queen were included in it. But there is also the overwhelming presence of Northumberland, who arrives in the midst of the sad rituals of farewell to dominate the scene and force the separation of the lovers before they are ready. And Northumberland clearly stands for Bolingbroke, the exponent of the practical Machiavellianism discussed in the opening chapter, though it is difficult not to feel that Bolingbroke would have handled the situation with greater tact. To let the queen continue to be Richard's wife, says Northumberland, "were some love, but little policy" (V.1.84). Like Blanche in *King John*, whose pitiful response to the political dealing in which she is a helpless pawn is the line, "They whirl asunder and dismember me" (*King John* III.1.330), Richard's queen is figuratively dismembered by the ruthless efficiency of a political approach utterly unknown in Richard's reign. Richard's Machiavellianism of the opening scene

18. Mildred Hartsock, "Major Scenes in Minor Key," *SQ*, XXI (1970), 53–61.

was fumbling and ill-planned. Bolingbroke's is the very opposite. The queen is the victim of political change in a world increasingly dominated by the Machiavellian outlook. Thus is her function in the play nothing if not political, and thus does she help provide the emotional climate for our shift in sympathies. With the conclusion of the last meeting between Richard and his queen, our sympathies are as much with the suffering monarch as they were against him at the time of Gaunt's death; and the queen has been second only to Richard himself in bringing the change about.

It is Richard, though, not the queen, who must chiefly evoke both our deep compassion and our guilt. He does so through the cumulative impact of four well-known, much-discussed scenes, all of which have roughly the same kind of emotional effect upon us. The basic subject of these scenes is Richard's unwilling acceptance of his increasing vulnerability, and the tone in all of them is established by the unceasing irony he sees in his condition. In the earlier discussion of *Edward II*, I compare one of these scenes (V.1) with the deposition scene in Marlowe's play from which I feel all take their basic tone. Richard's deposition scene will not be examined again in this context, but it will be considered later in connection with Bolingbroke. In the following pages, I shall concentrate on the other three scenes in the group—Richard upon his return from Ireland (III.2), Richard at Flint Castle (III.3), and Richard at Pomfret (V.5). They add little new to Richard's misfortunes, but they intensify our compassion toward this king to a point which makes the play genuinely tragic.

More perhaps than any scene in the play, with the possible exception of the deposition scene, III.2 has been the subject of critical discussion, and most seem to feel that it continues our earlier image of inadequate monarchy by revealing the far-ranging, excessive self-pity of which Richard is capable. Certainly Richard is articulate in this scene. The weak king as seen by Shakespeare possesses great verbal skill and a rich imagination. But the circumstances of the scene must be carefully identified before our accusations of enfeebling self-pity become too enthusiastic. Despite the bishop's admonitions, it is unreasonable to suppose that Richard has any real resources with which to fight Bolingbroke at this point. Let us not forget his long, arduous

Irish expedition and his disastrous sea voyage back. All we know and learn suggests that the prospect of raising an army now simply does not exist. Those around him know it, and their counsel that he be firm in his determination to fight is best understood as little more than well-meaning reassurance in a situation where any real alternatives have been foreclosed. Bolingbroke has already established his military and even political dominance.

In effect, Richard has already been deposed at the beginning of III.2; both his language and attitudes from this point on suggest not so much self-pity as the realization, arduously but richly prolonged through Richard's fertile sense of irony, that there is no *divinity* that *hedges* a king. If Richard seems to overdo his response, what he is responding to is the crux of all these plays. It is the one point on which author and audience seem fixed in consternation: that this royal figure, whom everyone has been taught all their lives to regard as a divine being quite beyond human necessities and feelings, can be defeated in battle like an ordinary lord, can be outwitted and outplayed as a commander, can be easily stripped of the outward symbols of dominance which were always thought to be part of his physical makeup. A king this fragile imposes the frightening thought that the seeming fortress of the state itself, and hence the safety and well-being of everyone, is fragile. It best represents a kind of audience fixation —seemingly ever to be repeated, never resolved. It represents the political point the audience of the 1590s cannot get past. How can a king not be a king?

> If we be not, show us the hand of God
> That hath dismissed us from our stewardship;
> For well we know no hand of blood and bone
> Can gripe the sacred handle of our scepter
> Unless he do profane, steal, or usurp.
> [III.3.77–81]

Richard here speaks to the audience and for them. It is they who want to "sit upon the ground" and hear "sad stories of the death of Kings" as much as it is Richard who wants to tell them— both responding to the awful reality of his unbelievably swift downfall. But it is that same audience (that same "they") who earlier shared with the lords the desire to put down that infamous inadequacy called the king. They have marched across the countryside with Bolingbroke, have thrown their hats in the air at his appearance—and, what is worse, they have had good reason to do it. They are outraged and helpless at the very forces within themselves and in the king that brought this reality to the fore. The tragic central figure of the weak-king plays, that honorable figure who must suffer, perhaps endlessly, for his own weaknesses and indecisions, is as much audience as monarch. The real impact of the history play is felt by viewers deeply involved with its central problem. Richard is not overdoing his reaction. The audience needs every bit he can provide to help purge them of their own emotions, their extreme fear and pity at the fall of the weak king.

If *Richard II* has a defect as a play, it is that nothing really changes in Richard's responses following III.2. Great emotional vacillation and the endless ironies that his mind produces to make the intolerable situation somehow tolerable characterize all the very memorable scenes that follow. The kingly tone of Richard's lecture to Northumberland at Flint Castle exists against the same basic acknowledgment of the king's total helplessness as does Richard's soliloquy at Pomfret, so that at no point can one say Richard's lines are free of irony—except when he breaks down altogether and openly confesses that helplessness. Sometimes the irony is subtle, as it is at Flint Castle, sometimes open to the point of hysteria, as it is in the deposition scene. But irony it is at all times.

At Flint Castle, Richard's defiant tone simply cannot be taken seriously:

> Yet know my master, God Omnipotent,
> Is mustering in His clouds on our behalf
> Armies of pestilence; . . .
> [III.3.85–87]

Both he and his adversaries are play-acting—as Northumberland crudely reveals by his oversights (failing to refer to Richard as king and later failing to kneel in his presence) and Bolingbroke by the iron quality of his decisions which have already been made and have little to do with what is going on. Skillful as Richard is at his act, he cannot maintain it long. As his sense of helplessness later takes over hysterically at the end of the deposition scene, it does so more philosophically here. First he acquiesces unexpectedly to everything he has vowed to defy. Then: "[To Aumerle] We do debase ourselves, Cousin, do we not,/To look so poorly and to speak so fair?" (III.3.127–28). Richard is more in control of himself here than he was at Barkloughly or will be in the deposition scene, but his basic situation is not different. His comparative calm results from his being between the first rude blow of truth and the later terrible apparition of Northumberland demanding that he read a public "confession" of his crimes. But he is powerless against the inevitability of Bolingbroke's takeover, and he knows it here as well as he ever will.

In Richard's death scene (V.5), much later in the play but quite in harmony with the two scenes just looked at, Shakespeare almost seems to want consciously to correct the impression made by the closing scene of Marlowe's *Edward II*. The final suffering the weak king endures in Shakespeare does not come from outside tormentors as in Marlowe, but from inside, from the "still-breeding thoughts" that endlessly "people" his enclosed world. Since no new experience can enter at Pomfret, these thoughts must be the ever-recurrent, and still unacceptable, ironies of his fall, spun now, as by the spider, into a complex network. Building upon Edward's response to deposition, "Which fills my mind with strange despairing thoughts,/Which thoughts are martyred with endless torments" (*Edward II* V.1.79–80), Shakespeare takes us far into the storehouse of those thoughts, now become a closed society of their own, a "generation" ever increasing its number but never getting any closer to a solution to the problem.

But something like an insight into his condition does appear before Richard's death. Unlike the previous scenes, this one approaches genuine tragedy, not because of Richard's extreme introversion, but because he finally shows some signs of new self-awareness. The king in *Woodstock* is quite consumed by guilt, but he cannot be tragic because he is not conceived in large enough terms. His realization of his crimes is really as paltry as were those crimes themselves. The anonymous author gave whatever tragic quality he had to the character of plain Thomas. King Edward II learns nothing, quite possibly because Marlowe was unsure just what it was he needed to learn. Faced with the prospect of expanding the introspection of Edward's deposition scene, Marlowe would turn to King Edward's murderers with gratitude. But Richard does learn. Almost lost in a characteristically extended figure, Richard confesses that he wasted time. Nothing more. And nothing more is needed, because, boiled down, that is most of what the crimes of the weak king come to. Realization of the nature of time is what brings *Richard II* to the edge of tragedy:

> And here have I the daintiness of ear
> To check time broke in a disordered string,
> But for the concord of my state and time
> Had not an ear to hear my true time broke.
> I wasted time, and now doth time waste me.
> [V.5.45–49]

Had he his reign to live again, he would try not to waste time. There is no suggestion of specific revision in his kingship, but he would think about time in its two basic senses: the one suggesting order, the other suggesting imminent decay. The insight may be slight. Certainly it is by comparison with the insights in *Lear*. But it is enough to distinguish this play from all the other plays considered here.

But even at his moment of insight Richard falls back upon the ironies of his downfall.

> But my time
> Runs posting on in Bolingbroke's proud joy
> While I stand fooling here, his Jack-o'-the-clock.
> [V.5.58–60]

Self-awareness has only been glanced at. In his final scene, he is still chiefly what he has been since III.2. And the emphasis is not so much on self-pity and inaction as on a fixed inability to escape the self-contradicting conception of the *deposed king*, an inability shared by those watching the play. In effect, each scene in which Richard appears from III.2 on represents the same image: the pathetic fall of the weak king. Whatever his faults before, in the end he arouses our compassion and our sense of guilt at having hated him earlier makes us vindictive toward his enemies. But we must still acknowledge that he has been terribly weak as a monarch and probably would always be.

Bolingbroke

The shadowy figure of the play, as everyone agrees, is Bolingbroke. While recent critics have come to closer agreement in seeing Richard roughly as I have, as a figure toward whom our divided sympathies reflect strong ambivalence toward the prescription that a subject be loyal to corrupt or incompetent monarchy, Bolingbroke's role has promoted no such agreement. He is generally identified as a Machiavel of sorts, but whether that be for good or for evil as far as England is concerned, we seem no farther ahead than Tillyard. As in Tillyard, Bolingbroke is still a bundle of contradictions: a strong, silent, competent, blackhearted, brutal usurper whose desperately needed accession was the cause of nearly a century of division and bloodshed. Any consideration of him tends to thus overwhelm and confuse. Yet he is also a believable, consistent character. Wilbur Sanders has come closest to identifying what Bolingbroke stands for. Although Richard's history suggests to Sanders that "a tolerable sore is better than . . . a dangerous remedy," there is underlying the whole play the sense of "a kind of historical necessity against which even the best type of conservatism is utterly powerless— the necessity is called Bolingbroke."[19]

Bolingbroke's Machiavellianism has been viewed in recent years across a broad spectrum, ranging from Brents Stirling's description of a calculating opportunist whose clearly conceived assault upon the crown is implicitly evident from his opening lines, to the recent contention of A. L. French that Bolingbroke never intends to depose Richard and never does depose him, but suddenly finds himself unwillingly and unwittingly ensconced

19. *The Dramatist and the Received Idea*, p. 157.

upon the throne of England.[20] One thing he is not, everyone seems to agree. He is not a stage Machiavel of the Richard III– Young Mortimer stripe. Any similarity with that figure exists only in his relation to the king, not at all in his own personality or even deeper motives. Yet there also seems to be unanimity on the fact of the Machiavellianism itself. Bolingbroke's is a shrewd, newly conceived approach to the old problem of how to become king of the hill and hold that position. He is not legal successor, he does get the throne, and his motives in getting there are success- fully hidden. Above all, he does a superb job of obeying the Machiavellian axiom that the greatest skill a politician can have is the knoweldge of how to wait, to observe what is going on, and either to strike at the proper time or at least to be available when that time arrives.

I share the view of those who feel Bolingbroke is basically an active figure who is most instrumental in bringing about his own success. Stirling is correct in saying that what the seeming restraint in Bolingbroke's ambition indicates "is that opportunism, of which he becomes the living symbol, is essentially a tacit vice: that although the opportunist is aware in a sense of the ends to which his means commit him, he relies on events, not upon declarations, to clarify his purposes."[21] While Shakespeare and his audience may be undecided about the rightness or wrong- ness of those purposes, the purposes themselves are clearly iden- tified in the play and have been somewhat mispresented by recent critics such as French. Stirling finds Bolingbroke's propensity to majesty evident even in the opening scene, and while that can be no more than an impression, it seems true. Bolingbroke is identifiably a usurper from the point of his arrival back in Eng- land. From II.3 on, he is treated as *de facto* king of England by almost everyone. And it is as *de facto* king that he speaks to others. The tone, for example, of his response to the somewhat impertinent Hotspur at their first meeting is nothing if not regal:

> I thank thee, gentle Percy, and be sure
> I count myself in nothing else so happy

20. Brents Stirling, "Bolingbroke's 'Decision,'" *SQ*, II (1951), 27–34; A. L. French, "Who Deposed Richard the Second?" *EIC*, XVII (1967), 411–33.
21. Stirling, p. 30.

> As in a soul remembering my good friends.
> And as my fortune ripens with thy love,
> It shall be still thy true love's recompense.
> My heart this covenant makes, my hand thus seals it.
>   [II.3.45–50]

All that is needed is the royal *we* to complete the effect. Even without it, Bolingbroke's graciousness in these lines is that which a king accords a subject.

Bolingbroke increasingly assumes the royal manner as the play progresses. Certainly York feels as much and obviously fears his nephew. York was earlier compared with Marlowe's Earl of Kent and plain Thomas in the anonymous play as barometers of audience sympathy for or against the king; when York berates Richard for seizing Gaunt's lands, for example, he closely parallels Kent and Woodstock. But in II.3 a new element enters: that of expediency. York is suddenly concerned for his safety. He starts by chastising Bolingbroke as he earlier chastised Richard:

> Grace me no grace, nor uncle me no uncle:
> I am no traitor's uncle, and that word "grace"
> In an ungracious mouth is but profane.
> Why have those banished and forbidden legs
> Dared once to touch a dust of England's ground?
>   [II.3.87–91]

And even Bolingbroke's standard disclaimer that he seeks only his inheritance leaves York unshaken as to the treasonable nature of his march across England. But suddenly York gives way—in a fashion most unlike the barometric shifts of Kent in *Edward II*. York's reasons are pragmatic. He lacks arms and men:

> Well, well, I see the issue of these arms.
> I cannot mend it, I must needs confess,
> Because my power is weak and all ill left.
>   [II.3.152–54]

But more, he is intimidated by Bolingbroke's iron fist under the velvet glove.

When Bolingbroke intends that something be done without question, somehow everyone, especially his victims, knows his intent before he makes it explicit—and knows he had better obey. Bolingbroke rarely says much, but his presence alone, dignified and seemingly forbearing, has the power to break men's wills. York simply capitulates under the subtle pressure of Bolingbroke's manner:

> *Bolingbroke.* But we must win your Grace to go with us
> To Bristol Castle, . . .
> . . . .
> *York.* It may be I will go with you. But yet I'll pause,
> For I am loath to break our country's laws.
> Nor friends nor foes, to me welcome you are.
> Things past redress are now with me past care.
> [II.3.163–64, 168–71]

Bolingbroke needs York at Bristol Castle, and there is no doubt that York will go to Bristol Castle. Lords demanding only an inheritance do not make such demands of their peers. Nor do lords who have no royal ambitions normally take upon themselves the public execution of royal favorites. Gaveston, it will be remembered, is surreptitiously murdered by a conspiracy in which the guilt is shared. Bolingbroke's conduct in the executions of Bushy and Green can only suggest royal prerogative.

Bolingbroke's kingly designs and manner are most evident in III.3, at Flint. Northumberland's blunder in failing to refer to Richard as king tells us something about Northumberland but more about Bolingbroke. The omission is the result of assumptions Northumberland has come to make as a result of his association with Bolingbroke, who is by no means an incidental observer here. When Bolingbroke speaks at length in this scene, he unwittingly gives himself away, this time by protesting too much the limit to his ambition:

> Henry Bolingbroke
> On both his knees doth kiss King Richard's hand
> And sends allegiance and true faith of heart
> To his most royal person. . . .
> [III.3.35–38]

Need Bolingbroke kneel "on *both* his knees"? Northumberland

neglected to kneel altogether. Simply kneeling would be enough
to suggest subservience, but both knees can only indicate hypocrisy. Ironically, these lines, which contain the clearest suggestion
so far of Machiavellian deceit, are frequently quoted to show
that Bolingbroke has no ambitions for the throne. Throughout this
scene, Northumberland and others hop to Bolingbroke's com-
mands, even Richard finally. That Bolingbroke is *de facto* king
is a foregone conclusion, and it is not a situation he has backed
into. It seems correct to infer that quietly he has engineered everything that has happened thus far.

The brief episode opening IV.1, immediately preceding Richard's deposition, contributes subtly to the dilemma created by
Bolingbroke's leap for power. In it, Bagot and Aumerle accuse
and assail each other much as did Bolingbroke and Norfolk at the
opening of the play. There is no indication that either side is
right, though Aumerle (like Norfolk earlier) probably is guilty
as accused of complicity in the murder of Gloucester. But the
point made by the episode is that Bolingbroke's word is law, and
that there can be no recourse to violence, as there was earlier.
Bolingbroke will "repeal" Norfolk and bring the whole matter
under review before the opponents can vent their spleen in combat which can only bring division to the kingdom. Richard in Act
I also made a decision to forbid combat, but at the wrong time.
Bolingbroke here knows how and when to take his stand. But
somewhere in the midst of all this must come the realization that
Bolingbroke is not king. Bolingbroke is behaving every inch a
king while the question is ostensibly still unsettled. It is, of course,
not really unsettled. He is quite willing here (IV.1.113) to crown
himself because he is already as much *de facto* king as he will be
when Richard openly abdicates later in the scene. And he has
arrived at this position by a carefully executed assault upon the
crown. But the bishop of Carlisle's sudden appeal to a divine
sanction everyone else has safely overlooked unnerves Bolingbroke and directly precipitates the deposition ritual which follows.
And the swift arrest of Carlisle suggests Machiavellianism in its
more ruthless form—one which Bolingbroke uses sparingly, but
uses nevertheless. Northumberland speaks the lines, but again no
more than as Bolingbroke's agent: "Well have you argued, sir,

and for your pains,/Of Capital treason we arrest you here" (IV.1. 150–51).

The deposition scene itself is a public ritual, a state function attended as part of their official responsibilities by all the important lords of the realm, both secular and ecclesiastical. Protocol is intended to govern it, and everything that is to happen bears an official stamp. Richard's assigned function is to abdicate in almost as formal a rite as that in which he was crowned. His famous tantrum, then, is comparable to such a tantrum at a coronation itself. Richard acts to disrupt a convocation the likes of which he has presided over throughout his reign. His performance is highly emotional and expressed in very personal terms, but it is hardly the adolescent outburst Bolingbroke and some of its critics try to make it. It is essentially a political outburst in which the deposed king focuses on the intolerable realities of a situation the usurper seeks to obscure. The deeply personal, brilliantly imaginative ironies of Richard's complaint figuratively keep him in the ring with Bolingbroke. So smooth has this takeover been, wrought with such obvious "political" mastery that even Carlisle's impassioned recitation of Tudor divine-king doctrine has only slightly defaced Bolingbroke's brilliant armor. But while Carlisle's speech does not lack spontaneity, its very length, its formal clichés, and its homiletic tone make it far less affecting than the intensely human image of fallen monarch Richard creates. Richard speaks with an abandon which make his remarks unexpectedly piercing and aggressive.

Earlier, I indicated that something like brainwashing is attempted on Richard and Edward. This is true insofar as each man ultimately yields voluntarily to a pressure exerted from within rather than from without. The tragic potential of both lies in their awareness of the essential, sinful humanity beneath the pomp, and this more than anything else makes the physical tortures which might be necessary for lesser men unnecessary here. But Edward yields in a private scene—a scene which we might well imagine for Richard as one of perhaps several earlier sessions with an interrogator resulting in York's happy news that Richard "with willing soul, Adopts thee heir" (IV.1.108–109). We see here how "willing." The brainwashing is only partially successful

because Richard refuses to follow the script. He directly accuses
and attacks Bolingbroke in a situation where form, ritual, and
protocol absolutely prohibit such expression—as Richard knows
better than anyone. He alone is willing—now without the assistance of Divine Providence—to tear the mask from the usurper's
face: "Here, cousin, seize the crown" (IV.1.181). Bolingbroke's
mask is infinitely clever because its features show only what Bolingbroke is anyway—a highly competent, strong, attractive, but
also wily lord, with all the earmarks of kingship. By being himself,
but focusing his attention at all times on the crown, Bolingbroke
has moved toward it in unbroken line—unbroken, that is, until
Richard, who is not given to brevity, identifies briefly and pointedly what Bolingbroke has been doing. Richard's chief concern,
of course, is with himself, and that awful apparition of self that
he sees finally breaks his own will. But at all times he keeps a
spotlight shining on the fact that he is being forcefully deposed:

> K. Rich. Mine eyes are full of tears, I cannot see
> And yet salt water blinds them not so much
> But they can see a sort of traitors here.
> . . . .
> North. My lord—
> K. Rich. No lord of thine, thou haught insulting man,
> Nor no man's lord. I have no name, no title,
> No, not that name was given me at the font,
> But 'tis usurped.
>   [IV.1.244–46, 253–57]

Clumsy Northumberland, who has a penchant for doing the
wrong thing, pulls out the confessions just when it is abundantly
clear that Richard will have no part in the rituals of abdication.
Thus Bolingbroke must call Northumberland off, but he does so
less from sympathy than from fear that, out of control, Richard
may mar an otherwise perfect *coup*. Bolingbroke's single concern
now is to get Richard peacefully back to his cell, to which end he
helps with Richard's imagery over the broken mirror: "The shadow
of your sorrow hath destroyed/The shadow of your face" (IV.1.
292–93). But Richard, far quicker, turns Bolingbroke's mock-
understanding into a mockery of itself:

> Say that again.
> The shadow of my sorrow! Ha! Let's see.
> 'Tis very true, my grief lies all within.
>
> . . . .
>   I thank thee, King,
> For thy great bounty, that not only givest
> Me cause to wail, but teachest me the way
> How to lament the cause.
>   [IV.1.292–95, 299–302]

Wit, however, was never Bolingbroke's weapon. Rather, he achieves his ends through sheer power. This scene closes, like Bolingbroke's others, with a ruthless, irrevocable command which bears little relation to the subject being discussed but tells us clearly how things are in the new order. And it burgeons suddenly and brutally out of his seeming compassion:

K. Rich.	I'll beg one boon,
	And then be gone and trouble you no more.
	Shall I obtain it?
Boling.	Name it, fair Cousin.
K. Rich.	"Fair Cousin"? I am greater than a king.
	For when I was a king, my flatterers
	Were then but subjects. Being now a subject,
	I have a King here to my flatterer.
	Being so great, I have no need to beg.
Boling.	Yet ask.
K. Rich.	And shall I have?
Boling.	You shall.
K. Rich.	Then give me leave to go.
Boling.	Whither?
K. Rich.	Whither you will, so I were from your sights.
Boling.	Go, some of you convey him to the Tower.
K. Rich.	Oh, good! Convey? Conveyers are you
	That rise thus nimbly by a true king's fall.

                                       [IV.1.302–18]

Richard is genuinely delighted by this flash of iron under the velvet, for it reveals, as nothing else has, that he has won this little confrontation.

Henry Bolingbroke has indeed seized the crown, and only Richard has the skill and courage to tell him so to his face. But the ambition which Bolingbroke represents is not thereby made incontrovertibly an evil one. The play suggests no final opinion as to whether he was right or wrong in doing what he did. And that he was a "tragic necessity," as Sanders claims, the play only faintly intimates. Bolingbroke's very silence may indicate more than his Machiavellianism. It may also reveal the genuine uncertainty of author and audience over just how politically necessary Bolingbroke is. His silence may be our silence over his motives and methods. He is spared a true characterization because the author is uncertain what kind of character to give him. He obviously has qualities of leadership Richard lacks, but whether those qualities are enough to justify the deposing of a weak king is not decided in this play.

There is no joy that Bolingbroke has become king, and there is great dismay that Richard is deposed. But just as Shakespeare has Richard reveal Bolingbroke for what he is in Act IV, Shakespeare revealed Richard for what he was in Act I. There is no ameliorating Richard's flippant tone, his acutely self-centered irresponsibility, or his complete indifference to the land which he fondles lovingly in III.2 but had rented to the highest bidder a few scenes earlier. The contradictions are all there and the divided response as deeply felt as it can get in these plays. But *Richard II* ends in question: What about Bolingbroke? The final image is not of a dying king but of a worried, uncertain usurper, whose abilities are undeniable but whose actions are morally unresolved. And the unresolved question is not Bolingbroke himself so much as it is the Machiavellianism for which he stands— the tempered, respectable Machiavellianism which had come to underlie the *modus operandi* of political life in the 1590s and which the "history plays" are a response to just as they are a response to the weak king.

The plays examined in the remaining pages of this study deal first one way then another with that new Machiavellianism, both in its effect upon the image of the weak king and in its ultimate, grudging acceptability to the popular audience of that day. *Richard II*, through Bolingbroke, shows only the surface. *Henry*

VI, in violent opposition, and *King John,* in less than violent opposition, reflect a public reacting to and seeking to come to terms
with a political philosophy which was officially anathema but, in
terms of everyday, practical government and political maneuver,
was already routine.

The form which links *Woodstock, Edward II,* and *Richard II*
is an articulation of public reaction to the burden of monarchy.
In the balance was the system itself, though it is doubtful that
either playwright or audience would have acknowledged or
even been aware of it. The king must be divine, the king will be
man; as the two are mutually exclusive, the two halves of each
play tend to cancel one another out. The other plays are more
complex in their construction, and this may be because they are
concerned with the relationship between the weak-king syndrome
and other major political problems of the day—notably the new
Machiavellianism. Thus, whereas the outline of the three plays
just discussed seems reasonably clearcut—the human king of the
first part countered by the martyred king of the second—that of
those which follow seems confused. We see a king vacillating
between weak and strong images almost from scene to scene, and
the plays have the extremely detailed effect of a medieval tapestry.
Nevertheless the motive force seems the same throughout: the
inevitable frustrations and contradictions associated with the royal
image. The plays to follow suggest a public grappling with the
problem rather than just a response.

III *The Meek King*

Shakespeare's three parts of *Henry VI*,[1] which are of course among his first plays, stretch to its limits the dilemma over whether an inadequate monarch ought to be deposed. For Henry's inadequacies result in part not from his desire for sensual pleasures but from his love for his fellow man and his desire to do good in the

1. For those who have not read these plays recently, the following brief summary may facilitate the reading of this chapter.

King Henry VI is in trouble from the start of his reign. Having become king as an infant following the untimely death of his legendary hero father, Henry V, he is thrust into the middle of several massive political conflicts before reaching an age when he might have even the slightest awareness of his kingly responsibilities, and he never knows sufficient peace to attempt to stabilize his tottering kingdom. The central lordly personages of the three plays are all at some time during the roughly forty years covered by the plays (1422–61) committed to a struggle for power which ultimately brings about the downfall of each. Duke Humphrey, Henry's protector, tries vainly to keep order, but he is ensnared in a plot laid for him by his old enemy Cardinal Beaufort and by the ambitious Queen Margaret. They are assisted by the duke of Suffolk, Margaret's lover, who had earlier won Margaret ostensibly for King Henry but really for himself. But chief among the conflicts are those known as the Wars of the Roses, a simple and direct account of which is A. L. Rowse, *Bosworth Field* (Garden City, N.Y.: Doubleday, 1966). These conflicts pit the House of Lancaster—which includes the unwilling, pacifistic king and his warlike queen, aided by a variety of noblemen (Somerset and Clifford the most important)—against the House of York, which includes the duke of York and his three sons (among them the deformed, fierce young Richard, years later to become the notorious Richard III). The Yorkists are ably supported by the powerful earl of Warwick and a large assembly of allies. York claims the throne by right of legitimate succession, and since that claim goes directly back to Bolingbroke's deposing of Richard II, even the truth-loving king comes to have doubts about his legitimacy; these doubts give sufficient fuel to the rebellion to result, after many long, see-sawing battles, in victory for the Yorkist cause. Though York never becomes king, having earlier been captured and ruthlessly murdered by Queen Margaret and Clifford, York's oldest son is crowned King Edward IV. Even that victory does not settle the issue, though, for when Warwick changes sides because he feels betrayed by King Edward, King Henry temporarily regains his throne. But in the end Edward is triumphant, and Henry (among others) is murdered by the bloody Richard, now duke of Gloucester, who keeps the audience informed throughout of his own plans to get the crown.

76

world. He has other failings to be sure—a measure of vindictiveness and a willingness at times docilely to be led by others—but his downfall results as much from his adherence in political life to traditional Christian virtues as it does to those shortcomings. Henry's experience in these plays has suggested to many that adherence to those traditional virtues is probably as much an invitation to political disintegration as excessive desire for sensual pleasures. But there is also more than a suggestion in these early works that given the chance Henry could have been successful, in spite of his ordinary human weaknesses, and that the troubles of his kingdom really result from the nobility's crude but exclusive acceptance of deceit and violence as their political equipment. While it is clear that the king's failure results in part from his Christian nature, it is equally clear that only the virtues associated with that nature could have saved the country from the disaster it experiences in these plays. The political evil in these plays is not so much the king's weakness as the attempts to appear strong on the part of those around him. The dilemma might now read: Should a weak but Christian king be deposed by a seemingly strong but Machiavellian nobility? Although the answer implicit in these plays may appear to be no, neither Henry's personal failings nor the seeming practical ineffectiveness of Christian leadership are glossed over. In the last analysis, a dilemma similar to the one which underlies the plays previously looked at underlies Shakespeare's *Henry VI*.

Over the past thirty years, though two seemingly opposed outlooks toward the *Henry VI* plays have been predominant, that opposition has been more over attitudes toward the nature and purpose of historical drama in the late sixteenth century than over the nature of the plays themselves. The apparent gulf that separates the views of E. M. W. Tillyard and Jan Kott basically concerns whether or not Shakespeare's history plays are part of a providential view of English history in the fifteenth and early sixteenth centuries. Tillyard's work in the forties long convinced most critics of the providential view, even in the face of numerous passages in the plays suggesting that man alone, and not Divine Providence, is the perpetrator of the events in them. More recently, Kott's view that what is represented in all the history plays is savage and corrupt man revealing his nature in the chaotic world of power politics has gained support. The difference between the two views, then, depends chiefly on whether or not one accepts or rejects the providential view.

The most influential single essay on the plays in the 1960s—J. P. Brockbank's "The Frame of Disorder—'Henry VI' "[2]—in effect fuses the two theories. With imagination and verve, but less than complete clarity, Brockbank talks about the political disintegration in parts 2 and 3, which focus on the fall of Humphrey, duke of Gloucester, and its anarchic results. But though Brockbank's emphasis is on the shape of governmental chaos, he adheres in some measure to Tillyard's view. England is being punished for her sins. The providence involved may be seen in nothing more than the presence of "governmental restraints and authority," but it operates from above to instruct men of their moral obligations in political life as well as on the hierarchical patterns they must observe. What Brockbank calls the "Machiavellian idea," which makes catastrophe "the consequence of weakness" is suggested in the plays but is countered by "the sacrificial idea" which makes it "the consequence of sin." In short, Tillyard's Divine Providence prevails.

Nevertheless, I suspect Brockbank has been more influential in working against Tillyard's approach than he may have intended. He calls the plays' contending nobility "murderous automatons whose reactions are predictable in terms of certain quasi-Hobbesian assumptions about human nature: when argument fails men resort to force: when an oath is inconvenient they break it: their power challenged they retort with violence: their power subdued they resort to lies, murder or suicide: their honor impugned they look for revenge: their enemies at their mercy, they torture and kill."[3] This is a picture of a human jungle which no kind of rationale about Divine Providence can easily dispel.

When Brockbank speaks of the "Machiavellian idea" that catastrophe is "the consequence of weakness," the weakness he refers to is the king's, and its form is the preachment and practice

2. J. P. Brockbank, "The Frame of Disorder—'Henry VI,' " *Stratford-Upon-Avon Studies 3* (London: Edward Arnold, 1961), pp. 73–100.
3. *Ibid.*, p. 94.

of Christian virtue. Machiavelli himself, as it happens, describes this kind of weakness quite explicitly:

> Our religion has given more glory to humble and contemplative men than to active ones. It has, besides, taught that the highest good consists in humility, lowliness and contempt for human things. . . . If our religion does ask that you possess some courage, it prefers that you be ready to suffer rather than to do a courageous act. It seems, then, that this way of life has made the world feeble, and given it over as a prey to the wicked, who are able to control it in security, since the generality of man, in order to go to Heaven, think more of enduring injuries than in defending themselves against them.[4]

This description not only fits Henry VI as though the Florentine had Shakespeare's king in mind; it is a theme echoed by other characters in the trilogy and (sometimes unwittingly) by many recent critics. To Richard of York he is "feeble Henry," "bookish," possessing "church-like humors." To Queen Margaret and Clifford he is timid, an incorrigible appeaser. To twentieth-century commentators he is "pious, amiable, and ineffective," "wanting in the public virtues," a "sort of weak, self-centered ruler," or even an "affected aristocrat" whose "flat, fatuous speech" (on the molehill) and sententious attitudes suggest that Richard of Gloucester "is almost justified in getting rid of such a bore."[5] At best he is considered a decent sort, occasionally gifted in his perceptions but utterly unfit to rule; at worst, as much an enemy to England in his faint-hearted humility as is Richard in his ruthless ambition. These remarks suggest a view of political effectiveness on the part of most important characters in the trilogy, and even on the part of many of its interpreters, which can, in the general sense discussed in the opening chapter here, be called Machiavellian.

4. From Machiavelli's *Discourses on Livy*, II, in *The Prince and Other Works*, trans. by Allan H. Gilbert (Chicago: Packard and Co., 1941), p. 295.

5. Quotes are, respectively, from J. A. R. Marriott, *English History in Shakespeare* (London: Chapman and Hall, 1918), p. 186; Irving Ribner, *The English History Play in the Age of Shakespeare* (New York: Barnes & Noble, 1965), p. 110; M. M. Reese, *The Cease of Majesty* (New York: St. Martin's Press, 1961), p. 167; and H. M. Richmond, *Shakespeare's Political Plays* (New York: Random House, 1967), pp. 50, 57.

In considering the Machiavellian influence in *Henry VI* the ambivalence, or "dualism," which Felix Raab, in *The English Face of Machiavelli*, finds characteristic of response to Machiavelli in the age is extremely important. Political leaders were victims of a kind of double-think whereby they sincerely believed themselves true and devout Christians at the same time that they felt increasingly justified in ignoring Christian precepts in political dealings. What once might have been considered hypocrisy was coming to be thought of as *policy*. The anti-religious attitudes of *The Prince* might be vehemently rejected, but methods of behavior suggested there eagerly adopted. Men who sought to apply Machiavellian practices in political life, while personally remaining sincere men of faith, dominated government offices of the 1580s and 1590s and as a class were the likeliest models for the majority of characters in the history plays. And while in some of these plays their Machiavellianism might be of minor importance, in *Henry VI* it is of fundamental importance.

Throughout the three parts of *Henry VI* there are the stage Machiavels, of course, whose attitude toward Christian morality, it may fairly be said, is knowingly and basely hypocritical. Aside from Richard, there is Joan la Pucelle and her replacement Margaret of Anjou, as well as Margaret's English allies Suffolk and Beaufort. And of course, Jack Cade. They are villains, and if the world of *Henry VI* were clear of them, it ought to be a better world. Ought to be, but would it be? Leaving aside the minor French figures of Part 1 (they are villains simply because they are French), what of the duke of York and his sons Edward and George; what of Warwick and the Salisbury of Part 2; what of Clifford and Oxford; what of the Somersets and Buckingham; of Vernon, Basset, Northumberland, and Hastings; what of Dame Eleanor (Humphrey's wife)? Which of these is not at some time motivated by the lust for political advancement to employ nearly any form of deceit or violent action to attain it? Yet these figures do not seem Machiavels, as do those mentioned earlier. The more important ones confess their true motives in soliloquy, but for the most part they only occasionally reveal what they are and what they are really after. But when they do, those motives are unmistakable, and the incidents involved give us glimpses, however brief, of just how ruthless a world this is. Early in Part 2, Somerset and Buckingham exchange the following comments on Duke Humphrey:

> *Som.* Cousin of Buckingham, though Humphrey's pride
> And greatness of his place be grief to us,
> Yet let us watch the haughty Cardinal.
> His insolence is more intolerable
> Than all the princes in the land beside,
> If Gloucester be displaced, he'll be Protector.
> *Buck.* Or thou or I, Somerset, will be Protector,
> Despite Duke Humphrey or the Cardinal.
>   [*2 Henry VI* I.172–79]

Buckingham's ambition is obvious enough, but note Somerset's "let us watch." The key to all Machiavellian design is patience, the knowing when to act. Other instances may be added: York's maneuvers in the attack on Duke Humphrey in Part 2, Clarence's switching of sides in Part 3. For the most part the nobles speak and act like moral men, but their motives are anything but moral. All scheme endlessly to achieve a political invulnerability which proves most elusive. Some succeed better than others, as the success of young Richard and the failure of his father attest. York honors an oath too long and thus is caught in Margaret's trap. His son makes clear he would have no qualms about breaking an oath. Warwick at one time seeks to save his own skin. Young Richard is all brutal courage in battle. So, the lesson seems to state, the better the Machiavel, the more cunning and swift in deceit and violence, the better the chances of success.

Out of the lives and actions of the contending nobility in *Henry VI* there emerges something like a perverse moral code. This code is hardly very complete as a working philosophy, but it is the standard by which most of the peers (and some recent critics as well) judge the king's effectiveness. And that it is a Machiavellian code is indicated as follows. The chief overriding good is the ability to take, and retain, power—and only vaguely and at times does this good have anything to do with unifying the nation. To achieve this good, it seems agreed by the contending nobility, one must be patient, alert, swift in action, courageous, physically strong, and ruthless. One must use deceit with great skill, since it is the chief tool at one's disposal, and one must use violence, at the right time, since it is the only type of activity which gets results. Following from this, the bad is indifference to the taking and retaining of power and, of crucial importance as far as Henry is concerned, the absence of deceit and lack of inclination to violent action. One must also be convinced that others are motivated by the same goals and are using the same methods. No man should be trusted, and the prospect of sudden violence from the outside must always be guarded against. Significantly, retaining power one already has (inherited or seized) requires the same skills as taking it. When York says he is better suited to wear the crown than Henry, he means that he would be able to hold it more securely by the means indicated above. He is not referring to the good deeds he would do as king or to the general welfare of his people except insofar as a stable monarchy might improve their lot. That word *stable* is the one usually used today, and it means planted so firmly at the top of the hill that one cannot be pushed off. But opponents will be constantly trying—backhandedly and frontally—and one can hold his position only by being both more devious than his opponents and a warrior of greater prowess. And by such a standard, of course, York is indeed far better suited to the throne than Henry. One of York's sons, though, is still better suited.

By the Machiavellian standards which govern almost everyone else in the play, Henry is surely the most wretched king in "Christendom." Not only does he fail to use the techniques presumed indispensable for retaining power, he also fails to exploit that ancient sense of a divinity that hedges a king. Such divinity is viewed as so much window dressing by the Machiavels, but useful window dressing in creating the illusion of invulnerability which clearly assists in the actual achievement of that invulnerability. Henry is no showman. He simply cannot and will not behave as though he were invulnerable when he is not. At times, he makes a feeble effort to be a real king, but always that effort is both ineffective and short-lived. Were pity allowed, he might be pitied.

But pity by others might reveal weakness on the part of the one doing the pitying, and so must be avoided—at least according to the code. All Henry wishes is "a heart untainted" (*2 Henry VI* III.2.232), and this, the plays protest with savage irony, will never do.

Henry's first bad move—and from a Machiavellian point of view the most damaging—is inheriting the throne as an infant. Infants are notoriously poor at deceit and violence. What saves Henry at all throughout the greater portion of Part 1 is that an older breed of nobleman still is in command—a breed who either eschews or does not know the newer political techniques. To these men the old chivalric myths and theories about kingly divinity are still meaningfully related to how one behaves politically. Brave Talbot possesses physical prowess, certainly, and as we see in his encounter with the countess of Auvergne is not without craft. All his talents, however, are used to benefit king and country. He is a well-oiled, smooth-functioning part of a divinely conceived hierarchical machine and is unable to comprehend anything other than the machine and his function in it. Humphrey of Gloucester is more sophisticated and gifted in intellectual terms we shall shortly consider, but he, too, genuinely devoted to king and country, thoroughly accepts his place in the hierarchical framework.

The Machiavels are around from the start, though. In England there are Beaufort and the participants in the Temple Garden debate, where "law" and "right" are first seen as only veneers of a raw, crude power-rivalry. By the time Henry is old enough to tell the time of day, some of the Machiavels are well-entrenched and others will be shortly. Exeter seeks to explain their rise by Henry's youth—"'Tis much when sceptres are in children's hands" (*1 Henry VI* IV.1.192)—but there is no reason to suggest a grown Henry might have countered their rise except by using their same Machiavellian methods: that is, by being one of them. The heroic non-Machiavels Talbot and Duke Humphrey are, after all, both crushed by the new politicians.

Henry early proves ill-suited to his role. The qualities of the true Machiavel may be learned, but Henry shows little aptitude. In his first appearance he foolishly believes Beaufort's assurances that Beaufort will cease his attacks on Duke Humphrey. Then he restores to Richard Plantagenet his land and title of duke of York, which the family had been deprived of since Henry V executed York's father for high treason. Both actions mark Henry as exceedingly gullible, a pathetically easy mark for a usurper's aim. And indeed he would be, if it could be determined who would be the usurper. Far from quickly removing Henry from his throne, the Wars of the Roses keep him on it for an unbearably long time.

The gesture in which Henry fails most evidently to show any promise as a "politician" is his random selection of a red rose in Part 1 IV.1 to point out the folly of the developing feud. Its effect is precisely the opposite of what he intends. He is suddenly committed to one faction in a quarrel the simplest Machiavellian king would shrewdly remain apart from—and further, as king, he must willy-nilly be leader of that faction. His reasons for selecting the red rose mean nothing to his listeners, since they are convinced men in such circumstances never speak what they mean. To them, Henry has simply blundered by showing his hand at the wrong time and perhaps by choosing the wrong side. Finally, Henry allows himself to succumb to Suffolk's descriptions of Margaret, revealing a weakness no capable monarch would ever disclose in such a manner. But, then, by this time, no one really considers him capable.

From a Machiavellian perspective, Henry's crucial mistake is in "allowing" Duke Humphrey's condemnation and murder by his enemies in Part 2. If youth and inexperience are unavoidable, then at the very least he must follow and protect the best advisors he has. And Humphrey, though no Machiavel himself, is alert and experienced enough to keep Henry from harm. The trouble is, Henry apparently cannot keep Humphrey from harm, and has been roundly condemned for it since. His Machiavellian options would have been many. Following reports of Dame Eleanor's treason, he could have feigned readiness to see Humphrey imprisoned but worked behind the scenes to obtain his release and, most important, Suffolk's downfall. Surely a king should be strong enough for that. Suffolk ultimately falls on the strength of Henry's anger. Why could Henry have not moved against him sooner?

Why could he not handle his power-seeking French queen in the manner of his ancestor Henry II, whose Eleanor spent most of her conniving days in prison? His failure to do these things is the surest evidence of his over-all incompetence, by Machiavellian standards.

Part 3, then, presents the inevitable fate of kings who will not outwit and/or overpower their enemies. In dismay they must seek withdrawal from the active life, yielding power to the faction strong enough to win it. Henry becomes contemptible to many in cravenly disinheriting his own son before York's threats. He does not even rage, as Edward II and Richard II rage, but yields mouse-like to his enemies' demands before stealing away from the wrath of his shrill queen. Having lost his kingly authority, he is refused permission by Margaret and Clifford to participate in the verbal confrontations that *pro forma* precede battles and is relegated to sit dunce-like on a molehill as alarums sound, fathers slaughter sons, and sons slaughter fathers. And while many (though not all) critics have praised the substance and tone of his remarks upon that occasion, those remarks are seen as at best a pastoral vision of an other-worldly life which we all may wish for but know can never be. In effect, what Henry says is considered by most as politically irrelevant—as Henry himself is looked upon as irrelevant by Margaret, Clifford, York, and Warwick.

Shakespeare's irony in his treatment of the relations between Henry and his nobility has been recognized by surprisingly few commentators. Not that anyone actually admires the contending barons; but most critics reject Henry outright as a political leader, and in terms of the alternatives the play represents, they unwittingly accept the barons' methods when they reject Henry. No mid-point or compromise, such as is implicit in *King John* and *Henry V*, is suggested anywhere in the *Henry VI* trilogy. If the actions of the king are evaluated by the Machiavellian standard discussed here, then its only successful character is its arch-villain, and it is against young Richard that all other characters should be measured. If we say Henry is "bad" because he is utterly without the ability to govern by force or guile, and the lords have their "weaker moments" because they fail to be sufficiently patient, alert, or self-centered, then we must call Richard, who is all force and guile and who has no weaker moment, "good."

Richard, the chief stage-Machiavel in the *Henry VI* plays, is nothing more than an extension of the watered, inconsistent Machiavellianism of the other nobles—notably his father and his brother. He will never fall into the traps of error, lust, or compassion that they do because, he tells us quite clearly, he can suppress his humanity:

> *Queen.* His sons, he says, shall give their words for him.
> *York.* Will you not, sons?
> *Edw.* Aye, noble Father, if our words will serve.
> *Rich.* And if words will not, then our weapons shall.
> [Part 2 V.1.137–40]

He counters his brother's qualms about the report of their father's death with the cold insistence that he will "hear it all," and in baiting contests preceding battles he outdoes even the articulate Margaret. His superiority in deceit is most explicitly acknowledged in his well-known soliloquy in Part 3 (III.2.124–95)—itself a logical extension of his father's soliloquies in Parts 1 and 2—but it is most effective dramatically when seen in practice. We recognize him best at the court of Edward IV (Part 3 IV.1) in the guise of humble, plain-dealing realist, who knows better than his brother George on which side to put his money. Less often observed is his subtle pretense in persuading his father to break the oath made to Henry and seize the crown at once (Part 3 I.2). To Richard the crown represents total, unadorned power—an end in itself—and his only concern is its attainment. But he recognizes that his father needs to be tempted and lured to seize it, and to this end he employs Marlovian rhetoric, a kind of language notably absent from his later, famous soliloquy:

> And, Father, do but think
> How sweet a thing it is to wear a crown,
> Within whose circuit is Elysium
> And all that poets feign of bliss and joy.
> [Part 3 I.2.28–31]

Thus, as Richard out-Machiavels Edward in determination and Margaret in spleen, he out-Machiavels his father in duplicity by making York, the erstwhile knave, the gull. He dupes his father into renewed hostilities, the need for which (in Machiavellian terms) is made all too apparent for York in the following scene. Accepting this inverted morality as that of the play, Richard has been a "good" son who is too late to save his temporarily mal-functioning father. But he has learned all he knows from his father's world, that "world of affairs" in which he was born and schooled. In the end he has become its most successful product.

Richard of Gloucester is Shakespeare's first great character, and his portrayal in *Richard III* is brilliantly anticipated in *3 Henry VI*. So great is he that critics tend at times to find the incredible "alacrity of spirit" which makes him the most memor-able of stage Machiavels an adequate substitute for morality itself. But even the temptation to do this does great harm to *Henry VI*. Shakespeare the beginning playwright has in these plays no ambivalence toward the new Machiavellianism. The proof that it is detestable resides in the creature that it breeds. It is difficult to imagine Shakespeare's reaction to an attitude which suggests that somehow Richard's evil is so engaging as to make him gen-uinely attractive. Two recent interpretations do almost approach a kind of Richard-worship rooted in the contempt which he possesses for the slovenly incompetence of most men of affairs.[6] But the effort which has gone into the creation of this character has been to suggest the effect of carrying to their logical con-clusions the seemingly quite practical aspects of evil represented in a new, tantalizing, man-centered morality, particularly evident in Shakespeare's day in the ambitions of an emerging new govern-ing class discussed by Raab, Neale, and McCaffrey.[7]

What Harold C. Goddard said of Henry VI still stands. He is "the most critically neglected of Shakespeare's kings."

> Henry was simple and sincere, a morally courageous and gen-uinely religious man and king. He is the only one of Shakespeare's kings whose public and private personalities are identical. As he himself reminds us, he was only nine months old when he came

6. I have in mind the views of H. M. Richmond, *Shakespeare's Political Plays*, pp. 19–98, and John Bromley, *The Shakespearean Kings* (Boulder, Colo.: Colo-rado Associated University Press), pp. 29–40.

7. Wallace McCaffrey, *The Shaping of the Elizabethan Regime* (Princeton, N.J.: Princeton University Press, 1968).

to the throne, and the situation in which he found himself later was not of his making. That he was frequently bewildered by the problems thrust upon him and willing to shed political responsibility is true. But he was childlike—not childish. No other king in Shakespeare had the good of his kingdom so at heart or suffered so keenly at the sufferings of his subjects. When he declares that he would give his life to save them, we do not doubt his word for a second.[8]

Creating "the good" in dramatic terms is a fantastically more difficult problem than creating evil, as Una Ellis-Fermor among others observes in *The Frontiers of Drama* (London: Methuen, 1964), and if Henry is not so successful a characterization as Richard, the task of creating him is of much greater dimension. Shakespeare did not attempt to come to grips with anything like it until he wrote *King Lear*. Shakespeare must somehow strike a balance between the sententious and the human in Henry, and given this problem, he succeeds, as Goddard seems justified in claiming.

In terms of moral standards, it seems obvious but necessary to state that a traditional Christian view of good government underlies the Henry VI plays. It is not Henry who is out of step, who is inadequate, who is ill-suited to govern—but just about everyone else. Without bitterness, cynicism, or guile (which would be the signs of maturity in Machiavellian terms), he remains childlike throughout the three plays. And his childlike image is that of the Nicodemus parable rather than that of Marlowe in the figure of the child-King Edward III or of Shakespeare in that of the child-King Henry III (*King John*), who are not children at all but midgets endowed with superhuman qualities. Those who wish Henry VI to be more effective are wishing for a different character and one impossible in human terms. Henry is quite effective in his love, understanding, and trust. It is the others who need thus to be more effective. He is the only character who sees the full horror of civil disorder, and he sacrifices his family honor to prevent its continuance. He alone believes in justice and the triumph of truth. In his actions and responses, he alone believes

8. Harold C. Goddard, *The Meaning of Shakespeare* (Chicago: The University of Chicago Press, 1951), pp. 30–31.

in the natural dignity of man. If man has betrayed that dignity, it is insufficient to say that the terms of the betrayal must therefore be the terms by which men are led and governed.

Shakespeare had a world of medieval and humanistic tradition from which to draw the virtues the good king ought to possess, and with these qualities he richly endowed Henry. Goddard observes that Henry alone possesses all Malcolm's requisites of a good monarch in *Macbeth:*

> . . . justice, verity, temperance, stableness,
> Bounty, perseverance, mercy, lowliness,
> Devotion, patience, courage, fortitude.
> [*Macbeth* IV.3.92–94]

But imagine trying to make such a figure something believably living. The problem is solved in *Macbeth* by few words and an early death for Duncan. But Henry must remain alive until the very end of *3 Henry VI.* The key to understanding King Henry is Goddard's own observation that he is inconsistent.

Making the good king a human king results in the same problem associated with the royal personality in *Woodstock, Edward II,* and *Richard II.* I speak now not in terms of the standards by which the Machiavels judge him, but of those by which a Christian humanist, an Erasmus or Thomas More, might judge him. Henry avoids being the stick-figure saint of medieval statuary precisely because he often fails to live up to the image he inherently has of himself. In other words, our sympathy toward him shifts considerably in the course of the three plays—and quite independently of the Machiavellian question. He is not a Machiavel, and in contrast to the contending nobles he is indeed a saint. But set against the ideal image of a Christian king, he falls short. He is a human king and thus, just as much as Edward II and Richard II, a weak king. In his striving to "govern better" he is to be praised, perhaps beyond any king in Shakespeare, but because of his inescapable human weaknesses as king, he must fail—and our feelings toward him must vacillate. Henry's perceptions throughout are those Lear comes to only following his agony on the stormy heath, but his actions frequently fail to suit those perceptions. He is the weak king in a more perplexing sense than the others because it is insufficient to call him unsympathetic when he is invulnerable and sympathetic when he is vulnerable. Far more honest about himself and the nature of his royal prerogatives than Richard II, he at times governs very well, even when he is seemingly secure, and at times he falters. Similarly, his reactions when he is under attack sometimes seem highly creditable and sometimes not. The shifts in appeal to our sympathies are more frequent, but their effects are not so final as in the other plays. Over-all, he emerges as a much better king, but still the weak king—weak because he is human, better because he is trying to govern better.

When Henry says in Part 2 that he wants to govern better, he says nothing about the standard of good government he has in mind, but it is more evident in the personality and actions of his famous protector. To more fully understand Henry and the ethic by which he lives requires consideration of the key role of good Duke Humphrey. For it is Humphrey who stands for the Renaissance political idealism associated with Erasmus, Thomas More, and the whole early sixteenth-century humanistic tradition; and it is Humphrey who must be destroyed before the Machiavellians can really begin to undermine Henry's royal stability.

DUKE HUMPHREY

If there is an idealized figure in the plays, it is Humphrey rather than Henry. The historical Duke Humphrey was a fifteenth-century Christian humanist, one of the first in England, who spent much of his lifetime collecting classical manuscripts and inviting important Italian scholars to England, subsidizing their visits for the edification and improvement of the English nobility. As Samuel Pratt makes clear in his discussion of the origins of Duke Humphrey's characterization in 2 *Henry VI*,[9] the image of the Christian humanist would be the first one to come to mind for a late Tudor audience, even though in the plays not much is made of this facet of his activities except in the reference to him as

9. Samuel Pratt, "Shakespeare and Humphrey Duke of Gloucester: A Study in Myth," *SQ*, XVI (1965), 201–16.

"clerkly." But it is immensely important to the play's underlying issues. As humanist and scholar Humphrey would be quickly identified with that considerable group of humanists and scholars who were so important in the political life of Henry VIII's reign: men who followed Erasmus in relating a new spirit of intellectual self-reliance to traditional Christian theology and values, men like More, Thomas Elyot, and Cardinal Reginald Pole. Some were loyal to Rome, others to Henry, but in loyalty to learning and reason they stood together. Humphrey of course predated these men, but he was in his humanist role their spiritual predecessor. And it was such men whom Henry VII and Henry VIII, both innovators, found fit royal counselors.

The influence of Christian humanists in sixteenth-century political life and institutions gave way to more sinister descendants. It was the Machiavellian brand of the new humanistic spirit which grew in influence following Henry VIII's divorce in the 1530s and was widespread by the end of the century. It may or may not be relevant to this discussion that Thomas More was martyred for his beliefs. It may not be relevant that Pole and Thomas Starkey were discredited. Nevertheless, the men in positions of importance in Tudor politics increasingly had more the look of Thomas Cromwell than of Thomas More.

But the image of the great humanists, if faded, was not forgotten in late Elizabethan England. Obviously, Erasmus and his followers were read in the universities, but the existence of the *Play of Sir Thomas More* suggests that they were still popular heroes as well. Erasmus himself, it should be noted, is a character in this anonymous work. He and More never discuss philosophy in the play, though they are once on the point of doing so. What they actually said would not be of that much interest to an Elizabethan popular audience. Rather, they are simply revered as great sages of the past. And since the touchiness of the issues involved precluded any direct reference to religion, the humanist More emerges in the play as a political martyr. Similarly, the humanist Duke Humphrey in *2 Henry VI* is murdered for political reasons. And also similarly, the specific content of his humanism is less important than his downfall. To the theatre audience of the 1590s the image of the humanist is that of a loser in politics.

And those to whom he was losing were the new Machiavels, the fresh, young faces coming into positions of political power during that period.

Shakespeare's Duke Humphrey is the ideal protector. Employing his wealth of knowledge and experience, confident in his own intellectual resources, he serves his king with total commitment born of his unshakable belief in a hierarchical order in which serving the king is his means of serving God as he has been ordained to serve Him. The humanistic balance between self-reliance and belief in a divine order is the guide by which he lives. He is also shrewd, not in a Machiavellian way—he is always honest himself—but in his quick understanding of the deceit of others. As has been observed many times, the most significant example of Duke Humphrey's great value to Henry is his unmasking of the imposters Simpcox and wife during the hawking episode at Saint Albans (Part 2 II.1). Of a similar nature is his swift removal of York as regent of France the moment doubt is cast on York's loyalty (Part 2 I.3). But he will not connive to save himself or his foolishly ambitious wife, though he knows they will both be destroyed. He is as honest and eminently courageous to the end as he is outspoken about the envy and deceit of his enemies.

Those enemies are, of course, the Machiavellian majority who are the antagonists of the Henry VI plays; and that they make common cause in opposing Humphrey is extremely significant. Before the opposing factions can enter upon their self-serving quest for power, they must briefly work together to destroy the now-aging humanist—and thus a tradition wherein individual reason and knowledge are put to the service of God, not man, through unfailing loyalty and service to king and country. Moreover, Humphrey must be murdered. He cannot be bought, he is too shrewd to be deceived, and the only way they can overcome him is through a temporary alliance which each is committed to destroy once the protector is out of the way. The "stop Humphrey" movement actually begins early in Part 1 with Beaufort's, that is, the medieval Church's, opposition to him (one thinks of Erasmus' difficulties with Rome), and is vitally strengthened by the alliance of Suffolk and Margaret, who join with the hated Beaufort ("Although we fancy not the Cardinal") early in Part 2. The key to their operation, though, is "grumbling York," Margaret realizes. York at first seems agreeable to supporting Humphrey (I.1.242) but is suddenly found to have switched sides. His being the officer who discovers Dame Eleanor consorting with witches (I.4) is hardly accidental. Even though York and Suffolk have been severely at odds over the French regency a scene before, it is obvious that York is playing both sides. He actively joins the conspiracy following (not preceding) Humphrey's imprisonment, and actually urges his murder, stopping short of volunteering to perform the act. But significantly his sworn ally Warwick is the first man on the scene following the murder as spokesman for an enraged public, which has assembled with surprising haste in III.2. York and Warwick, in other words, have out-maneuvered (out-Machiavelled) Suffolk, Margaret, and the cardinal at the crucial moment, thus reaping all the political benefit of Humphrey's murder while sharing none of the blame—York now of course being safely off in Ireland. Humphrey's downfall, then, leads directly to York's Machiavellian leap for power.

Many have observed that the Cade rebellion in *2 Henry VI* is a grim parody and anticipation of the Yorkist rebellion to follow, but few have mentioned that it also emphasizes the larger implications of Humphrey's murder. As Cade and his Kentishmen, we are told explicitly by York, are stand-ins for York and his followers, Lord Say is almost as obviously Humphrey's replacement. In IV.7, the victim's credentials as Christian humanist are specifically identified; and his murderers, with their crude, irresponsible lust for power, are the contending Machiavels of the play obscured only by a thin veneer of lower-class language and manners. Say's plea is practically a humanist manifesto:

> When have I aught exacted at your hands
> But to maintain the King, the realm, and you?
> Large gifts have I bestowed on learned clerks
> Because my book preferred me to the King,
> And, seeing ignorance is the curse of God,
> Knowledge the wing wherewith we fly to Heaven
> Unless you be possessed with devilish spirits,
> You cannot but forbear to murder me.
> [*2 Henry VI* IV.7.74–81]

His greatest crime for Cade is not that he speaks Latin and has great learning, but that using these talents he wishes to put country over self in the service of God. He is utterly courageous in facing the mob, both to gain time and, he hopes, to win them over (which he nearly does). Cade must mock Say's rational responses lest his reason prove mightier than the emotion Cade has aroused in his peasants. By the same token he must have the old lord murdered before his humane qualities win their hearts. So, too, Humphrey's reason and humanity necessitated his brutal murder, since the force of his mind and personality might well have brought his just acquittal in a trial.

Interestingly, it is the humanist, who has neither force nor guile at his disposal, who most frightens the Machiavels. He is the first one they must dispose of. (Even before the Lord Say episode, Cade has a poor clerk murdered for his ability to read and write.) It is not so much that literacy is a sign of high birth, as H. M. Richmond suggests, as that literacy is identified with the entire humanist tradition; and that tradition, which puts so much stress on individual talents in the service of God, is an obvious threat to those who would hoard their talents, denying service to others in order to serve themselves. Machiavellianism in the Henry VI plays is seen as a gross perversion of what the humanists stood for. The self-confidence of York, Cade, and young Richard is a perversion of the self-confidence of Duke Humphrey and Lord Say. A blinding, youthful anger at the destruction of the Christian humanists and their morality, as well as at a corrupt interpretation of humanistic individualism, seems the most potent motive force of these plays; and nowhere is that rage felt more than in the Jack Cade episodes.

2 *Henry VI*, then, is principally the story of the protector's fall and murder followed by its reenactment in an illustrative view of social and political turmoil in the kingdom. Its implications are large because what has been defeated is a political viewpoint rooted in faith in man's capacity to serve God through his own independent moral strength and intelligence. Humphrey, despite his fierce emotion, is unchanging. His farewell to Eleanor is charged with feeling, but he is unflinching in his conviction that she must be punished for her crimes. Even in his outrage at Beau-

fort and his later accusers, he says what is appropriate in an articulate, forceful manner. And as he is never uncertain, our sympathy toward him remains constant throughout.

It is Henry who prompts the shifts in our sympathies, but it is also Henry in whom, following Humphrey's death, the sole counterforce to the Machiavellian onslaught resides. It is his progress through the three parts which must be considered in detail. His is the downfall of the weak king who tries to govern well in a world dominated by a new political morality which denies him the chance. He is pusillanimous in many respects, yet frequently he is strong, and, at those very points the other characters and some critics condemn him for his pusillanimity, he is strongest of all.

HENRY

Unless we share the Machiavellian perspective of the lords, it is difficult to have any feeling about King Henry in Part 1. We may have a sense of his absolute innocence as a background against which the first deceptions, contentions, and betrayals take place, but we also share Exeter's regret about infant monarchs. Henry does not appear, of course, until III.1, at which time he acts as one would have him act. That scene's two adversaries—Duke Humphrey and Bishop Beaufort—sound alike in angrily presenting their grievances to the young king; but since Humphrey's accusations are just—we have already witnessed the bishop's brutal treatment of him at the Tower—and since it is the hated Rome to which Beaufort says he will turn for "remedy" (1.51), the king rightly calls Beaufort, not Humphrey, to account. As it is obvious that the "uproar" was "Begun through malice of the Bishop's men" (1.75), it is also obvious that Humphrey, not the bishop, seeks to restrain his men in this scene. And it is the bishop who tells us in asides that he is lying when he agrees to a reconciliation. In this scene, "the right" prevails through the force, clarity, and insistence of Humphrey's protestations. But, then, Humphrey is protector, and Beaufort's crudely Machiavellian

designs are not likely to make much headway here. More significant, perhaps, is the calmer portion of the scene, in which Henry
restores the young Plantagenet his birthright, creating him duke
of York. Were Humphrey and Henry motivated like the others,
this would never happen, since York's father had been proven
guilty of treason. But they are not so motivated, and the protector
counsels the king justly and explicitly to restore to York what is
rightfully his. The betrayal that follows is the result of York's
perfidy, not Henry's folly—unless we are to see the events from
the Machiavellian perspective considered earlier. So, following his
protector's sound advice, Henry governs well in this encounter.

But Henry's true stroke of political genius in Part 1 is, by
Machiavellian standards again, his biggest mistake. I refer, of
course, to his putting on a red rose in IV.1 to indicate the folly
of the contention brewing so swiftly in his kingdom. Far from
being a foolishly sudden, inappropriate act, it is the means by
which Henry honestly seeks to demonstrate the folly of decision
based exclusively on political expediency. His forthright gesture
brings him all kinds of trouble later, but it is the basic, simple
logic of his statement and its complete freedom from subterfuge
that points the accusing finger at the connivings and pretenses of
the lords:

> I see no reason, if I wear this rose,
> [*Putting on a red rose.*]
> That anyone should therefore be suspicious
> I more incline to Somerset than York.
> Both are my kinsmen, and I love them both.
> As well they may upbraid me with my crown,
> Because, forsooth, the King of Scots is crowned.
> But your discretions better can persuade
> Than I am able to instruct or teach; . . .
> [Part 1 IV.1.152–59]

Henry assumes they all think as he does and, thus, that their
"discretions" will serve as better teachers than he can; but the
lords are already so mired in false-seeming, in flattery, in subtle
forms of communication (cues, hints, implications, and the like)
that their "discretions" are obscured and Henry's wisdom is received incorrectly. Henry here reveals a gift for leadership which

could save England from the disaster that lies before it—but no one is listening, or if they are they understand him deviously, in their own fashion, rather than directly, in his fashion. They will not "learn" from him, and they can no longer learn from themselves.

Otherwise Henry is a neutral quantity in Part 1, acting under the sound guidance of his protector—until, that is, the play's final episodes. In those episodes, we see the first of his truly weak moments—moments in which he acts in a manner less kingly than we would like but in which he is, as elsewhere, unashamedly open and honest. Throughout the earlier portions of the play the envious, contending lords have been too busy destroying monuments of past honor (Talbot their chief victim) to be concerned about assaults on the power of the crown itself. The first to jump at supreme power has notable if temporary success because he hits upon a stratagem both Henry and Humphrey are unprepared for —Henry because of his youth and Humphrey because his mind is so occupied with matters of immediate political import that the great potential of Eros as a political force fails to occur to him in time. Suffolk is the master of the situation in Part 1 V.5. Through his description of Margaret he alone knows the place to undermine Henry where Humphrey cannot protect him. Humphrey might be able to counter a Margaret-in-the-flesh, but not a Margaret of "wondrous rare description," and Suffolk does not allow Henry to see his bride until after the proxy marriage. Suffolk denies the king a living princess. Rather, he belies her "with false compare." But that is more than we need to be aware that Humphrey has no chance. Suffolk's fish takes the bait.

But the fault is not entirely Henry's, despite the claim first stated by Edward of York in Part 3 that Henry's big "mistake" was having married Margaret. The *fault* is Suffolk's. If we blame Henry for not listening to Humphrey's advice, then we must listen to his own ingenuous response:

> And you, good Uncle, banish all offense.
> If you do censure me by what you were,
> Not what you are, I know it will excuse
> This sudden execution of my will.
> [Part 1 V.5.96–99]

The king says in effect that he is too young and inexperienced to withstand the onslaught of a super-subtle troubadour, a master of erotic description. We have seen Suffolk wooing Margaret for himself, and we know the force of his persuasions. Can we honestly imagine one so gentle, callow, and trusting as Henry resisting them? Henry is not the criminal here. He is less than we would wish in a king; that is, he is human. And he is Suffolk's victim, as he will be the victim of each of the play's leading Machiavels in succession.

The episode is understood best when contrasted with the episode in Part 3 which parallels it. There, too, the king of England (Edward) betrays his closest adviser (Warwick) who is seeking a good political marriage for him in France (Lady Bona) by marrying someone else (Elizabeth) for whom his erotic impulses have been aroused. The circumstances are the same, but the motives of the characters and the effects are quite different. In the one case they are innocent, in the other worldly and corrupt. Far from being won by the force of quasi-erotic rhetoric, Edward marries Elizabeth when he cannot bribe her to satisfy his lust. Edward is a hardened sensualist, Henry an impressionable novice. Edward always satisfies his appetites—in one way or another. Henry's hard lot is to know not a single moment of earthly pleasure. Warwick, to avenge the insult to his personal honor, deserts his king, and briefly achieves the Machiavel's dream. By shifting sides he increases his political power; in effect, he becomes king. Humphrey, on the other hand, whose honor has been just as insulted as Warwick's, remains as unflinching in his loyalty to his king as before. What we see in the first scene is the successful temptation of innocence in a world still dominated by trust and honor, in the second, creatures seeking to outdo each other in Machiavellian deception and animal lust.

Henry's innocence is the quality for which he is condemned here and elsewhere, but his innocence is what makes him Henry. It is a sign of human weakness in this scene, but in other situations it is also his strength. Through it we see how men of authority in a Christian commonwealth ought to behave. Henry possesses no miraculous powers—only trust, gentleness, and honesty. But these are powers by which men and societies may survive and which are deteriorating in a state increasingly entranced by the illusory practicality of Machiavellian methods.

The strength implicit in Henry's innocence is revealed in the fall and murder of Duke Humphrey in Part 2, an episode in which his actions have been roundly condemned by characters and critics alike. In the face of the many accusations made against the protector early in the second play, Henry has two choices. He can either engage in the Machiavellian practices suggested earlier, or he can agree, as he does, to a trial by Humphrey's peers which he is confident will reveal Humphrey's innocence.

> My Lord of Gloucester, 'tis my special hope
> That you will clear yourself from all suspect.
> My conscience tells me you are innocent.
> [Part 2 III.1.139–41]

The conspirators are also confident that a trial will reveal Humphrey's innocence; hence they feel Humphrey must be murdered. Henry is not guilty of inaction. He protests his faith in Humphrey with great emotion, but the appearance that he is weak results from his inability to use Machiavellian tactics. He instead relies on the legal machinery of his state and his own conviction that right will triumph. He receives a rude shock as a result.

That Henry is disillusioned in Part 2 III.2 by Humphrey's murder is not surprising. What is surprising is that he does not really change. He continues to be uncynical, trusting, and gentle. Revenge never enters his mind when he banishes Suffolk. He is clearly above revenge. But he is extremely angry and terribly sad. And if he does not change, he does learn. While each of the others is engaged in furthering a deception whereby his or her cause will be advanced by Humphrey's death, Henry, bewildered with grief, is searching for the reality in the situation—and he finds it.

Characteristically, Henry says far less in this scene than others do—notably Margaret. Suffolk sends out smokescreens of righteous indignation on one side, Warwick on the other. Margaret, who sees the greatest threat to her position from Suffolk's downfall, makes her long, impassioned complaint on Henry's indifference to her, which, were it not for our knowledge that her amatory needs have been amply satisfied by Suffolk from the start, might indeed evoke pity at the plight of a scorned, rejected queen. But we do know what Margaret has been up to and thus that the emotion being generated over Henry is a cover for her fear of losing Suffolk. That she is genuinely attached to Suffolk is made evident by the total bloodiness of her thoughts following his death, but her long passionate speech here (III.2.73–121) is purely histrionic display intended to take Henry's mind away from the murdered Humphrey.

Surprisingly, perhaps, and unnoticed by many, Henry comes through all the smoke like a beam of bright light. His first instinct (III.2.39–48) is to blame Suffolk, and he does indeed finally banish him on the basis of circumstantial evidence. But he tries to fight off the conclusion the circumstances and his distraught emotions point to so clearly. And he dwells at length on the murdered duke, in whom Henry sees his own "life in death."

Throughout the long and angry interchange between Suffolk and Warwick that dominates the middle of this scene, Henry says nothing. Then he speaks four lines which seem almost irrelevant to the situation at hand but are in fact most relevant to it and to the entire trilogy:

> What stronger breastplate than a heart untainted!
> Thrice is he armed that hath his quarrel just,
> And he but naked, though locked up in steel,
> Whose conscience with injustice is corrupted.
> [Part 2 III.2.232–35]

The lines are apothegmatic, and the success achieved in keeping Henry sounding human results largely from the near total absence of the sententious in his lines. But his few moral pronouncements are important. Henry's lines here are clearly a response to something, but not to anything the contending Suffolk and Warwick have just been saying. His last previous utterance, some eighty lines earlier, was his memorial to the qualities of the dead duke. During the succeeding quarrel, Henry's thoughts, not the quarrel itself, are what prompt the lines quoted above. Those thoughts must have to do with whether or not it is worth trying to lead the kind of life Humphrey led, since the conclusion stated in the lines is that truth and justice are inherently stronger attributes than falsity and injustice—appearances to the contrary. Thus while others may be content with stratagems and threatened force, Henry resolves to defend himself solely with the "breastplate" of "a heart untainted" in the troublesome days that lie ahead. It is a direct ruling out of both force and deceit from all his endeavors, and is most important in judging Henry as he will later appear.

Henry becomes no saint following these rather saintly lines. He appears from time to time uncertain, frightened, and even paltry. Our sympathies continue to vacillate. The lines quoted above represent only what he has learned from the experiences of his life thus far. The question often implied in commentary about Henry is: "When will he ever learn?" But what can he learn from the behavior of those around him other than to be like them, which constitutionally he could not do even if he wanted to? Rather, he learns from Humphrey and the manner of Humphrey's death that he must be faithful only to truth and justice—or try to be. Like the other kings, he is a man. That is to say, he is weak and will make errors which can only make him look terribly weak as king. But here he has the insight that the sole approach to genuine strength is unceasing adherence to the simplest verities. Such adherence, perhaps, looks easy enough in the stone and wood of medieval statuary, or in plays about ideal kings, but it proves almost impossible for Henry, who is in no way more than human.

The remainder of Part 2 is, in the crude, obvious terms of the Cade rebellion, mostly a restatement of what has happened and a foreshadowing of what is to come. Henry mildly follows the course he set for himself following Humphrey's murder. I say *mildly* because it is not his nature ever to shake earth and heaven, and thus our attention is easily drawn away from him by his much louder associates, but what he says and does is important to the central issue of these plays. He refuses to judge the dying Beaufort, despite the horrible death that prelate's seething guilt causes (III.3); he genuinely laments the prospect of putting Cade's Kentishmen to the sword (IV.4); he is considerate of York's inflammatory disposition in preparing for negotiations with him (IV.9); and his chief concern in the face of his many difficulties is that he "learn to govern better" (IV.9.49). But his Machiavellian adversaries are far more effective in immediate, practical ways than he. York is determined to have his war, and Margaret frustrates whatever hope Henry might have of defusing York by her own release of Somerset (V.1), whom Henry had temporarily imprisoned as York's price for negotiations. Margaret's action shows her to be precisely as guilty—no more, no less—as York. Nothing on earth can prevent the outbreak of hostilities, so determined is each side to have them. Henry meanwhile maintains his "breastplate" of "a heart untainted" throughout the battles which ensue.

The most severe test of audience sympathies toward Henry, as it is the most severe test for Henry, is the opening episode of Part 3. The chief difficulty here is that he seems so utterly craven even though he is rationally so utterly right. A few scenes into the play Shakespeare assigns Henry lines which make his responses in Part 3.I.1 reasonable and plausible; but in the situation itself he seems helpless, almost crushed by his fear. Our sympathies toward Henry in the scene are certainly divided, but the elements that go into the scene must be considered carefully.

In Hall's chronicle, the events of Part 3 I.1 never take place. There, following York's victory in battle at Northampton, a parliament attended by York, but not by Henry, proclaims that Henry shall reign for the remainder of his days, to be succeeded by York. Henry, in prison, is forced to accede. Shakespeare makes of this affair of state a personal confrontation between the two sides. York, surrounded by his followers, defiantly sits on Henry's throne, while the Lancastrians in the vestibule angrily demand that he be forcefully removed. The Yorkists thus invite a bloody test within the palace walls to assure their hold, and Clifford is ready to fight them, despite the certain outcome provided by the circumstances. Exeter says if they slay York, his troops will "quickly fly," but when York is later slain, his forces regroup and subsequently triumph. And there is little possibility here that they can even get at the duke.

Henry, who is the first to express his outrage, is also the first to see the realities of the situation: "Ah, know you not the city favors them,/And they have troops of soldiers at their beck?" (Part 3

I.1.67–68). And few could fault his determination to avoid blood-shed in this location. Henry seeks to make headway with verbal exchange, but he is no thunderer and anything but a spellbinder. In political negotiations, as in everything else, he stumbles over his old infirmity: absolute respect for the truth. York handles him with consummate Machiavellian skill. Rather than threaten him—Henry is a passive man but hardly the coward he is made out to be by everyone—York again rehearses his hereditary claim. And Henry, faced with irrefutable facts, can only retreat: "I know not what to say, my title's weak" (*3 Henry VI* I.1.134). No Machia-vellian would so hesitate, but Henry is no Machiavellian. *His title is weak!* If Henry is to wear the "breastplate" of "a heart un-tainted," this must be admitted. And it is the confusion over commitment to honesty or crown which gives him the appearance of uncertainty and cowardice through the remainder of the scene. Since Henry's position is not a secure one morally, he does not know how to react. As king of England and head of the House of Lancaster, he has a natural desire to retain his throne and is grateful for Clifford's defiant words. But commitment to truth provokes a terrible dilemma, which the changing sides by the long-loyal Exeter greater intensifies. That York is doing the very thing for which he here condemns the long-dead Bolingbroke makes no difference to Henry. Both York now and Bolingbroke then are Machiavels, but Henry is dedicated to truth and justice. His instinctive loyalty to his crown and his house is thus power-fully challenged by the fact of his tainted title.

What lies behind Henry's divided response is the whole ugly tale of deception and violence that ended the reign of Richard II and prepared the way, not for the legitimacy of York's claim, but for the total absence of an untainted title in Henry's time. The ruthless act of an earlier Machiavel in a previous age pro-duced the state of affairs Henry is faced with, and its renewal can only result in total chaos—a chaos caused exclusively by hu-man irresponsibility, not Divine Providence. In groping for a solution, Henry is not so much concerned for himself as for his country. His confusion and uncertainty are not fear, but his reaction to the shock of realizing that his breastplate of truth is marred by his own birth, that he is willy-nilly as corrupt as those around him. At the same time he cannot suddenly throw off the inborn conception of himself as rightful king of England.

Henry's decision to "unnaturally disinherit" his own son is not the result of selfishness and cowardice but a fruitless attempt to right the wrong done Richard II so many years before. This attempt is quite in keeping with his desire in Part 1 to right the wrong done York's father. But abdicating would do another wrong. As legitimate successor to his father and crowned king of England, he is both *de facto* and *de jure* monarch, and he would be breaking his own sworn oaths were he to relinquish the crown. Under duress, he seeks a solution honorable for both houses, though such a solution is no longer possible. He has told us that he longs "to be a subject," but he is also deeply and instinctively resentful of the "proud Duke" who would usurp his throne. Hoping for peace and unity, Henry acts selflessly and against instinct in adopting York as his heir. It is of course a useless gesture since it accomplishes none of its ends. Neither peace nor unity results, and Henry feels very bad after it has been done. Again, the Christian king has been victimized by the Machiavellianism of ambitious men, this time including one who lived well before the king was born. The Bolingbroke of old provokes Henry's dilemma here more than York, and Henry's attempt to resolve it fails both in personal and political terms.

If our sympathies toward Henry vacillate in this episode, it should be after his pact with York rather than during his excruciating perplexity before it. Henry's response to Margaret is weak because, with York gone and his son before him, his instinctive resentment and hurt immediately dominate him. Margaret calls him a coward, and he believes he has been one:

> Had I been there, which am a silly woman,
> The soldiers should have tossed me on their pikes
> Before I would have granted to that act.
> [Part 3 I.1.243–45]

But being tossed on the soldier's pikes would have achieved nothing except to bring bloodshed to the palace and intensify the civil conflict. The line between cowardice and natural horror at bloodshed is a difficult one to draw. To say Henry is a coward is to say he is naturally meek, and that is true. He is not dishonorably a coward—but literally Falstaff's "coward upon instinct." Henry's whole personality is so unmistakably tied to those scriptural inheritors of the earth that it is meaningless to condemn him for cowardice when any violence on his part would necessarily link him to that whole rapacious society his very being opposes. Yes, Margaret would be tossed upon the pikes, but so would Margaret consort with a ruthless lover to become the real master of England and taunt a helpless enemy with a cloth soaked in the blood of his slaughtered son. Henry's human weakness is evident in saying that York "enforced" him and in hoping Margaret may be revenged "on that hateful Duke"; he is not weak in attempting by naming York his successor to resolve an irresolvable, ugly dilemma not of his own making. But Henry is a human king and thus a weak king. Were he to respond very differently to Margaret, he would be an idealized king, a wish-fulfillment—and this he clearly is not.

Any lingering doubt as to Henry's motives in Part 3 I.1 should be resolved by his responses in II.2 as he is led to battle, literally as prisoner of Margaret and Clifford. First, in response to Margaret's asking whether he is not pleased to see the head of the slain York above the town gates, he answers:

> Aye, as the rocks cheer them that fear their wreck.
> To see this sight, it irks my very soul.
> Withhold revenge, dear God! 'Tis not my fault,
> Nor wittingly have I infringed my vow.
> [Part 3 II.2.5–8]

Then Clifford, scandalized by such a response from the titular leader of the government side in a civil war, respectfully but severely berates him for unnaturally refusing to fight and, worse still, for refusing to protect the rights of his son. Throughout his speech, Clifford draws images from the animal world for parallels to the point he is making. And the animal world is the appropriate one, for it is the animal world Henry is set against when he insists upon virtue and morality. The animal nature of man is represented in the sight of York's head upon the gates. Henry would leave his son something better:

Full well hath Clifford played the orator
Inferring arguments of mighty force.
But, Clifford, tell me, did'st thou ever hear
That things ill-got had ever bad success?
And happy always was it for that son
Whose father for his hoarding went to Hell?
I'll leave my son my virtuous deeds behind,
And would my father had left me no more!
[Part 3 II.2.43–50]

If Henry seems ahead of his time, it is ironically because he takes seriously the notion that in Christianity man has taken a step beyond the beast. Seen through the *Henry VI* plays the new Machiavellianism is but rationale for the step back to bestiality.

With this scene, *3 Henry VI* takes the shape all the events have been pointing toward since the final scenes of Part 1, and the direction which it maintains the rest of the way. The scenes of cruelty and relentless bloodshed are the pillars on which the play rests: Clifford's murder of Rutland, Margaret's murder of York, the death of Clifford and the desecration of his body, the death of Warwick, the slaughter of Prince Edward, and Richard's murder of Henry. Henry watches it all, not so much from the outside as from above, like the angel in an Italian Renaissance painting. His position on the molehill suggests this. When Margaret and Clifford deny him the right to be heard late in II.2, he ceases to be part of the immediate political world of the play. But that immediate political world is one of pure bestiality. Henry becomes more important than ever to what the play reveals about political behavior and leadership. The qualities represented by the play's competent men are Machiavellian qualities which result in ever-increasing horror for the kingdom. Henry's so-called inadequacies are in fact his desire for honesty, justice, and peace. He does not relinquish his authority. It is taken away from him, first by Margaret and Clifford, who insist that he speak their feelings, or be silent. Thus, on the molehill, Henry longs for escape, the shepherd's life. But Henry's famous speech in this scene (II.5) suggests the very qualities needed in king and kingdom which are so rudely rejected by the others. The time-honored image of the virtuous leader is that of shepherd tending his flock. What Henry longs for in his pastoral idyll is what the country longs for: the ordered, simple life under a humble, virtuous leader:

> So many hours must I tend my flock,
> So many hours must I take my rest,
> So many hours must I contemplate,
> So many hours must I sport myself;
> So many days my ewes have been with young,
> So many weeks ere the poor fools will ean,
> So many years ere I shall shear the fleece.
> [Part 3 II.5.31–37]

But the wolf now stands in the shepherd's stead, and the standards by which the wolf lives have been accepted by the sheep.

That Henry's way is the right way is attested to not only by his own words and presence but by the worldly men themselves at the point when each has been mortally wounded or otherwise fully expects death. In a pattern originating in medieval *De Casibus* literature and carried out so relentlessly in *Richard III*, each acknowledges the folly of earthly success in his death speech: "Why, what is pomp, rule, reign, but earth and dust?" (V.2.27). But here "pomp, rule, reign" have a more specific and contemporary point of reference than in the old medieval exemplum. Here they express the way of the Machiavel, the old game of "king of the hill" now philosophically defended. Moreover, the *De Casibus* tone makes a distinction between the worldly and the spiritual. In Henry they are fused. He is not a bad king who happens to be a good man. He would be as good a king as is humanly possible if men would let him. But they would rather have their kings of stratagem and force, regardless of the accompanying bloodshed and hardship, and they pronounce sadly the doom of a king of peace, honesty, and mercy—who is, they say, unfit to rule. As humans, all kings are weak—and our feelings toward them must vacillate. Most kings refuse to acknowledge this and thus normally are unsympathetic until vulnerable. Henry acknowledges it with his every move, and thus while our superficial feelings fluctuate, even sharply, in the long run (and *Henry VI* is a "long run") he is the one king who has the capacity to rule well—not a wish-fulfillment king, but a flesh-and-blood king. The point at which we realize this is the point at which our basic sympathies toward him shift. But by that time, the game of king-of-the-hill is in full swing —and in that game Henry possesses no ability and, with occasional lapses, wants none. Each dying Machiavel realizes, if not explicitly the wisdom of Henry's way, at least the folly of his own. But true to the *De Casibus* tradition, no one is listening.

Henry's way is perhaps best illustrated in Part 3 III.1., in which two gamekeepers capture him and take him to the newly crowned King Edward. Henry here is frequently pictured, in dramatic productions as well as criticism, as bewildered and abjectly forlorn, but he conveys a quite different image to me. His key lines are those made in answer to the first keeper's asking where his crown is:

> My crown is in my heart, not on my head;
> Not decked with diamonds, and Indian stones,
> Nor to be seen. My crown is called content,
> A crown it is that seldom kings enjoy.
> [Part 3 III.1.62–65]

More than simply the pastoral wisdom of the exiled Duke Senior in *As You Like It,* these lines are a political comment on the proper humility required of the Christian king. Henry is as intelligent and resourceful in this scene as he is patient and compassionate. His concerns in having lost his crown are in having lost his freedom to enjoy the land of which he has been the incarnate symbol, in having lost the responsibility which he has sworn to fulfill in the eyes of God, and in having lost the ability to help petitioning subjects:

> No, Harry, Harry, 'tis no land of thine.
> Thy place is filled, thy scepter wrung from thee,
> Thy balm washed off wherewith thou wast anointed.
> No bending knee will call thee Caesar now,
> No humble suitors press to speak for right,
> No, not a man comes for redress of thee;
> For how can I help them, and not myself?
> [Part 3 III.1.15–21]

Richard II, acknowledging Bolingbroke's ascendancy at Flint Castle, begins with a similar lament, but he significantly omits the

last part. Henry's conception of his function as "Caesar" is that
of benefactor and judge. Richard lived mostly in the adulation
and ease of majesty, little in its responsibilities. Henry cared
little for the ease and had the responsibilities, which he welcomed,
largely denied him—well before he was deposed.

Henry's essential relationship with his subjects is briefly enacted in the exchange which follows. He does not plead with
them, as might at first be supposed. Rather, he instructs them—
and then is compassionate toward their limitations, submissive in
the face of their ignorant force. He at first resorts to the interrog-
atory method of the patient teacher, later to example:

> *Hen.* But did you never swear, and break an oath?
> *Keep.* No, never such an oath, nor will not now.
> *Hen.* Where did you dwell when I was King of England?
> *Keep.* Here in this country where we now remain.
> *Hen.* I was anointed King at nine months old.
> My father and my grandfather were Kings,
> And you were sworn true subject unto me.
> And tell me, then, have you not broke your oaths?
> *Keep.* No, For we were subjects but while you were King.
> *Hen.* Why, am I dead? Do I not breathe a man?
> Ah, simple men, you know not what you swear!
> Look, as I blow this feather from my face,
> And as the air blows it to me again,
> Obeying with my wind when I do blow
> And yielding to another when it blows,
> Commanded always by the greater gust,
> Such is the lightness of you common men.
> But do not break your oaths, for of that sin
> My mild entreaty shall not make you guilty.
> Go where you will, the King shall be commanded;
> And be you kings. Command, and I'll obey.
> [Part 3 III.1.72–93]

Henry's paraphrase of Christ on the cross and his concluding
charity and forgiveness should indicate, if nothing else does, that
he, not the keepers, is in command of the situation. And his final
line—"And be you kings"—lights up the whole play. The way of
the Machiavel indeed makes the keepers kings, as much as it

makes Edward IV king or Richard of Gloucester king (or Henry Richmond king, though Shakespeare did his utmost to muffle that clear resonance).

But Henry is far from a uniformly ideal figure of wisdom and detachment. Perhaps more than ever before, he is pictured late in Part 3 as resentful at the usurpation of his throne. At the beginning of III.1 he wishes Margaret well in her appeal for aid from France, despite his feelings about her methods; and his joy at Warwick's defection to the Lancastrian side prompts him in IV.8 to refer to that Machiavel as "my Hector and my Troy's true hope." Again, our admiration based on his patience and Christian submission is shaken by his desire to be victorious in worldly terms and his joy at finding a worldly champion. Again we find Henry weak. Or, better, again we find him human. The king who could put aside entirely his earthly desires, who could maintain indifference to a crown he has held from birth and is more his right than anyone else's, tainted title or no, would not be a human king but a superhuman one, typical of the plays in which a king can do no wrong. Henry's rapture at Warwick's presence in III.1 is similar to his rapture at Suffolk's description of Margaret late in Part 1. Warwick here is as devious in his motives as Suffolk was then. Moreover, now in the pattern of the other plays, the king is less admirable when he is less vulnerable and more admirable when he is more vulnerable. At this moment of seeming recovery in Henry's fortunes he is weak by his own Christian standard in flattering Warwick and weaker still in yielding Warwick kingly prerogatives; but when challenging Clifford and instructing the keepers, he is anything but weak.

In Henry's final appearance, he is murdered by Richard, now duke of Gloucester. True to form, here Henry is strong and heroic. John F. Danby correctly considers it the confrontation of sainted king and detested Machiavel,[10] only it is not so much a confrontation of ideas as of the contrasting personalities in which those opposed ideas most happily reside. The episode represents the murder of "pity, love, and fear" in political life by cold, ruthless pragmatism, but it is Richard who makes this explicit following

10. John F. Danby, *Shakespeare's Doctrine of Nature* (London: Faber and Faber, 1968), pp. 58ff.

the murder. Henry, knowing well what the appearance of Richard
means, is nevertheless occupied with the death of Edward his son,
whose well-being he has been accused of neglecting. Henry's
detailed use of the classical image of Icarus here is particularly
significant:

> I, Daedalus; my poor boy, Icarus;
> Thy father, Minos, that denied our course;
> The sun that seared the wings of my sweet boy,
> Thy brother Edward, and thyself, the sea
> Whose envious gulf did swallow up his life.
> [Part 3 V.6.21–25]

The function of individual actors in the story is identified:
Prince Edward with Icarus, Minos with York, the searing sun with
King Edward, and the drowning sea with Richard. But most important is Henry's identification of himself with Daedalus, who
possessed rare skills denied other men yet who could not avoid
the wrath of the jealous Minos. Henry's rare skills are those of
the virtuous governor, but they are not of a kind to be forced on
subjects. They must be freely accepted. Daedalus by tradition
was crippled and awkward, but his gift was rare. So Henry
appears crippled as governor in this strife-filled world, but he
understands deeply the uses of those rusting agents of good
government: justice and mercy. Prince Edward—Icarus—sought to
succeed his father but learned little from his mother about the
requisites of good government. Blood-curdling as his murder is,
he dies as one more Machiavel defying many. Henry laments his
son's passing nevertheless, both because Edward was his son and
also because of Henry's hatred of cruelty and bloodshed of any
kind. Witness again his response to York's head in II.2.5–8.

Following, Henry foresees disasters to result from Richard's
ascendancy, which are all to be borne out in *Richard III*, and
describes the horror of Richard's existence in terms later to be
picked up by the Lady Anne. As Henry seems on the threshold
of stating the larger implications of Richard's hellish earthly
mission, Richard gives him the death stroke—in mid-sentence.
Henry dies asking God's forgiveness for his own sins and pardon
for Richard, which may be in character but is surprising neverthe-

less. Imagine the dying York forgiving Margaret or the dying Clifford and Warwick forgiving Richard. Henry does not speak bitterly and his words betray no irony. They are a mark of benevolence beyond anything else we see in these plays. He forgives one of the worst villains in Shakespeare. No one does as much for Iago, or even the dying Edmund, who so desperately wants to be forgiven. But Richard at the start of his bloody rise is forgiven by the holiest man he kills.

Richard's victim here is more than Henry the deposed king of England. It is the "older cultural solidarity" of which R. S. Berman speaks. Henry, says Berman, is "a re-creation of medieval faith in the will of heaven."[11] Even the worst of the Machiavels have heretofore paid lip-service to the old Christian morality. But not Richard. He is refreshing to some in killing Henry the way he does, partly because he has put aside even the façade of that old morality; it is this new freedom from pretense that carries him along so much farther than earlier, lesser Machiavels like his father York. After all the pretenses and self-deceptions we have witnessed going all the way back to the Temple Garden scene (1 Henry VI II.4), we are grateful for his underlying honesty, which takes the shape here of undisguised adherence to Machiavellian means. It is his proud assertion that he has successfully suppressed all human feeling which allows his disdain for even the formalities of Christian sentiment and the conventions of honorable behavior (such as letting Henry finish). And it is a long time in Richard III before that quality in Richard is finally tested. His father led the way, but the struggle in York's nature with the modicum of honor he possessed kept getting in the way and finally destroyed him. Richard is the first one who seems fully able to deny that Christian (or human) motives need deter him in the least.

There is no doubt that a part of us is with Richard in this scene. A part of us is gratified to see unvarnished evil, so vital and engaging, destroy the good king, who in the final analysis perhaps is something of a bore. But it is that part of us which can tempo-

11. R. S. Berman, "Power and Humility in Shakespeare," SAQ, LX (1961), 413. See also David Riggs, Shakespeare's Heroical Histories (Harvard University Press, 1971), pp. 93–139.

rarily shut out the vivid images of a strangled lord, a slaughtered child, and even the innocent life's blood that spurts out on Richard's dagger in the scene before us. It is that part of us which can temporarily shut out compassion. And the temptation to be with Richard is great because humanity and compassion tend to be a bore, having no guide or means of operation other than seemingly impractical, certainly tedious, moral virtues. Above all, acknowledgement of human response also involves that which we wish to deny most of all—human weakness. Richard offers an escape from the essential burdens of life, as *The Prince* did to a new, spirited Renaissance youth reacting against the restrictions imposed by a medieval view of man's existence. The temptation to be indifferent to the blood of Henry on Richard's dagger is great. But the sight of human blood violently shed is finally hard to be indifferent to, as Antony knew well in the Forum, and even Tyrrel and the murderers in *Richard III* learn.

Ultimately, of course, Richard himself must yield before the pressure of human response. As Sanders observes in his far-reaching discussion of *Richard III*,[12] Richard's real nemesis in that play is conscience, and the play thus tests the deeper moral implications of Machiavellianism. His true adversary is not Richmond, a stick figure whose nature is dictated by Tudor propaganda, but the moral force that underlies the responses of Clarence's murderers, Tyrrel, and Richard's own suppressed humanity which suddenly surfaces late in the play. For one speech, V.3.177–206, Richard III is the weak king. But that speech only indicates forcefully that Richard, too, is human; it is not sufficient to shift the play's appeal to our sympathies. For once a king seen in a genuinely political context succeeds in preventing the persistent vacillation that accompanies our response to the other kings. He avoids the appearance of being the weak king. But Richard can avoid that appearance only by unrelenting commitment to evil, only so long as all stops of "pity, love and fear" in his nature can be kept closed.

Henry VI, on the other hand, no less than Edward II, Richard II, and John, is the weak king—in his case, more clearly than else-

12. *The Dramatist and the Received Idea*, pp. 61–109.

where, because a human king must be weak. Wantonness and cruelty play no part in his weakness, and he is genuinely governed by Christian motives. Yet, he succumbs to Suffolk's description of Margaret, he frequently and inadequately adopts defiant tones, he is sometimes more concerned with the loss of his prestige than with what that loss means, he allows guilt at his son's disinheritance to confuse him about his own motives, and he succumbs to the image of Warwick as a champion and savior. These are Henry's weaknesses, but what would we have without them? We would have a stick figure less plausible even than Henry Richmond. We would have the shape of saintliness seen in the bas-relief in the niches of a medieval cathedral. Essentially Henry has the qualities to be a truly good king, but just as essentially he is grossly capable of error. This is the way kings are! The best of them, like Henry, to the worst of them, like John—all, that is, who acknowledge their humanity. The villain in *Henry VI* is not the king's humanity. It is the inhumanity, or the struggle toward inhumanity, of his nobles. And in the presence of that inhumanity Henry's inevitable human weaknesses drag him down. But a Henry VI might also overcome those inevitable human weaknesses. His reign could succeed through his mercy, truth, and justice—but he would have to be supported by subjects equally human and willing to face their limitations honestly. Henry's lords seek other means to deal with their limitations. They reject mercy, truth, and justice in favor of power achieved through force and deceit. By rejecting the Christian virtues in favor of newer, seemingly more practical methods of political behavior, they bring about a state of affairs in which the worst inherent human weaknesses prevail.

The Henry VI plays are not so much a cry of frustration against the inevitable shortcomings of monarchy as against the combination of deceit and force by which men of affairs seek advancement or unchallenged power. These plays are not proposing hard political solutions. They are only vaguely plays of ideas. The anger that lies behind them is intense, but except that the shameful underside of political life is shown, they are not entirely clear in their direction. They feed an audience state of intense frustration, and relief from the frustration is nowhere to be found, unless it be in the catharsis successful dramatic experience produces. But that catharsis here is less probable than in the plays discussed earlier, where our own ambivalence is being excited and our confusion purged. Unless we recognize in the behavior of the Machiavels our own political disposition, which is of course quite possible, we are likely to be more frustrated at *3 Henry VI* than at the end of the others. The Machiavellian victory is clear. We are not left in a state of divided sympathies. In retrospect, there is nothing to consider but the whole frightful cacophony all over again. Nothing is likely to occur to us that is not readily apparent while it is happening. There seems nowhere to go from here, and though the plays follow on to a redemption in Henry Richmond, that is a redemption necessarily rooted in Tudor political propaganda. The greatness of *Richard III* hardly lies in its ending. With all Henry VI's virtuous qualities, one cannot construct an image of him reigning successfully in this world. No man has a better chance, perhaps, but that still does not make him plausible as a leader of those who refuse to yield their greed and duplicity. The Christian king cannot win with a Machiavellian nobility, and there is little chance of that nobility changing its ways, as there was little chance of that parallel actual nobility of the 1590s changing its ways.

The Henry VI plays are written in anger at political realities as Shakespeare and his audience knew them. Gradually both would become sufficiently inured to those realities to think that they might serve better ends than they serve here. The plays which follow suggest the sad acknowledgment by late sixteenth-century Englishmen that in one form or another Machiavellianism was there to stay.

IV *John*

The Machiavellianism to which the Henry VI plays respond is the same political force to which *King John* responds, but the response is quite different. And though we can never precisely know the reasons for the difference, we can guess at them through the play itself and through its relation to its immediate source, *The Troublesome Reign*. Despite the idealism expressed through the character of King Henry, the Henry VI plays hardly espouse a political way of life which could seem viable from any politically modern vantage-point in the 1590s. The Machiavellian approach was not something about which politicians were uncertain; they had quite accepted it. The uncertain ones were members of the audience—and the playwrights who articulated their uncertainty. Faced with the inevitability of the weak king, the appeal of a consciousness which (among other things) fostered the creating of an illusion of effective monarchy as an alternative to the endless inadequacies of actual monarchy was in the end too much. Machiavellianism, so detested in the Henry VI plays, had to be made to appear acceptable on the stage; the way was to subordinate the brutality and to glamorize the deceit.

If the dramatic image of an acceptable Machiavellianism is finally that which emerges from the *Henry IV–Henry V* trilogy, as many today are coming to feel, the transitional play is *King John*. In *King John* the Shakespearean terms of a rapprochement with the new political methods are first set forth and will be the major theme of this chapter. Seen in the context of the weak-king plays, *John* assumes a clarity of direction it has rarely possessed in other interpretations. Certainly, the reasons for its many ambiguities and seeming contradictions can be better understood, including the eternally puzzling characterization of the Bastard. But the play which apparently led Shakespeare to consider the possibilities John's reign provided for achieving his ends was *The Troublesome Reign*. It is that anonymous work we must look at first, before considering the very significant changes Shakespeare made in it—changes which point directly to the attitudes underlying the final trilogy.

THE TROUBLESOME REIGN

The *Troublesome Reign of King John* (henceforth referred to as *TR*) is a weak-king play—or, perhaps, two weak-king plays, since the work was written in two parts, each of which may be treated as a separate, if truncated, play. Most of the irritation with the play found in twentieth-century comment results from failure to recognize the strongly ambivalent response it invites toward the king. Since as everyone agrees, Shakespeare makes John more sinister in *King John*, with more attention focused on his usurpation and his tragic infirmities, most critics settle for John in *TR* as the anti-papal hero, the "Warlike Christian and Your Countryman" of the play's Prologue, and give little attention to his gross inadequacies, which are little less virulent really than in Shakespeare. It is hard, for example, to reconcile the heroic John of the Prologue of the anonymous play with the John who later orders the torturing of an innocent child.

The identification of John as a heroic figure in *TR* results, of course, from his defiance of the pope and from the admirable qualities thereby assigned him in Bale's *Kynge Johan* and Foxe's *Book of Martyrs*. John R. Elliott and John Elson both trace the central figure of *TR* to such sources.[1] But since sixteenth-century opinion itself was divided—Polydore Vergil was anti-John and Holinshed was noncommittal—there is room for difference of opinion as to how John might be seen in drama of the 1590s. Thus, the critics have tacitly acknowledged this division by finding John heroic in *TR* and a good deal less than heroic in Shake-

---

1. John R. Elliott, "Shakespeare and the Double Image of King John," *Shakespeare Studies*, I (1965), 64–84; and John Elson, "Studies in the King John Plays," in *Joseph Quincy Adams Memorial Studies* (Washington, D.C.: Folger Shakespeare Library, 1948), pp. 183–97.

speare's play. I find him a figure whose appeal to our sympathies shifts radically in both.

Most scholars have overlooked John's image in other plays of the 1590s, popular plays which were thus as Protestant in orientation as *TR*, yet in which there is no hint of John as a Protestant hero. I refer to the *Robin Hood* plays and to *Look About You*, which derive from legends of the Fulk Fitzwarin prototype of Robin Hood, who lived during the reign of John and whose stories in folklore and ballad see John as a constant in unremitting villainy.[2] In *1 Robin Hood*, John is clearly an evil usurper who must be removed from the throne to make place for the rightful King Richard I. In *2 Robin Hood*, he is just as bad in his pursuit of the unfortunate Mathilda (Maid Marion). In *Look About You*, Prince John's consummate evil, taken for granted by all other characters in the play, is the focal point for the jests and farce which constitute the major part of the play's action. Against this background, the assumption that John's defiance of the pope necessarily changed his traditional image for the author of *TR* or Shakespeare is unfounded. Rather, the use of that Protestant heroic aspect of his reign in their plays suggests an attempt to represent the shifting perspective from which this king, as another in a growing series of weak kings, must be viewed. The religious issue as such plays a small part in either work.

The weak-king plays reveal and reflect audience uncertainty about submission to a monarch whom his subjects see as inadequate. The pattern in *Woodstock*, *Edward II*, and *Richard II* was one of sympathy with the king's opponents up to the point at which those opponents get the upper hand. Then sympathy shifts to the king and gradually builds until it culminates, in *Edward II* and *Richard II*, in our deep pity toward his tragic demise. *TR* reflects the same ambivalence, but it does so more in the manner of *Henry VI*. Our sympathies shift back and forth between and even within scenes. Our indecision seems perpetual, though it is of course resolved at last by kingly penitence and the king's death, which are intended to evoke shame and guilt in the viewer. The concluding scenes and statements do not, however, sum up

2. See Maurice Keen, *The Outlaws of Medieval Legend* (London: Routledge & Kegan Paul, 1961), pp. 39–52.

the play. They may pacify the censor and leave us sympathizing with the crown, but it is the total effect of the play that goes home with its viewer for reflection—some of that reflection no doubt as seditious as that heard from the rebellious figures in the play.

The zig-zagging pattern of our sympathies in *TR* goes something like this: When we first see John, he looks and sounds the strong monarch answering a challenge from a foreign king, and our feelings would be quite positive were it not for certain disturbing factors. One is that the French challenge in question is made on behalf of Prince Arthur, son to John's older brother and therefore legal successor to the throne. Shakespeare at this point makes more perhaps of John's dubious title, but it is strongly suggested in both plays, and even the suggestion of usurpation jars the impression of stable monarchy. Equally jarring is the importance, if not the dominance, of Queen Elinor in the opening scene. History and folklore give one a glimpse of this eternally fascinating ambitious queen who made life hell for a husband and four children. The legendary scheming and bad will of this lady play an important part in both John plays. In both, her presence throughout the first half of the play casts John as a royal figure flawed by maternal dominance; as such, the John we first see in *TR* is not an image of unmarred royal stability and competence, as some have suggested.

Our second impression of John is similarly mixed. Listening to the counter-claims to the inheritance of Sir Robert Faulconbridge by his two sons, John seems the soul of sober kingly responsibility, dealing justice to his subjects with patience and sympathy. This action of course launches the hectic, and in *TR*, confusing career of the Bastard and does not appear to focus directly on John. As in Shakespeare, John justly and wisely decides in favor of the claims of an elder brother, despite unsupported accusations of that brother's illegitimacy. In retrospect one might reflect, however, that Arthur, legitimate heir to John's older brother, has been dispossessed by John. So even the apparent image of John here as wise, unbiased judge is not unmarred. We do not really know what to make of him in Act I.

If in the first act our reaction to John is mixed, in the second act our sympathies toward him actually vacillate—and violently before it is over. In John's first meeting with King Philip of France, his image is that of the heroic, defiant English king. But when the citizens of Angiers enter the picture, John quickly begins to lose stature. The shrewd indecision of the citizens and the indecisive battle between John and Philip which results from that indecision reflect our own divided response to John. But when the citizens propose the "deal" whereby Lewis will marry Blanche to resolve the conflict, John's stock plummets. For dowry he yields five French provinces, nearly half of his kingdom. The implicit blow to English prestige is immense. In acquiescing to the marriage and yielding the dowry, he has acted in a puerile, selfish manner which directly affects the lives of others (especially the Bastard, who has already wooed and won Blanche for himself) and the welfare of his kingdom. The hero of *TR*'s prologue hardly jibes with the indecisive, hypocritical, and paltry figure we have thus far seen here. Then Pandulph enters.

It seems that Elizabethan anti-papal sentiment is exploited in *TR*, as in Shakespeare, to provide periodic *foci* of sentiment favorable to John in the play, thereby creating that ambivalence toward him which the audience has toward the other weak kings. History and legend could provide little that was admirable in his nature or his actions. Yet he is not viewed in these plays as a Richard III-type monster, and one reason he is not is his radically improved image in Protestant propaganda of the Tudor period. The image of the anti-papal hero created by John Bale, a Protestant fanatic of Henry VIII's reign, and preserved in John Foxe's quite biased survey of anti-papal martyrs, served admirably to provide a counterweight for John's horrendous crimes and thus the uncertainty about the monarch which is central to these plays. The author of *TR* thus uses the pro-Protestant bias of the times as a device to keep the audience off balance in its assessment of the monarch.

Shakespeare would later perform the difficult task of making the weak, guilt-ridden monarch and the defier of the pope a consistent dramatic figure, but the author of *TR* was hardly so well-equipped a writer. Just as the first signs of a penitent, reforming king seem awkward and out of place in *Woodstock*, so the signals that the anti-papal hero speaks in *TR* are woefully out of harmony with what surrounds them. A special diction is heard when John speaks of Rome in *TR*, one which joltingly shifts the play's gears in appealing to audience sympathies. Earlier, John interrupted the sober resolution of his departure for France with an abrupt suggestion of how his battle expenses would be paid:

> I'll seize the lazy abbey-lubbers' lands
> Into my hands to pay my men of war.
> The Pope and popelings shall not grease themselves
> With gold and groats that are the soldiers' due.
> [I.1.327–31]

Later, he will break the dignity of his post-battle moralizing by instructing the Bastard to "take some order of our popelings there,/That swell with pride, and fat of laymen's lands" (II.5. 1161–62). Similarly, the whole abbey scene (III.1), in which the Bastard extorts money from the friar and discovers a nun hidden in the money-chest, is grossly unsuited to the rest of the play. So, here, with the appearance of Pandulph, a different John flashes forth—suddenly not the cringing, mother-dominated introvert but the snarling lion of England defying the serpent of Rome. The monarch who has just yielded half his territories in a shaky bargain to keep a shaky throne speaks with very different effect:

> Know, Sir Priest, as I honor the Church and holy churchmen, so
> I scorn to be subject to the greatest prelate in the world. Tell thy
> master so from me, and say, John of England said it, that never
> an Italian priest of them all shall either have tithe, toll, or polling
> penny out of England; but as I am king, so will I reign next
> under God, supreme head over both spiritual and temporal; and
> he that contradicts me in this, I'll make him hop headless.
> [II.1.1018–26]

This, the brightly-lit signal reads, is the anti-Catholic hero. Now you must cheer him.

For a brief time, then, John enjoys the success which fittingly is afforded the enemy of Rome. In battle he defeats King Philip, who has broken oaths now to both claimants to the English throne, and he prepares to return to England in triumph with Arthur, the source of all his troubles, as his prisoner. But no sooner is Arthur brought back into the picture, and Rome dropped out of it, than John's image again declines as suddenly as it rocketed with the appearance of Pandulph. Shakespeare of course makes far more of his sinister suggestion to Hubert, but the author of *TR* rather deftly projects John's old evil image with the Janus-headed instruction:

> Hubert, keep him safe,
> For on his life doth hang thy sovereign's crown,
> But in his death consists thy sovereign's bliss.
> Then, Hubert, as thou shortly hear'st from me,
> So use the prisoner I have given in charge.
> [II.5.1176–80]

The undoubtedly whispered mid-portion is all that is needed to dim John's success as commander of God's side in a holy war.

Two scenes later in *TR* (only one in Shakespeare, who mercifully omits the abbey sequence), the kingly image declines farther than in any of the other weak-king plays. That John's original call for Arthur's death is unaccountably changed in the charge Hubert receives that the child be blinded may indicate that the author of *TR* is guilty of carelessness which Shakespeare did not bother to correct, but I suspect both knew what they were doing. Although Shakespeare makes a radical modification in the effect of the scene, he let the supposed oversight stand. He apparently approved of the change from outright murder to blinding. (It is hardly something he would have missed.) John's decision in both plays is undoubtedly prompted, as is later implied, by his wish to avoid the accusation of having murdered Arthur while at the same time hoping his victim will die, the same motive which prompts Cornwall and Regan to blind Gloucester in *Lear*. But whereas a Gloucester might survive such treatment, a child hardly could. The author of *TR* has thus introduced an element which for some makes John (here and in Shakespeare) more terrible than Richard Crookback, who orders his princes murdered, not tortured. Furthermore, the murder of the princes in *Richard III* is only reported to us by the murderer, not shown. John's attempt to avoid the accusation of murder only increases the implicit deceit and in no way mollifies the crime. What follows is the painful scene in which Arthur prevails upon Hubert to spare him, a scene which will be alluded to in specific terms in connection with Shakespeare's treatment of it. This is the nadir of John's reputation in this play as it is in Shakespeare's and, it seems, utterly destroys any argument that would seek to defend John's "heroism" in either play.

The most confusing episode in both *TR* and *King John* is the long, chaotic affair following the Hubert-Arthur scene. Here John responds to a host of developments, including some which seem quite extraneous to the play's action. But the very chaotic nature of the scene makes it most characteristic of the play, because in it our feelings toward John lurch from utmost contempt to genuine compassion. While most of what happens makes John appear deceitful and cowardly, what finally happens makes him appear victimized and penitent.

At the start of III.3, we hear John discussing his proposed second coronation with the chief lords of the realm. (In Shakespeare their discussion comes later, with the coronation already an accomplished fact.) John attributes his decision to be crowned anew to his relief that the "Abbey-lubbers" have been suppressed, and he peremptorily rejects Pembroke's reasonable thesis that the second coronation will suggest a weakness in his title which supposedly does not exist. It clearly does exist, though, and despite the extent of John's boasting about the pope, the religious issue here is a red herring:

> But now for confirmation of our state
> Sith we have pruned the more than needful branch
> That did oppress the true, well-growing stock,
> It resteth we throughout our territories
> Be reproclaimed and invested king.
> [III.3.1558–62]

The real subject of this scene is still Arthur, and the "more than needful branch" John has "pruned" is the child whose murder he has ordered and assumes is being carried out. But to be crowned anew following news of Arthur's death would be too obvious. Hence John's timing and the papal red herring.

The arrival of the Bastard with Peter the Prophet and the news of his success at extortion among the "ease-bred abbots" complicates the scene, but the basic theme remains unchanged. Arthur is still the chief subject of the scene. Following the hurried coronation—it takes place briefly between two speeches—John again explains that its cause was the growth of "ambitious weeds" in the kingdom, which superficially refers to the abbots but also obviously applies to Arthur. He speaks of abbots as "false intruders," but the abbots have been there right along; the only "intruder" has been Arthur. John does everything he can to keep the lords' minds off the boy. As evidence of his gratitude, John bids the lords ask anything at all of him, and he will grant it. But the lords focus on the issue that has been dominant all the time, obscured by John's endless drill about popelings and abbots. They request Arthur's release. John's answer is unexpectedly confessional: "Your words have searched the center of my thoughts." He seems ready to acquiesce (confident perhaps that Arthur is dead) but is forestalled by an utterly unprepared-for development. Five moons suddenly and mysteriously appear in the sky.

There seems little reasonable explanation for the moons at this point, other than that they are reported in the chronicles and hence are reported here. Shakespeare apparently felt their irrelevance to the scene as it appears in TR and changed it with a stroke. Instead of having them refer to England and the other nations of Catholic Europe, as in TR, Shakespeare makes them omens of Arthur's death, thus tying them directly to the underlying subject of the scene. Like John's earlier fulminations against the clergy, they serve in TR to again obscure the Arthur theme. It almost feels as though John's attempts to suppress the thought of Arthur in this scene are mirrored by the events of the scene themselves. Until its end, everything that happens takes our minds away from the prince. But it is the prince who remains throughout the underlying issue of the scene.

Audience sympathies, already rudely shuttled between John the abbot-baiter and John the child-torturer, are more severely jolted than ever by the scene's conclusion. First we sympathize with the lords' rebellious exclamations at the news of Arthur's "death." We know Arthur really lives, but even the thought of such a crime makes us share the shocked response of the barons.

But by the time John has finished his long lament which follows, we are well on our way back to sympathy with him. In deep penitence, he now curses both his crown and his birth:

> But now they shun me as a serpent's sting,
> A tragic tyrant, stern and pitiless,
> And not a title follows after John
> But butcher, bloodsucker, and murtherer!
> . . . .
> Curst be the crown, chief author of my care—
> Nay, curst my will that made the crown my care;
> Curst be my birthday; curst ten times the womb
> That yielded me alive into the world.
> [III.3.1785–88, 1793–96]

Since Arthur is in fact alive, John's penitence actively reawakens the Tudor conscience concerning royal deposition, and Hubert's "confession" that Arthur lives which closes the scene makes us ready to condemn those lords who have just before served as choric spokesmen for our own hostility. John is now once more restored in our sympathies.

But not for long. The king's image declines again sharply with Arthur's cruel death in the first scene of Act IV (beginning Part II of the play). John is not absolved of guilt, either in *TR* or in Shakespeare, even though he is innocent of outright murder. Shakespeare adds the thought that John's "spirit" resides in the stones upon which the boy leaps to his death, but the addition only puts what is already implied in *TR* into sharper focus. There is no earthly doubt that Arthur would be alive but for John, and the image of the dead child must affect us as it does the lords. What seemed convincing penitence on John's part at the end of III.3 becomes groveling, whining evasion in IV.2. The image of the hysterical king peremptorily hanging the prophet and rashly giving orders, then revoking them, prompts the Bastard's just exclamation: "My lord, these are the passions of a mad man." John's obvious culpability in Arthur's death prepares the way for his final ignominy: yielding to Rome.

M. M. Reese in *The Cease of Majesty* (p. 274) makes much of John's "dissembling" with the cardinal, of the fact that his submission to Rome is made under duress. Shakespeare clearly indicts John far more in this situation than does the author of *TR*, but submission to Rome is submission to Rome. Even in Bale's play, John is hardly praiseworthy in this situation. It is, in fact, John's one weak point in Bale and contributes to his downfall. John's words later in *TR* clearly tie his downfall both to his murder of Arthur and to his submission to Pandulph here: "Since John did yield unto the priest of Rome,/Nor he nor his have prosp'red on the earth . . ." (V.5.1131–32). The cardinal's words cannot be trusted, and John trusts them. What saves him for the time is the Bastard, the weather, and the confession of the French lord Melun—not the cardinal. John may reveal contempt for himself in his frequent asides here, but his submission is ignominious nevertheless. That John knows this and knows moreover that he is far from the anti-papal hero he would like to be is indicated by the self-accusing lines immediately preceding his meeting with Pandulph, which underlie the entire interview with the legate: "Thy sins are far too great to be the man/T'abolish Pope and popery from thy realm" (IV.2.305–306).

That the speech goes on to predict the success of Henry VIII in his struggle with Rome need not identify John with Henry. It is saying that a weak, sinful king cannot be a Protestant hero like Henry VIII, and that while he would like to be one, his weaknesses will inevitably undo his good intentions—as they do here in his capitulation. John's royal image seems unredeemably weak following his sell-out to Pandulph.

Nevertheless, in keeping with the other weak-king plays, our sympathies in the last act return to John and intensify with the agony of his death. And the final shift takes some doing. First, late in Act IV, the Bastard in the language of straight Tudor doctrine makes his long plea for loyalty to the crown. John's name is mentioned once, when the Bastard absolves him of guilt for Arthur's death. Otherwise, only "the king" is referred to. God will reward those who obey "a king anointed by the lord"—even admitting that "the wrongs" he is accused of "are true." Gaunt could say it all more concisely in *Richard II* I.2, but no more explicitly. But, as with Gaunt's lines, the Bastard's lines taken out of the context of the play are one thing. They are a homily on obedience, nothing more or less. But in the play the Bastard's logic runs smack into the fact of a proposal to maim and murder an innocent child, "untimely butchered by a tyrant's means," says Essex. The issue is not fully resolved even by Tudor doctrine and the force of the Bastard's rhetoric.

Next (in V.2), the lords who have left John because of Arthur's death swear allegiance to Lewis, directly paralleling John's own sworn allegiance to the pope. Coupled with the Bastard's Tudor logic, this image helps prepare the way to our final shift in sympathies. If we are not yet ready to sympathize with John, we now fall out with the barons, who here appear no better than he. And Melun's dying confession helps these feelings along by introducing guilt as part of the barons' responses—and by extension of ours. As in Shakespeare, Melun serves solely as a catalyst in transferring our sympathies back to John.

Finally, and most important, is John's fever and his poisoning: the psychological and physical agony of his death. Fever and poisoning are admirably suited to John. History provided the appropriate instrument for his death, and the author of *TR* made good use of what he was provided. Throughout the play, John poisons himself and others with evil thoughts and then is tormented by the fever of guilt. But if the means of his death is appropriate, that death also strongly evokes our sympathy. The Bastard's homily may have affected intellectual loyalties, but pain and suffering affect deeper loyalties than those. What the Bastard's logic cannot quite do, the sight and sounds of an English king suffering the throes of a particularly painful death can do. The final scenes of *TR* are most similar in kind if not in degree to the conclusion of *Edward II*. Sympathy for the king finally is prompted by the horrors of a physically painful death. But the progression to that final sympathy has not been steady. It has involved constant uncertainty and vacillation.

One scene in the last act seems out of place. Yet Shakespeare keeps it, reducing it to twenty-two lines from its already abbreviated fifty-five in *TR*. Its function is clearer in *TR*. It explicitly concerns Lewis of France, and since its contents are reported in the final scenes of both plays, there seems no apparent need for it in the plot. What we see is Lewis trying to cope rapidly with four distinct, contradictory pieces of information: (1) the French military victory over the "daunted" Englishman at St. Edmund's Bury; (2) Melun's death and the defection of the English lords; (3) the grounding and loss of the entire French army in the Channel; and (4) the loss of the English army "in the tide" on Lincoln's Washes ("as Pharoah erst within the bloody sea"). Fifty-five lines in *TR*, twenty-two in Shakespeare. Lewis in *TR* is left gasping. ("Was ever heard such unexpected news!") By intent of the author or not, the scene metaphorically represents the central movement of the entire play. Chaotic reversals are the nature of our experience with this play. The dilemma of the weak king is presented in such a way as to leave us gasping, like Lewis. It is both in the action and in our feelings toward the central figure that the reversals take place. Lewis responding to the different pieces of information about his fortunes is like the audience responding to different pieces of information about John's. The play has been a tumult of events and feelings all pointing up the dilemma of the weak king.

Despite the patriotic utterances with which the Bastard concludes the final scene, the end is just one pinnacle in the up and down movement of our sympathies toward the royal figure. Our sympathies for John just before Arthur's death were almost as high as they are now. Yet they fell at an alarming rate. So could they again. This is not to say there is doubt cast on young Henry in the play. Far from it. He is the strong king: the Edward III–Henry V–Henry VII figure; in short, the wish-fulfillment. But the severe oscillations of our feelings toward a king who is of this world—a weak king, a human king—are our central response to this work. The glance at the bewildered Lewis just before the end may be seen as a glance at ourselves.

E. B. Everitt is correct in calling *TR* "a parable of dishonor."[3] But it is more than that. It sets in opposition forces engendered by the desire to be honorable without resolving the chaos which results. In an article published in 1966, Sigurd Burckhardt[4] finds

3. E. B. Everitt, ed., *Six Early Plays Related to the Shakespeare Canon, Anglistica,* XIV (Copenhagen: Rosenkilde and Bagger, 1965), 143.
4. Sigurd Burckhardt, "King John: The Ordering of this Present Time," *ELH,* XXXIII (1966), 133–53.

Shakespeare's *King John* built about the counter-pull of "mighty opposites": the axiomatic Tudor view of hierarchical obedience set against the dilemmas which result. To whom is one obedient, asks Hubert, king or God? To whom does one swear allegiance, ask the citizens of Angiers, *de facto* king or *de jure* king? In whose name are oaths taken, asks King Philip, God's or the pope's? These dilemmas obviously are present in Shakespeare's play, but they are far more pointed in *TR*, and Burckhardt's observation would be better directed toward it than toward *King John*. The "so-called" Elizabethan world picture, he says, cannot endure divided loyalties. In *TR* loyalties are severely divided, culminating in that ultimate division in the audience between king and conscience. Nothing is resolved by the last scene, really. The Bastard may speak of England being true to itself, but wherein lies that being true? In fealty to a child-murdering usurper? The nobles were wrong to defect to France, but their motives seemed justified. There seemed little alternative at the time. In retrospect, they were countenancing Arthur's death by remaining loyal, John's death by defecting. They are damned both ways. The ending brings the *deus ex machina* in the form of the successor. But this resolves nothing. The contradictory feelings of the weak-king plays seem nowhere more deadlocked than in *TR*. And this may have been the chief element in its appeal to Shakespeare.

KING JOHN

The relationship between *TR* and *King John* has been discussed in the past, sometimes at length. Many of the changes Shakespeare made have been singled out and the possible reasons for them discussed. One senses a conscious, determined effort on Shakespeare's part to follow the outlines of the earlier play and just as determined an effort to modify details, right down to the order in which speeches—many of them precisely the same in substance—are spoken. The language is altered with unusual thoroughness throughout the play, even when one feels an echo would be the most natural thing in the world. M. M. Reese and others indicate how few words or phrases in *TR* appear in passages of the same sense in *King John,* yet the events are nearly identical throughout the first three acts, and little less so in the last two. The opening of II.1 in *King John,* for example, and I.3 in *TR* have nothing to distinguish them in content. Both present King Philip, Lewis, Constance, Arthur, and Austria discussing their challenge to John, followed immediately by the appearance of John and his retinue. Each character has approximately the same things to say. But not only is the language—with exception of one line out of two hundred—entirely modified, so too is the order of the speakers and of several conversational exchanges. All the alterations can be explained on artistic grounds. Reese in *The Cease of Majesty* (pp. 268–70) shows clearly the way Shakespeare tightened and accentuated the poetry and action opening Act I. But this still does not explain the seemingly unrelenting alteration of language, something which is quite uncharacteristic in the relationships between Elizabethan plays and their immediate sources. It is almost as though Shakespeare were concerned about copyright. The seeming stubbornness with which Shakespeare has retained the outlines of plot and action in *TR* but altered the language gives one the sense that he felt quite strongly about *TR* —strongly enough to have wished the play subsumed by his own. And in fact, most modern readers I have talked with who are familiar with *TR* have difficulty remembering it. When they relate it to Shakespeare's play, some obvious changes in particular scenes and additions in the role of the Bastard emerge, and that is about all. *TR,* which has blank verse as good as that in *Woodstock* at least and a plot that is logical and coherent by late 1580s standards, simply disappears. One must persist in returning to the text to remind oneself of its existence. Shakespeare not only improved *TR;* he nearly obliterated it.

The weak-king play that is *TR* is practically the *same* weak-king play that is the main plot of *King John.* But in *King John* the weak-king play is not the whole play. It is eventually overshadowed in dramatic terms by a new political vision, one which makes *John* the transition, as J. F. Danby observed some years ago,[5] between Shakespeare's first tetralogy and the *Henry IV–Henry V*

---

5. J. F. Danby, *Shakespeare's Doctrine of Nature,* pp. 67–80.

cycle. In drama Shakespeare could not have found a better example of uncertainty and ambivalence toward the dominant political question of the day than *TR*, and he used its shape intact to represent in a work of art the alternative being accepted in the 1590s to the frustration that inevitably accompanied the kingly image in all the plays examined so far. In rhythm practically identical to that in *TR*, the appeal to audience sympathies toward the king shifts in *John*, though the extremes have been intensified. John seems more genuinely heroic in facing down the cardinal and blacker than ever in his relations with Prince Arthur. The intensification is something more than merely the natural outcome of Shakespeare's superior art. It makes the endless emotional oscillation and sense of futility in these plays more pointed than it has been thus far—even in *Henry VI*—and provides the background of emotional chaos against which Shakespeare's vision of another approach to political life is projected.

In the first act, Shakespeare prints the same actions and the same king as in *TR* more deeply into our imaginations, and this sets the pattern for much of what follows. Despite Elinor's explicit indication of John's illegitimate possession of the crown, the king here seems not quite so mealy as his counterpart in *TR*, and this is the result of Shakespeare's sharpening and focusing of his lines. No change in his characterization is intended. In the dispute between the brothers Faulconbridge, he is the same fair adjudicator, though Shakespeare makes him appear more supple by the suggestion of a sense of humor. The effect is that he seems a more urbane figure. But the thematic undertone of the scene is still the irony implicit in John's decision for the older brother in view of his own treatment of Arthur.

Similar intensification continues throughout the confrontation between John and Philip and their responses to the proposal from Angiers. Both kings begin bravely, but their chivalric decorum declines as the issue continues unresolved and neither can win a military victory. Both emerge from battle calling names, boasting victory, and otherwise descending to the level of Elinor's drawing Constance into a catfight. Then, as in *TR*, John suddenly plummets in our estimation, yielding the five provinces as part of the Angiers deal. But so, too, does Philip, whose desertion of

Arthur and subsequent double cross of John draw more attention by far in Shakespeare than in *TR*. The reasons for this will be discussed later in relation to the character of the Bastard. The overall effect (as the Bastard emphasizes) is one of the extreme shabbiness of political affairs. The impression of these scenes in *TR* has been considerably deepened.

That Shakespeare can dignify John's defiance of Pandulph after all this, that he can make it part of a coherent characterization (which John obviously is not in *TR*), is to say that he is Shakespeare. He does it by radically changing the tone of John's speeches, but not in the manner of *TR*. John, who in *TR* descended to the worst kind of anti-papal name-calling and braggadocio, speaks to Pandulph with greater force and dignity than we have ever heard from him (or ever will again):

> What earthy name to interrogatories
> Can task the free breath of a sacred king?
> Thou canst not, Cardinal, devise a name
> So slight, unworthy, and ridiculous
> To charge me to an answer, as the Pope.
> Tell him this tale; and from the mouth of England
> Add thus much more: that no Italian priest
> Shall tithe or toll in our dominions;
> But as we, under Heaven, are supreme head,
> So under Him that great supremacy,
> Where we do reign, we will alone uphold
> Without the assistance of a mortal hand.
> So tell the Pope, all reverence set apart
> To him and his usurped authority.
>   [III.1.147–60]

This speech, and one to follow it, are all that John says to the cardinal, and they are followed by the extended trial of Philip's oath and conscience. Pandulph's appearance has fallen like a bombshell on the proceedings, yet John has unexpectedly proved up to the challenge. Why? Because John is ready for it. Because such a blast from Rome is something he expects at any point. (Why else the reference to the otherwise irrelevant Stephen Langton affair?) Literally or figuratively, the speech seems one John has in his vest pocket, ready to be delivered at any time.

It is as rehearsed as it is concise. It also jolts our sympathies for John suddenly upward—as suddenly as Pandulph's entrance itself is sudden. John is now the strong English king opposing Rome. It is a single image, and once it has been flashed upon our imaginations, the scene gets to its business of investigating Philip's corroded conscience. As far as John's heroism goes, it is convincingly and emphatically there in an instant—and it lasts just about that long in the play. The next we see of him he is plotting Arthur's murder.

The first two acts, then, create severely ambivalent feelings in us toward John. When he seems most competent in Act I, we are deeply aware of the hypocrisy underlying his decisions; when he seems most debased and malleable in Act II, we are suddenly confronted with his anti-papal heroism. Rather than first being invited to condemn this king, later to admire him—as we are with Richard II and Edward II—our feelings toward him constantly vacillate. Similar vacillation is prompted, of course, by Henry VI, but John and Henry are very different. Both are human in the sense that they are inconsistent and guided by their emotions, but Henry's humanity is his saving; John's is his destruction. Henry is a believable human being trying to be a good governor. John cares little about good government. John's general incapacity to react forcefully and consistently to any challenge and his utter contempt for Christian morality (by which Henry sought vainly to rule) puts the problem of the weak king here in a quite different light. It is once more the question encountered in *Richard II* and *Edward II:* should an obviously incompetent monarch be deposed? And John is worse than Richard or Edward. He neither is legitimate heir to the throne nor does he have any personally redeeming qualities. We cannot depose him, yet we surely cannot endure him. Moreover the John of the three final acts becomes a figure who may reasonably seem worse to some even than Richard III because his evil is practiced so infirmly and with so weak a will, yet is so similarly horrifying and far-reaching.

Without the abbey scene of *TR*, John's evil becomes more focused in Shakespeare, and it is inspected far more minutely. In no play does Shakespeare lay the confused and infected motives of a king open to full view as he does the John of III.2 and IV.1.

First John instructs Hubert to murder Arthur; then Arthur prevails upon Hubert not to blind him. Only the latter scene held much interest for the author of *TR* and in terms specifically modified by Shakespeare and closely linked to John's instructions in the earlier scene. Throughout, Shakespeare's monster is a terribly human one. His thoughts and actions are familiar, and he is plagued with all-too-recognizable uncertainties and guilts. Those characteristics that bring him home to us most in human terms are what make him so debased a figure. We hear much about Richard III as true predecessor of Macbeth; we should perhaps hear more about John.

In *The Dramatist and the Received Idea* (pp. 205–307), Sanders contrasts the evil represented in Marlowe's *Doctor Faustus* with that represented in *Macbeth*. The dynamism in Marlowe, he finds, is limited by the playwright's confusion over medieval images of hell-horror and the new introspective sense of evil spawned by sixteenth-century Calvinism. In *Macbeth*, by contrast, says Sanders, evil has a "human face." It is a rich, varied, living presence which cannot be easily identified by investigations of medieval ethics and theology. A similar distinction can be made between the Hubert-Arthur scenes in *TR* and *King John*. In *TR* the scene is an exercise in medieval theological debate, with the side espousing loyalty to God taking precedence over loyalty to the king. Hubert in the earlier play is in his heart a true medieval Christian whose loyalty to John is demonstrated to be evil by the logic and force of Arthur's theology. Shakespeare makes of him a villain from the start whose evil wilts before the heat of Arthur's humanity. Rather than speaking in the language of theology, Arthur here speaks in that of familial affection. When Hubert's "head did but ache," says Arthur,

> I knit my handkerchief about your brows—
> . . . .
> And with my hand at midnight held your head, . . .
> [IV.1.42, 45]

The red-hot iron approaching his eyes, he says, "would drink my tears." And later, when Hubert has told him to hold his tongue,

> Hubert, the utterance of a brace of tongues
> Must needs want pleading for a pair of eyes.

Let me not hold my tongue, let me not, Hubert;
Or, Hubert, if you will, cut out my tongue,
So I may keep mine eyes.
[IV.1.98–102]

All this of course goes to support the terrible painful pity of
Hubert's responses to the boy. He is all father to him well before
he relents:

Come, boy, prepare yourself.
[IV.1.90]
Is this your promise?
[IV.1.97]
I can heat it, boy.
[IV.1.105]

And after:

Much danger do I undergo for thee.
[IV.1.134]

No logic, no ethics, no theology—just one seething mass of fierce
compassion which will not be denied. *Caritas.*

But so the face of evil is human, too. The intensely personal,
almost affectionate quality of John's earlier appeal to Hubert to
commit the crime gets under the skin—of a modern audience, at
least—as the splendid evil fabric of Richard III never quite does.
John literally woos Hubert to the deed. The terms are sincere,
the effect almost sensuous. A sense of the physical still predomi-
nates in the imagery:

Or if that thou couldst see me without eyes,
Hear me without thine ears, and make reply
Without a tongue, using conceit alone,
Without eyes, ears, and harmful sound of words;
Then, in despite of brooded watchful day,
I would into thy bosom pour my thoughts.
But, ah, I will not! Yet I love thee well,
And, by my troth, I think thou lovest me well.
[III.3.48–55]

John thinks that human physical attributes are naturally the allies of the good and thus wishes those attributes suppressed in Hubert in order that he might be able to perform the deed. But human attributes are hardly suppressed in John, and they are in no way allied to the good.

The worst and perhaps most human part of it is that John thinks he is being the artful Machiavel, whereas he is actually being the more usual, incompetent variety, the kind found throughout the Henry VI plays. Richard III, who would bring this instruction off in a highly skilled set-piece, and Bolingbroke, who would do it with a nod, would both be contemptuous of John's performance. John openly reveals his uncertainty and his troubled spirit to Hubert. Good Machiavels do not do that. They may talk about "midnight bells" and the "drowzy race of hell," but as agents of the night they do not acknowledge the power of conscience, as John does in wishing to close off all avenues of human response. John is clumsy. He has done his hinting; he need not reveal his hand further. But John tells all. He completely undoes whatever Machiavellian deceit was left:

> Good Hubert, Hubert, Hubert, throw thine eye
> On yon young boy. I'll tell thee what, my friend,
> He is a very serpent in my way,
> And wheresoe'er this foot of mine doth tread,
> He lies before me. Dost thou understand me?
> Thou art his keeper.
>
> *Hub.*   And I'll keep him so
> That he shall not offend your Majesty.
> *John.*   Death.
> *Hub.* My Lord?
> *John.*   A grave.
> *Hub.*   He shall not live.
> *John.*   Enough.
>   [III.3.59–66]

John's evil is the more telling because of its incompetence, because it is so embarassingly, clumsily human.

The Hubert-John and Hubert-Arthur scenes (III.2 and IV.1) are of a piece. Shakespeare has made of John a living dramatic representation of Ivan Karamazov's child-torturer. And he does it the way Antony wins over the mob. He stresses the human and the physical rather than the intellectual or theological. No blood is shed until later, but the prospect of the red-hot iron and the affectionate child are more than sufficient to parallel the bleeding wounds of dead Caesar. These images jolt us "out of thought." They blind us in helpless compassion and rage. No weak king has ever received this kind of treatment. But still John is no devil incarnate—no Richard of Gloucester. Would that he were. He is man corrupted, and the image is far less attractive to watch. It seems impossible that this creature can be redeemed. But redeemed he must be and, because he is so grossly human, can be. The only Richard of Gloucester who could have been saved was the one of the "Richard loves Richard" speech in the last act. John is vile, but possibilities for redemption emerge from every sweating pore of his speeches. The manner in which he is finally redeemed, however, is by no means anticipated at this point in the play.

John's evil continues to be the subject of IV.2, the scene paralleling the long chaotic sequence of unexpected happenings and wildly shifting sympathies surrounding the second coronation in *TR*. In Shakespeare it is honed, compressed, tightened, unified, and poetically enriched—but not rendered essentially different in function or effect. The coherence of the scene is of course greatly enhanced by its beginning after the crowning rather than before it. Until the Bastard's entrance, there is no mention in Shakespeare whatsoever of the plundered abbeys. Rather, the space devoted to John's lengthy rationale in *TR* is taken up by an equally lengthy outpouring of protesting metaphors by the lords, all devoted to the folly of John's coronation:

> To gild refined gold, to paint the lily,
> To throw a perfume on the violet,
> To smooth the ice, or add another hue
> Unto the rainbow, or with taper-light
> To seek the beauteous eye of Heaven to garnish
> Is wasteful and ridiculous excess.
> [IV.2.11–16]

This is followed by a second series of more extended metaphors.

Such a sudden outpouring seems grotesque and is not typical of the language anywhere else in *King John*. But the effect of the passage is hardly unconsidered by the lords. All these metaphors refer to the superfluity of an action which the speakers all know may indeed not be at all superfluous. The very excess of figure in Salisbury's and Pembroke's speeches suggests their underlying irony. In short, the lords are being sarcastic. In the guise of concerned counselors, they are cutting their liege to ribbons:

> In this the antique and well noted face
> Of plain old form is much disfigured,
> And, like a shifted wind unto a sail,
> It makes the course of thoughts to fetch about,
> Startles and frights consideration,
> Makes sound opinion sick and truth suspected
> For putting on so new a fashioned robe.
> [IV.2.21–27]

Indeed, "sound opinion" is "sick and truth suspected." Salisbury here is castigating not only the second coronation but the present conditions of John's reign. "So new a fashioned robe" hardly seems an appropriate image for a crowning. The new fashion may invidiously allude rather to the other more troubling method John has employed to assure his title: child-murder. As in *TR*, the underlying image in the scene is that of Arthur, as the lords again shortly make explicit. Shakespeare has replaced John's religious red herring in *TR* with John's utter silence, an uncharacteristic silence born more of fear than "policy." But he does attempt to bribe the lords by granting anything they request, which leads them to what has been on their minds all along: free Arthur (if he is still alive). There is no grotesque spate of metaphors here. Pembroke now links Salisbury's earlier vague hints of startled and frightened "consideration" and the sickness of "sound opinion" explicitly with the imprisonment of Arthur, whose restraint "Doth move the murmuring lips of discontent/To break into this dangerous argument" (IV.2.52–54).

With the entrance of Hubert (1.67) bringing "news" of Arthur's death, the action begins to offer the same chaos of emotional shifting which characterized the scene in *TR*. We are one with the lords in their high dudgeon, and we slam the door with them as they leave. But we also stay behind (having no choice) to hear the waves of unexpected news and to experience the tumultuous reversals and counter-reversals of feeling to follow. The scene is almost too much to stay with. Even in Shakespeare, it runs the risk of provoking audience resistance. Too many counter-pulls are present. But, then, this all contributes to the underlying vision of the play which, unlike *TR*, looks, as we shall see, beyond the rudely shifting sympathies of the weak-king plays to an alternative beginning to be palatable to a public fed up with so unstable an image of monarchy.

By the end of the scene, we have forgotten the lords and are again John's faithful subjects—briefly. We are brought to this point by the severe jolts John experiences in the scene. Groveling, guilt-ridden John again comes through the thin regal veneer as he "repents" Arthur's murder following the stormy departure of the lords. It would be hard to imagine the hostile lords reaching the palace gate with their "fearful heads" still on in *Richard III;* but John, a would-be Machiavel most unsuited to the role, repents. Shakespeare next abandons John's long agonizing struggle with guilt and self-doubt of *TR* in favor of action showing John jolted by various sudden reports. The reports, until the final one, are all bad. France is set to invade, John's subjects are ready to rebel over Arthur's murder, and Queen Elinor is dead. That the last is the heaviest jolt to John's stability is revealed only in brief exclamations: "What! Mother dead!" The other news is superficially more shaking. Piling Pelion on Ossa, Peter darkly prophesies that John will yield the crown "ere the next Ascension-day at noon." But John is numb. After helplessly begging the Bastard to win back the lords, he reveals where he still is: "My mother dead!" (1.181). We are moved to pity John, and, as is the case in scenes involving the queen in *Richard II*, pity is one means by which our sympathies are shifted in these plays. Our slamming the door with the lords now seems lost in the past. We are prepared for Hubert's "confession," and for the first restoration of John to our sympathies since that very different episode involving the cardinal in Act II.

Were it not for history, this would be a good place to end a weak-king play, as the author of TR obviously felt in ending his Part I here. John has been through hell—in part an expiation of his crime against Arthur, as Hubert's report of the five moons bears out. Making the moons the omens by which the rebelling populace fears for Arthur's life ties them far more intimately to what is going on than they are in TR. Here they are a message from God to John. John heeds the message, is penitent, and assures Hubert they will both roast in hell for the crime. Then Hubert informs him that all is well; Arthur lives. Everything is suddenly reversed. John is saved, the lords will return, the populace will submit, the French will stay home, and we will once more be loyal, faithful subjects of a heroic Protestant king.

But a minute into the following scene (IV.3), and all that John has gained is lost, the fault still his. Arthur leaps to his death ("O me! my uncle's spirit is in these stones.") The heritage of the two-part structure of TR leaves even more telling the theme of unending fluctuation of our sympathies toward the weak king. Our sympathies are with the king at the conclusion of *Woodstock*, *Edward II*, and *Richard II*, which may suggest that there our sympathies should officially reside. In the John plays, we reach a play ending before the death of Arthur, and our wildly shifting sympathies seem to come to rest with John's penitence and joy at the news that Arthur lives. But it is all to begin again. There is no point of emotional stasis regarding the weak king. What is emphasized between IV.2 and IV.3 is that we seem condemned to endless vacillation toward this figure. And so it will continue. His death and the patriotic utterances which surround it—even the accession of a boy hero-king (the wish-fulfillment, as in *Edward II*)—are nothing more than one of the peaks along the way. More valleys, too, will follow. There is always the morning after the coronation. Arthur's death comes both literally and figuratively the morning after John's second crowning. The indignation of the lords at finding Arthur's body mirrors our own, and we are in no mood to determine whether John is directly or indirectly at fault. The irony comes not in the fact that Arthur should die just after John has "reformed," but that Arthur's death must begin the awful antiphony of our responses all over again.

And in addition, John has not reformed, as his infamous submission to Pandulph loudly protests.

For Elizabethan public sentiment, nothing like the Hubert-
Arthur scene was needed to debase John. Popular response would
automatically make yielding to the Pope the low point of John's
reign—as it is even in the pro-John work of Bale. Both Shakespeare
and the author of *TR*, in making of the Arthur affair a second
low point, provide the means whereby the violent, unpredictable
shifts in appeal to audience sympathies are emphasized. And as
Shakespeare has deepened the emotional effect of the Arthur
affair, he has made John's submission to Pandulph more damning
by showing it as a *fait accompli*, omitting all the agony the John
of *TR* goes through beforehand. The final portion of the play is
more compact and brief in Shakespeare, with less emphasis on
John's devastating guilt and more on his desperate helplessness.
But the elements are the same, and if Shakespeare omits or tele-
scopes many of John's reactions here, it is because the Bastard
and his reactions are assuming importance which is utterly
foreign to *TR*.

So in the final act, Shakespeare condenses everything but the
Bastard's role and the totally unexpected confession of French
treachery by the dying Melun. The latter is a thunderbolt, but
it has been a play of thunderbolts. Unexpected developments
have consistently jarred our expectations and our sympathies.
The monarch who opens the act *having* yielded his crown to the
hated Pandulph must be made a tragic figure by the end, and
only another surprise, bigger than the steady stream of surprises in
IV.2, can make us momentarily forget what we have just seen.
History (Holinshed) provided the author of *TR* with Melun, and
Shakespeare takes him over, practically intact. Melun's direct
appeal to loyalist sympathies in the audience is as important as
his informing the lords of Lewis' treachery. We are ready for
John's death scene (with recollections of Arthur and Pandulph
delayed until after the performance). Considering what a radical
shift in sympathies we are asked to make, all the patriotic fervor
implicit in Melun's confession is needed. Shakespeare's Bastard,
of course, also makes patriotic speeches in this act, but they have

a somewhat different nature and function. Melun, a character who exists just for the occasion, speaks clearly and directly to our confused and battered loyalties.

Shakespeare fuses the two Swinstead Abbey scenes of *TR* into one, omits of course the comic plotting of the monks, and considerably tightens all the action surrounding John's tragic demise. John is not underplayed at the end, however. If his death is not so magnificent a poem as Richard II's, it is nevertheless made genuinely tragic by its language:

> The tackle of my heart is cracked and burned,
> And all the shrouds wherewith my life should sail
> Are turned to one thread, one little hair.
> My heart hath one poor string to stay it by,
> Which holds but till thy news be uttered;
> And then all this thou seest is but a clod
> And module of confounded royalty.
> [V.7.52–58]

And the Bastard heightens the effect with his traditional ultimate pledge of the squire to the dead hero:

> I do but stay behind
> To do the office for thee of revenge,
> And then my soul shall wait on thee to heaven
> [V.7.70–72]

With the accession of a successor who promises all the strength and wisdom a successor always promises, *King John* ends on a heroic note. The king is dead, and his death has been tragic. Revere his memory—at least until you get home.

So, we have the weak-king play. Or do we? The play as dealt with thus far is essentially the earlier *TR* with broad changes in its language, but little change in overall movement or intent. But the play has been radically changed by Shakespeare's treatment of two characters only touched on here, and this change constitutes for the first time a solution to the dilemma of the weak king. The two characters are Lady Constance and the Bastard Faulconbridge.

Shakespeare greatly increased the size of Constance's role in *TR*. There, some thirty-eight lines constitute her response to King

Philip's betrayal of Arthur. Shakespeare inserts an entire scene of one hundred thirty lines, most of them Constance raging at Salisbury, a patient ally. Eight lines are all Constance has in *TR* to respond to Arthur's capture as against sixty in Shakespeare. On first reading *King John,* I shared the reaction of those who listen to her in the play: "Patience, good lady! comfort, gentle Constance!" "O fair affliction, peace!" (III.4.22, 36). Because she will not relent, they call her mad, but she is not mad. She "wishes to heaven" she were, so that she might forget her grief. Constance picks up where we left off in *Henry VI.* Her rage at what is done to her son is the same underlying rage we feel so strongly in the early trilogy—rage at the atrocities committed in the name of political necessity. She believes her son is the legitimate king and that justice demands he be put in John's place. She has accepted King Philip's oath that he will help as evidence of his desire to let right be done. She never considers other motives. When Philip deserts her, she rages at his perfidy, and never ceases raging through the remainder of the play. She never comes to terms with political realities and inevitabilities. We only hear late in the play that she has died "in a frenzy" (IV.2.122). The relentless quality, almost tedium, of her outcries and lamentations are the ultimate expression of rage and helplessness against the kind of behavior which characterizes political life. She will not be quieted, she will not submit, she is not mad. No one can do anything with her. And she can do nothing to counter what she is raging against. It is inexorable.

Our responses to *Henry VI* can be much like Constance's responses to what is going on around her. Either we rage as she does or we despair in silence because the only viable alternative to the weak king is the Machiavel: Richard III. So the solution is worse than the dilemma. In the plays examined thus far, the playwrights have done what playwrights must do with the underlying philosophical, political turmoils of their time. They reflect and echo. They sing the sufferer's song and by deepening and articulating the experience relieve him of some of his pain. But they may also go farther, and *King John* does go farther. It is the turning point in Shakespeare's "history" plays, as the 1590s were a turning point in public acceptance of a new view of political reality. It seeks the means by which Christian man can come to terms with "policy," by which the right men may somehow be able to bridge the gap between the moral and the possible. Finally, *King John* bridges the chasm that exists between the anti-Machiavellian *Henry VI* and the pro-Machiavellian *Henry V*, and it does so through the development of the character of the Bastard.

Largely, it would seem, because the book was written about *King Lear*, John F. Danby's *Shakespeare and the Doctrine of Nature* (in particular, pp. 57–101) has never received its due for what it says about the history play. Danby claims to be supporting Tillyard's then newly written *Shakespeare's History Plays*, and insofar as order in the state is the goal toward which the plays point, one can understand the claim. But Danby's order hardly jibes with the divinely inspired, providential order Tillyard is talking about. Danby is not concerned with the punishment of England or its redemption; nor is he really concerned with degree (hierarchy). He is concerned with what we might call the semblance of order: with men somehow living from day to day without endlessly going at each other's throats. And the solution he finds in Shakespeare represents political stability as hardly more than a set of *ad hoc* decisions and actions by the king intended to avoid civil bloodshed and keep people relatively satisfied.

Achieving even the semblance of order inevitably requires some of the actions of a Richard III, but performed by a far more attractive, craftier leader, one who genuinely wants to avoid killing fellow Englishmen. Danby sees the Bastard as the preliminary sketch for such a figure. Where I differ from him is in seeing the Bastard not as a figure who *has* come to terms with the system, but as one who is *in the process of* coming to terms with it, and in feeling that what we see in *King John* is the process.

In identifying the Bastard as the central figure in *King John*, the spate of excellent articles of recent years, beginning with Adrien Bonjour's "The Road to Swinstead Abbey,"[6] have all failed to come to grips with one important fact observed by

6. Adrien Bonjour, "The Road to Swinstead Abbey," *ELH*, XVIII (1951), 253–74. For others, see the Bibliographical Remarks.

Julia C. Van de Water in an article published in 1960. That fact is that, as in *TR*, Shakespeare's Bastard is not one character but two. "In the first three acts he is little more than a thinly disguised vice, and in the last two the embodiment of active and outraged nationalism: the English Patriot." And the break seems complete. "The vice," she says, "is simply replaced by the Patriot."[7] Any discussion of the Bastard which fails to be aware of the complete transformation in his character is simply not dealing with the play as a whole. Most discussions seek to explain his earlier tone in terms of the later one—or the later tone in terms of the earlier one. Thus, the implicit acknowledgment is required that either the shift in the Bastard's character must be explained or the play is the contradictory, confused affair that some critics find it. It is doubtful that the latter is the case.

It is difficult to agree with Miss Van de Water that Shakespeare, who had probably written several comedies and at least four history plays by the time he got to this play, would purposely intensify the contradictions in a character he found in his source— as it appears he did at first glance. The division in the Bastard's personality can be dealt with in terms that take cognizance of both the first three acts of the play and the last two. But in order to comprehend the "whole" Bastard, the play must be gone through yet once more, this time from his point of view. While he is, as some say, "outside the structure of the play" his observations and attitudes point directly to its central issues and finally shape its new direction. What frustrates a modern audience is that he does not comment on himself as he does on others—except at one critical yet confusing moment.

Insofar as the Bastard's attitudes earlier in the play are satirical and point out the ironies implicit in the actions and attitudes of others, he is like the Vice; but whereas the Vice is essentially faceless, a truly "motiveless" if delightful "malignity," the Bastard we first meet is by no means faceless. He conveys a very distinct personality. He is a soldier of fortune who is unwilling to see life in large philosophical terms. He is direct and offhand, and he respects this quality in others. What basically distinguishes the

7. Julia C. Van de Water, "The Bastard in King John," *SQ*, XI (1960), 137–46. Quotes taken from pp. 143 and 146.

Bastard of Shakespeare's opening act from his counterpart in *TR* is his humor and youthful cynicism. Both are attractive, but Shakespeare's character is "seized" by no mystical, ghostly report of his true parentage. He knows from the start that considerable doubt exists about his legitimacy. He is not seeking a legal right, but an instinctive one. He cannot abide men who are constrained and petty and hence cannot abide his brother. His claim to the inheritance is based purely on his opinion that his free and open spirit is much better suited to it. But he is quick to throw off one attraction for another which seems still more worthy of his inexhaustibly expansive spirit. His superficial cynicism is thoroughly engaging, but underneath he is callow. Whereas he can see through the courtier's pretenses and false attitudes because he is clear-eyed and intelligent, he is as yet unquestioning about larger moral or political issues. And he is as yet unquestioning about himself. His mother's confession delights him for the excitement and challenge his new life will bring him more than for his elevation in rank. He lives for that which will feed his incredible *élan,* and accepts Queen Elinor's offer in such a spirit. He would follow any great lady capable of so lively and forthright an offer as follows:

> I like thee well. Wilt thou forsake thy fortune,
> Bequeath thy land to him, and follow me?
> I am a soldier and now bound to France.
>   [I.1.148–50]

The Bastard does not question the justice of this soldierly voyage because such issues are as yet beyond his ken, no more than does the impulsive Hotspur examine the hard implications of the rebellion in which he takes part. And the parallel to Hotspur is not superficial. Both live by that chimera called "honor," which may be "plucked . . . from the pale-fac'd moon," yet have no very clear earthly correlative. Its existence goes no farther than the limits of its possessor's ego. One may "cavil at the ninth part of a hair" because of it, yet not really know why one is cavilling. Rarely are the issues that affect it ongoing. They are ephemeral—one today, another tomorrow. And rarely is the order and welfare of the state an issue. It concentrates more on piecemeal, short-term issues. Thus the Bastard would have no deep concern about John's usurpation and the controversy surrounding his reign, nor would he sense the deep irony in John's decision in favor of an elder brother as he senses the surface ironies in the humors of asthenic brothers, pretentious courtiers, and boastful foreign dukes. The Bastard's honor in Act I concentrates piecemeal upon immediate and ephemeral issues only.

Few have asked why this very vocal young man is so comparatively unvocal early in Act II. True, he loudly lampoons the unwary Duke of Austria, who suddenly becomes the great challenge to his Hotspurian honor; he also upsets the formal decorum of challenge and counter-challenge between John and Philip with exclamatory thrusts at his apoplectic adversary. But, strangely, as the claims of Arthur unfold and Elinor baits poor Constance, we hear nothing from the Bastard. For all we know, he is unaware that there is anyone else present, except possibly Limoges. But the dominant subject of the scene, that of Arthur's legitimacy, we shall shortly find, has been getting through to him.

The first evidence that the Bastard has been responding to what is going on in II.1 suggests that he has been listening intently and for some time. It is revealed in his aggressive reaction to Hubert's neutrality on behalf of Angiers. That the "citizen" who speaks to the two kings from the city's walls is not the faceless spokesman of *TR* but the terrible Hubert de Burgh has been finally established by Wilson and Honigmann and is quite important to the play at this point.[8] Up to the point of his "conversion" by Arthur, Hubert is a stock Elizabethan villain—that is, in outward appearance of dress, posture, and facial expression. The frantic John later makes this incontrovertibly clear. In his anguish, John charges in IV.2 that Hubert's presence prompted him to seek Arthur's death:

> How oft the sight of means to do ill deeds
> Make deeds ill done! Hadst not thou been by,
> A fellow by the hand of nature marked,

8. See J. D. Wilson, ed., *Shakespeare's King John* (Cambridge: At the University Press, 1954), pp. xlv–xlvii; and E. A. J. Honigmann, ed., *Shakespeare's King John,* New Arden ed. (Cambridge, Mass.: Harvard University Press, 1969), pp. xxxiv–vii.

> Quoted, and signed to do a deed of shame,
> This murder had not come into my mind.
>   [IV.2.219–23]

If this is the image of the spokesman on Angiers's wall, then what he speaks is not cool logic but active deceit. It has puzzled critics that the Bastard should become so angry at the city as to propose that it be leveled. What has angered him is the villainy of Hubert, evident in his dress and, if we know anything about Elizabethan acting conventions, his manner. But if Hubert is not neutral, but only pretending neutrality, then on whose behalf is he really speaking? Whose cause does his deceitful neutrality serve? It serves John's cause, because Arthur is the lawful heir to the English crown, and thus by rights Angiers should yield to Arthur. Regardless of Philip's intent, Philip stands for Arthur's right. Arthur should be king, and thus Hubert serves John's interests in his neutrality as Angiers's spokesman and certainly later in proposing the marriage of Lewis and Blanche. John later thanks him (III.2.29–33), but not so the Bastard. If the Bastard does not say outright here that Arthur's claim is just and Philip is honorable for defending him, then he makes this feeling abundantly clear in the Commodity speech, which is largely a castigation of Philip for later betraying the boy. Here he settles for the heated suggestion that the city and its insidious spokesman be destroyed.

To the obvious rejoinder that an Elizabethan audience would never side with a French king, one can only say that neither would they naturally side with a usurper, especially with the rightful heir available and on the scene. The succession here has not become clouded, as in *Henry VI*. Arthur is legitimate, John is not; and except for a will which Elinor claims to have discovered, there is really nothing but John's "strong possession" between Arthur and the crown—and Philip is ready to question that strength. Contempt for the Frenchman enters the picture when Philip betrays Arthur, not when he opposes John on Arthur's behalf. Philip is governed by greed, but in a just cause. John is governed only by greed.

John has everything to gain by Hubert's neutrality because anything but neutrality from Angiers would tip the scales. To declare outright for John would be too direct and less effective for Hubert. Hubert wishes to create an image of detachment which can play into John's hand without showing his own. Announcing his position here would weaken his later position as arbitrator. When the Bastard's suggestion about leveling Angiers seems about to be taken seriously by the kings ("I like it well," says John), Hubert is forced to come up with something better. Hubert is the kind of manipulator a ruthless king can count on in such circumstances. And the something better actually proves so beneficial to John as to suggest that even the whole idea of the marriage was cooked up beforehand. John's gratitude to Hubert in III.2 could cover a good deal. In sacrificing five French provinces, and provoking contempt of his audience, he gains unchallenged authority over the rest. Blanche is literally his pawn and he uses her as such—or Elinor does, who is by far the better Machiavel.

John, under Elinor's guidance, is a usurper and has been playing a crooked game from the start. But the betrayer, the agent of disillusionment, the one who comes out looking worse because he wore at least a mask of honor, is Philip. And it is Philip whom the Bastard is chiefly studying in this scene. A scene later (III.1), faced with Pandulph's insistence that Philip break his oath to John, Philip will undergo a struggle of loyalties which transcends anything in *TR* and, considered against the background of his betrayal of Arthur, is deeply ironic. Were it not for what has gone before, one might then feel compassion for Philip in his plight. But what troubles him is not his conscience. The whole issue of Philip's vows before God, brought up in III.1 as it is not when Philip breaks his vows to Arthur in the present scene, only masks his distress at losing the wealth and power the Lewis-Blanche marriage would bring him. When his vows to Arthur, which are just as binding in the eyes of God, are broken, Philip reveals no such scruples. Philip, who was genuinely confused in *TR*, is a shifting, smiling hypocrite in this play—an instinctive man of "policy" who will rationalize in moral terms any action that will increase his personal gain (which he construes to be national gain). And as such, it is he who, more than anyone or anything else in the play, opens up the Bastard's eyes to political reality.

The foregoing analysis in effect summarizes the Bastard's speech on Commodity. What is usually overlooked in this speech is that the Bastard takes John's perfidy for granted. Its existence is self-evident and no longer disturbs him. John fights in a dishonorable cause: "John, to stop Arthur's title in the whole,/Hath willingly departed with a half" (II.1.562–63). The Bastard, after what he has seen and heard, expects no other action from John. But the shock is at the one who said *Let Right Be Done,* then yielded to "that daily break-vow . . . That smooth-fac'd gentleman, tickling Commodity."

> This bawd, this broker, this all-changing word,
> Clapped on the outward eye of fickle France,
> Hath drawn him from his own determined aid,
> From a resolved and honorable war
> To a most base and vile-concluded peace.
> [II.1.582–86]

The audience may not have thought Philip was acting selflessly, but the Bastard had and that is the important point here. It shows how shallow his youthful cynicism had been, and the shock proves traumatic. His reaction is the utterly characteristic gesture of the disillusioned, sensitive youth:

> Not that I have the power to clutch my hand
> When his fair angels would salute my palm,
> But for my hand, as unattempted yet,
> Like a poor beggar raileth on the rich.
> Well, whiles I am a beggar, I will rail
> And say there is no sin but to be rich;
> And being rich, my virtue then shall be
> To say there is no vice but beggary.
> Since kings break faith upon commodity,
> Gain, be my Lord, for I will worship thee.
> [II.1.589–98]

It is important to look at the Bastard for a moment in the images and language of our own time, for we clearly empathize with him. We are caught in the dilemma posed by Constance and the Bastard: that between outright rebellion against "the system," or accommodation with it. The image of the Bastard at this point in the play is that of the sensitive young man "selling out." In becoming John's trusted lieutenant, he joins forces with his "Establishment." His alternative would be the way of Constance, whose response to these events immediately follows his, the way of endless, hopeless protest. His first reaction to his new consciousness is the sense of his own corruption and deep self-condemnation. But what follows in the play is not the utterly grasping existence the Bastard imagines here. There will be a place for conscience and truth within the system, so long as it is understood that they will take different shapes in different situations. The most guilty-seeming of men—Hubert—will prove to be the most compassionate. But the system will be corrupt, with its central symbol the king the most corrupt of all. And through that very corruption the Bastard will learn the need for a new political *modus operandi,* one which acknowledges the inevitability of human corruption. He will have come to understand the nature of the weak king and will build his own image around that understanding.

Beginning with motivation by "gain" rather than that vague "honor," the Bastard pledges himself wholeheartedly to the support of the *de facto* king of England, to a man whose title the Bastard has acknowledged is nonexistent and who is to plot criminally and brutally against the life of a helpless child whose title is as clear as it is possible to be in a system of hereditary succession. While the Bastard is ignorant of John's specific plot against Arthur, he now knows unmistakably that John is dishonorable and a usurper. "Gain" for the Bastard will mean unswerving if cynical adherence to Tudor doctrine, to that concept of obedience which the homilies have been fatuously espousing for some time but which is so at odds with existing reality as to provide the war of conscience which underlies all these plays. It will mean loyalty to the reigning king, come what may. It can be argued, of course, that the Bastard would hardly adhere to John if he were motivated first by profit and gain. Obviously, a gamble is involved, and those that are after profit must gamble. Recall that Richard of Gloucester took such a gamble (*3 Henry VI* IV.1) in supporting Edward IV when things looked bleak, when Clarence deserted the crown because Warwick's new alliance with

Margaret and the French king looked so promising. That Richard's loyalty to Edward is pretense is obvious. His real motive is that he guesses rightly (and this is part of what makes him a successful political figure) that Edward will come out on top. In Machiavellian terms, risk is essential to political success. Like Richard in *3 Henry VI*, the Bastard here realizes a gamble is necessary. His motives are like Richard's, and to a degree his success is comparable to Richard's.

What makes the Bastard's transformation difficult to analyze is that it involves in part his reluctance to discuss his first-hand responses with the audience. But, as we shall see, one potent glimpse of those responses in IV.3 is convincing evidence that this is the old Bastard still. Otherwise he gives us no indication of his personal feelings, and it is an essential part of his role that he does not do so. On his path to power, the identifying characteristic of Bolingbroke the politician is his silence. Until the final scene of *Richard II*, Bolingbroke says nothing about his motives, but we are constantly invited to speculate freely about them. They are an essential part of that drama, as his silence about them is an essential part of his personality. Prince Hal, Bolingbroke's successor in political method as well as power, soliloquizes about his motives early, but is silent about them later—like the Bastard. Hal's "I know you all" speech directly reveals his inner thoughts and feelings, but once he has assumed his role of committed political leader, we do not hear how he really feels again until the troubled king speaks to us in the night before Agincourt. This is not to say that his real feelings, or the Bastard's, are not important or that we may not speculate about them. We cannot have the same kind of understanding of them as we can have of their directly stated feelings, but we can have understanding nevertheless.

The shift from Vice to Patriot, then, that Miss Van de Water finds in the play is not the failure on the part of the author to render a consistent characterization. It is the author's attempt to show a man going through the Tudor version of selling out: relinquishing youth and its commitments to Hotspurian chimeras of honor and conscience in favor of "gain," here seen as adherence to a *de facto* king when a *de jure* king is alive and innocent. The "good" which results cannot be acceptable to one who feels that good cannot be qualified, and certainly Shakespeare was to review this question himself in the tragedies; but it is the end of the road in the history plays.

In his next appearance following the Commodity speech, the Bastard speaks with the same voice toward Austria as before, though now more in control of the situation. His use of Constance's "And hang a calve's-skin on those recreant limbs" as a magpie refrain to torment the duke is less explosive than his earlier responses—calculated to goad Austria into battle rather than simply elicit the duke's uncontrolled spleen. And following III.1, the change in his manner becomes marked. The Bastard we see now is no longer the sophomoric if skillful social critic of the first act. He is John's chief lieutenant. How he achieved the position is not important. He did not have it when they came to France, but he has it when they leave. His first assignment is to do John's bidding with the abbeys, to which his response certainly reveals, crudely at least, a new commitment to gain: "Bell, book, and candle shall not drive me back/When gold and silver becks me to come on" (III.3.12–13). And he is not seen again until the middle of the long, tumultuous IV.2, back from the abbeys with both gold and the voluble prophet Peter.

The Bastard we see in Act IV has become an Establishment lord and is so regarded by the others. It is not just a passing image but reveals the Bastard now operating in a thoroughly political sphere in which he is at home and is accepted by others. As such, he now lives by those same Machiavellian tactics which we have seen in a very different guise in *Henry VI*. Up or down in our sympathies, king and lords alike live by craft and appearances. Gain is certainly the chief motive of the nobles, though not their only one—as their sympathetic responses to Arthur indicate. Just how much of their pity is craft and how much genuine the play does not indicate. But in the alertness and vigor that are so essential to political success, the Bastard reveals himself far superior to the lords. He is, in short, the better Machiavel. He is quicker, more intelligent and has a stronger personality—like the Richard III who went before and the Henry V to follow. He alone has the presence of mind not to jump to conclusions about Hubert following the discovery of Arthur's body, and his will regarding Hubert's safety from the lords' wrath prevails. But the sight of the dead child has stirred the old call of conscience in him. If he does not join the lords in rebellion, it is not because his emotions have not been so aroused as have theirs. Nevertheless, he returns to the king, and the return is his gamble. It is governed by pure political expediency.

Danby finds the Bastard's second soliloquy the most important speech in *King John,* and I agree completely that it is a deep revelation of his real feelings—but not the only one of its kind we have heard. Its contents are of the same order as the Commodity speech, different as is its tone. In both, the Bastard is overwhelmed by the evil effects of "policy." The earlier speech was charged with rage leading to total disillusionment. This one is a sober, bitter lament at the sorry moral condition of political man. It is not a new discovery to him. It shows the sensibilities of old still with him—but resigned to the rapine operation of worldly affairs:

> I am amazed, methinks, and lose my way
> Among the thorns and dangers of this world.
> How easy dost thou take all England up!
> From forth this morsel of dead royalty,
> The life, the right and truth of all this realm
> Is fled to Heaven, and England now is left
> To tug and scamble, and to part by the teeth
> The unowed interest of proud-swelling state.
> Now for the bare-picked bone of majesty
> Doth dogged War bristle his angry crest . . .
> [IV.3.140–49]

Danby profoundly relates this speech to old King Henry's farewell to "pity, fear, and truth" before the unrelenting drive of Richard of Gloucester. Like Henry, young Arthur is the departed symbol of the "right and truth of all this realm." But if there is no political viability remaining but that of Richard of Gloucester, if we are doomed "To tug and scamble" for the "bare-picked bone of majesty," then there is, as William Matchett observes,[9] but one

9. William Matchett, "Richard's Divided Heritage in *King John," Essays in Shakespearean Criticism,* J. R. Calderwood and H. E. Toliver, eds. (New York: Prentice-Hall, 1970), p. 165.

way open to the Bastard: "I'll to the king." He must be part of the
"tug and scamble." He must use the tactics of the Machiavel, but
avoid, wherever possible, the bloodshed. He must strive to come
out on top, and the most effective means to achieve that end will
be the best.

Fortunately for all, the means the Bastard discovers are the
province of the theatre. They are visual and rhetorical. He does
not put aside deceit, though he employs it far more subtly than
Richard. He puts the headsman's axe on the shelf (to be used
infrequently and only when absolutely necessary), and he calls to
his aid the makeup man, the costumer, the tapestry-maker, and
above all the patriotic poet. He is determined to succeed where
Richard and Buckingham failed despite their most vigorous efforts
in *Richard III* III.5 and 7, where they try to take the kingdom
exclusively by means of their histrionic talents. In *King John*, the
Bastard is determined that the image of the weak king must die,
and in his place must emerge an image of the hero king.

The final act of *King John* is one of the most unexpected dramatic contrivances in Shakespeare, if we realize what the Bastard
is doing in it. John opens the act with his ignominious submission
to Rome, to which even the now utterly loyal Bastard can only
gasp, "O inglorious league!" And the rest of the act is spent ready-
ing the wretch for the tragic glory of his death. That is what the
weak-king script calls for, and all possible aids—Melun the chief
one—are summoned. But this weak king is such poor stuff that the
task is nearly ludicrous. Richard II was more than ready for the
occasion, poor Edward II well suited to the pathos of his terrible
demise. Henry VI reached true glory, the glory of heaven itself,
in death. But what can be done with John? The author of *TR*
provided guilt, guilt, and more guilt—and the result was credible.
Shakespeare's—that is, the Bastard's—tack is quite different. Rather
than trying to correct John's obvious weaknesses in the slightest,
the Bastard ignores them. He speaks to John, urges him to combat,
exhorts him to revenge as though he were the greatest king in
Christendom receiving encouragement following an unfortunate
turn of events. His stirring lines create the image of a strong king
as though there were no question that that is what John is and
has been all along:

> Be great in act, as you have been in thought.
> Let not the world see fear and sad distrust
> Govern the motion of a kingly eye.
> Be stirring as the time. Be fire with fire.
> Threaten the threatener, and outface the brow
> Of bragging Horror. So shall inferior eyes,
> That borrow their behaviors from the great,
> Grow great by your example and put on
> The dauntless spirit of resolution.
> Away, and glister like the God of War
> When he intendeth to become the field.
> Show boldness and aspiring confidence.
>   [V.1.45–56]

The Bastard further brushes aside John's attempt to justify his league with Rome and exhorts the hero king to hoist his French boy-enemy on his own petard. And if he thus remakes John's shriveling image in John's own unkingly presence, he redoubles his efforts to that end before the rebels. The image of the Bastard's resolute, all-wise monarch whom the rebel lords have offended makes Henry of Agincourt a stripling, proud Edward III a younker:

> Now hear our English King;
> For thus his royalty doth speak in me.
> He is prepared, and reason too he should.
> This apish and unmannerly approach,
> This harnessed masque and unadvised revel,
> This unhaired sauciness and boyish troops,
> The King doth smile at, and is well prepared
> To whip this dwarfish war, these pigmy arms,
> From out the circle of his territories.
>   [V.2.128–36]

The Bastard is painting John in the most heroic colors he knows because he has come to realize something about kings. They are all men, and thus they are all weak—some, like John, unspeakably weak. But even the best of them must be the weak king in terms of the inevitably fluctuating responses of his subjects to his actions. If the tools of the Machiavel are the only effective ones available to the politician, then he must use them boldly to counter the weak-king image. He must somehow forestall our endlessly shifting sympathies. The Bastard must be a king's image-maker. Later, in *Henry V,* the king will be his own image-maker, but the likes of John must have a promoter. And he is fortunate to have the Bastard, who discovers a technique to counter the weak-king image better than any before it—a technique which he happily passes on to Hal. He develops a special diction, a new, subtle, thoroughly engaging, occasionally inebriating kind of patriotic rant.

The first of the passages above (V.1.44–56), listened to several times, begins to have the ring of another far more familiar passage:

> Stiffen the sinews, summon up the blood,
> Disguise fair nature with hard-favored rage.
> Then lend the eye a terrible aspect,
> Let it pry through the portage of the head
> Like the brass cannon.
>> [*Henry V* III.1.7–11]

And the other quoted passages certainly have the same familiar ring as the following:

> And tell the pleasant Prince this mock of his
> Hath turned his balls to gunstones, and his soul
> Shall stand sore charged for the wasteful vengeance
> That shall fly with them. For many a thousand widows
> Shall this his mock mock out of their dear husbands,
> Mock mothers from their sons, mock castles down;
> And some are yet ungotten and unborn
> That shall have cause to curse the Dauphin's scorn.
>> [*Henry V* I.2.281–88]

The ringing diction here is no mere byproduct in the creation of the *Henry V* pageant. It is part of a new approach to royal diction, one which we have heard bits of before, but never in such rich tones and with such sustained energy. It is a music which is intended to and has for centuries succeeded in obliterating thought: seditious thought, perhaps, which grows out of reflections on kingly incompetence. It "sets the teeth" and "stretches the nostril wide." It stirs the blood, but it tranquilizes the mind. And it is possibly the least introspective language in all Shakespeare. Had Shakespeare been ready with it in *Richard III*, perhaps we would have heard it from the Richmond in Act V, whom he obviously wished to glorify. But Shakespeare wasn't and succeeding generations have commented on the thin brew that hero seems capable of turning out. Not so Henry V, and not so his predecessor, the Bastard. It is a special diction, in no way spontaneous. It is capable of being turned on and off. Hal, who had never used it earlier, suddenly turns it on following his coronation. One of its harmonies is homespun English amid the broad sounds of vowels, the rich imagery, and the regular, heavily stressed rhythms: "Not Amurath an Amurath succeeds,/But Harry Harry" (*2 Henry IV* V.2.48–49). Perhaps it is that homespun patch that most of all gives this diction its individuality. We have heard the vowels and rhythms, seen the images before in the oratory of challenge and boast in Marlowe and the *Henry VI* plays, and certainly in the contemporary plays of George Peele and Robert Greene as well. But not:

> For your own ladies and pale-visaged maids,
> Like Amazons, come tripping after drums,
> Their thimbles into armed gauntlets change,
> Their needles to lances, and their gentle hearts
> To fierce and bloody inclination.
> [*King John* V.2.154–58]

Not:

> And leave your England, as dead midnight still,
> Guarded with grandsires, babies, and old women,
> Either past or not arrived to pitch and puissance.
> [*Henry V* III.Prologue.19–21]

Or:

> We are but warriors for the working day.
> Our gayness and our gilt are all besmirched
> With rainy marching in the painful field.
> [*Henry V* IV.3.109–11]

It is hard, if not futile, to try to account for the salient quality of any special type of diction in Shakespeare, but this one cries out for such identification because it has become so powerful an instrument of political image-making. With it, the Bastard makes wretched John a king to strike fear into the hearts of his enemies and create admiration in the hearts of his subjects. I would go too far to say it brings the rebellious lords back—Melun does that—or that it drives Lewis out of England—the work of God and the English Channel do that. It wins no battles for the Bastard, nor does it save the English troops from the flood tide in Lincoln Washes. But it does create an ambience which can transform this play from a weak-king play, most relentless in its emotional shifts and frustrations, into a piece of studied patriotism which can suitably end with one of the most magnificently chauvinistic speeches in Shakespearean drama. It can transform an audience from sober empathy with rebellion to an intensely nationalistic mob.

It is hard to accept the Bastard's closing speech in exclusively calculating terms, and I am not sure it need be so accepted. The Bastard is using his new patriotic diction all right, but what he is saying applies to the whole play and not just its two final acts. English lords have failed to be true to England, but in a far deeper sense England has failed to be true to herself in her king, the living embodiment of the land. The weak-king play has told of John the usurper and child-murderer, of the defiance of Rome followed by submission to it, of many varied and atrocious royal weaknesses. In the end, under the Bastard's new management, John has just made it. But it has been a close call. And if John has been worse than most, his flaws have resulted from human weaknesses—man failure—and there is no hope that any being other than a human one will come to the throne of England. In late Tudor terms the need for what the Bastard represents was and would be great, very great. Like Henry V, Elizabeth was her own very adept image-maker, but the enigmatic royal figure waiting in Edinburgh for Elizabeth's demise might well be a different case. The public responding to *King John* was the same public responding to the expectation of James I.

In summary, in *King John* Shakespeare used the form of *The Troublesome Reign*—the weak-king play—to serve as the background action for a play about a young man coming to terms with an admittedly brutal, deceit-ridden political system. He does not come to terms happily with it. Danby is quite right about the Bastard's continuing horror in his speech before the body of Arthur at the realities of political life. But the Bastard comes to terms with those realities and will live them out regardless. Vaguely, there is even the implicit hope that he can make something better of them. The weak-king play against which the Bastard's personal history is enacted comes to be almost a series of grotesque gestures in which the king's strong moments almost disappear in the glare of his weak ones. The prospect for any type of satisfactory resolution to the dilemma of the weak king seems more remote in this play than it is in any. Yet the Bastard hammers it out. The play attests to man's capacity to live with a myth that is terribly divorced from reality. To this extent it is a compromise with Tudor doctrine, if a cynical one. Shakespeare is far from recovered from the revolutionary emotionalism reflected in the *Henry VI* plays. But he is seeking a way through to a dramatic view which will reconcile some sense of personal honor with political effectiveness. *King John* has been a most passionate treatment of this attempt at reconciliation. Creating a dramatic form for that reconciliation in the world of ideas, in terms of conflicting ideologies, becomes his artistic objective in the *Henry IV* plays. What is important here is that the Bastard is certainly Hal's ancestor. The Bastard of the earlier part of the play is the spirited Hotspur of youth, indignation, and total involvement with personal honor. Hal is another kind of youth, of course. A dropout, he is equally at odds with the way things operate in the political realm. His alliance with Falstaff is parallel to Hotspur's alliance with personal honor. What links Hal and the Bastard even more clearly, however, is the Bastard's conversion to the same kind of knowing but strong identification with the system. And the emphasis is finally vocal as well. *Henry V* successfully obscures our horror at political realities by its magnificent music. It is Shakespeare's most heroic play but inevitably his most superficial as well.

Henry IV and *Henry V* are to become Shakespeare's systematic, more dispassionate reworking, in full color, of the transformation so fiercely set forth in the black and white of *King John*.

V New Thoughts To Deck
Our Kings

Henry IV, says Danby, "takes over the assumptions that are left in *King John* once Prince Arthur is dead."[1] He might as well have included *Henry V* in this statement, since all three plays constitute a carefully reasoned, objective, detailed dramatic treatment of the coming to terms with Machiavellianism which dominated political life at the close of the sixteenth century. In *Richard II*, as we have seen, uncertainty about the Machiavellian ruler is not resolved. Bolingbroke leaves the question of the weak king open. As Machiavel and usurper, he has overcome some of the difficulties which destroyed his predecessor by being patient, alert, and ruthless, but his image remains clouded. Throughout both parts of *Henry IV*, rebellion continues to alternate with obedience in our responses. The unworthy ambition of the Percys is strongly offset by the attractions of their champion Hotspur, whose honesty and openness make us think twice about the troubled, crafty king. The political dilemma remains what it was at the conclusion of *Richard II* until the closing act of *2 Henry IV*, when Hal becomes king. *Henry V*, however, fully embodies the solution, hinted at throughout the preceding plays, which many Elizabethans feared but knew was inevitable. Following the lead of *King John*, *Henry V* explores the means by which Machiavellianism could be seen as attractive and even desirable as a guide to political behavior. In *Henry V*, the weak king is finally removed from public view, and the means by which this is achieved is the one the dramatist knows and understands best. Linguistic artifice, with all its connotative devices, is used by Henry and his aid the Chorus to con-

1. *Shakespeare's Doctrine of Nature*, p. 82.

vey the same effect of flawless monarchy the Bastard sought to convey by the same means in *King John*.

Relating the plays of the second tetralogy to the problem of the weak king involves one in a problem concerning the two parts of *Henry IV*. Purely as drama and in relation to the larger understanding of Shakespeare's art, these two plays are a good deal more important than *Henry V*. Certainly, they are more complex in language, in theme, and in their appeal to our emotions. But detailed interpretation of them in studies of the history play has frequently meant skimping on *Henry V*, and the direction of this study makes that impossible. Thus, any probing of the wide variety of human concerns in *Henry IV* must have the effect of digression here. What follows, then, should in no way be construed as a comprehensive analysis of Shakespeare's *Henry IV*. I am simply seeking the issues in those plays most closely identified with the issues of the plays that have been discussed—with the weak king and the coming to terms with English Machiavellianism. But these issues do not shape *Henry IV* in the way they shape the plays already looked at.

Henry IV, seemingly so lucid and simple a few years ago during the heyday of the order-oriented approach to the history plays, seems once again confusing and to some amorphous. What was only recently considered the story of the novel education of the perfect Tudor prince has once again become the story of an uncertain youth viewing the political chaos of a state ruled by a strong man whose precarious power makes his reign a period of endless intrigue and insurrection. Part 1 is devoted to the inevitable rebellion which accompanies illegitimate succession, and to mockery of the hypocrisy and pomposity of a political system in which the animal propensities of men are made to seem so admirable and important. Rebellion and mockery are focussed in the very attractive characterizations of Hotspur and Falstaff, but what those two memorable opposites both seem to invite is nothing short of anarchy. And as the plays progress, anarchy seems less and less an attractive force. The wasteland quality which pervades Part 2 itself suggests a kind of real anarchy. The accession of Prince Hal comes to be most longed for, both by the audience and by himself. We come to feel the need for new, strong leadership, rather than the non-leadership implicitly sanctioned by both the Percys' revolt and Falstaff's levity.

So Hal becomes king. But in his first appearance crowned, he makes no statement intimating a new political philosophy, nor does he say anything about a break with the past. What we do hear instead is a new diction which suggests a departure from what has gone before, even if no real departure is intended. Hal's reign will be basically similar to his father's. The desire for new, strong leadership implicit in the events and language of Part 2 is answered by an illusion of new, strong leadership. And this image is largely created through Henry's new language—a language which is, of course, the same language we heard from the Bastard in the last act of *King John*. The rich tones, the brightly vivid images, the even meters and balanced sentences, the carefully spaced repetition of words and phrases are all etched with native English sounds which achieve a magnificently regal effect accompanied by a uniquely homespun texture:

> This new and gorgeous garment, majesty,
> Sits not so easy on me as you think.
> Brothers, you mix your sadness with some fear:
> This is the English, not the Turkish Court;
> Not Amurath an Amurath succeeds,
> But Harry Harry. . . .
> [2 *Henry IV* V.2.44–49]

By the end of *Henry IV*, it is apparent that Hal's true "father" is none other than Philip Faulconbridge.

But the Bastard is father to more in *Henry IV* than simply the language of Hal at the end of Part 2. He is ancestor to the entire thematic development of *Henry IV* represented in its three leading figures. In Hotspur we see his first image in *King John*, in Falstaff his second, and in the crowned Hal his last. The sense of disillusionment and maturation which characterizes the basic thematic movement of *Henry IV* grows out of the disillusionment and maturation we saw in the Bastard in *King John*.

Hotspur is remarkably close to the Bastard we knew early in *King John*, the swashbuckling figure with the feverish lust for action which will test every fiber of his moral and physical being at every turn. Without ever using the word *honor* as Hotspur uses it, he caviled "at the ninth part of a hair" in challenging his brother over the inheritance, and "plucked bright honor from the pale-fac'd moon" in following Queen Elinor to France as Coeur-de-Lion's Bastard. But, like Hotspur, the Bastard had no real end in sight, only the ever-receding gleam of an honor which is reduced in all these plays to the "trim reckoning" Falstaff finds it. Following where his impulses led early in *King John*, the Bastard found himself in the same paltry world fighting paltry dragons (Limoges) as Hotspur finds himself, enmeshed in a plot to divide the kingdom hatched by a petty Machiavel (Worcester) who has little concern with anything but his own advancement. Like Hotspur, the Bastard early in *John* had the same hard eye for the stupidity and affectations of others, but no grasp of the ultimate emptiness of his own mercurial ambitions. Both can condemn the pretenses of their Owen Glendowers or Austrias, but both are victims of their own egomania. Honor revealed for the mere bauble it is in these plays proves an almost unbearable trauma, which Hotspur does not have to endure until he is fatally wounded but which the Bastard bitterly endures as he watches the king of France, for reasons of pure political expediency, betray the legitimate heir to the English throne.

Perhaps another word for that trauma is Falstaff. In the flash of a single instant near the center of *King John* (II.1.561ff.), the world assumes the proportions of a monumental joke, the result of a change in the Bastard's view of things radical enough to change his whole approach to life. The same vision of human folly, hypocrisy, and duplicity which was the driving force of the Bastard's "mad world" is the driving force of the mountainous exuberance which is Falstaff. The revelation of both is that any concept of honor at all is finally meaningless and worthy of ridicule. The Bastard's vision was obviously a sudden one resulting from the shock of disillusionment, but so, too, less obviously, may be Falstaff's—if we see him in the light of earlier plays. The disillusionment of course must be Shakespeare's. The Oldcastle business aside, Shakespeare's name for the fat knight is a variant of Sir John Fastolfe, the disgraceful fraud and coward of *1 Henry VI*. Between the Henry VI and Henry IV plays, without pushing biographical intimations too hard, there has been at the very least a realization that in a world dominated not by chivalry and honor but by Machiavellianism, "the better part of valour" may indeed be "discretion." The coward has become the sage. Through Falstaff we hear the same rage at political life which underlies the first tetralogy transformed into the boisterous, unrelenting laughter of the Boar's Head Tavern. The passion has not changed so much as the expression of it. The Bastard's image of "that smoothfac'd gentleman, tickling Commodity," who is "the bias of the world" provides a cross section of Falstaff's immense view of human corruption.

But Falstaff, of course, goes well beyond political life as such, and thus a concern so limited as the one in this book is much too limiting for him. Those who see in his activity only a satirical miming of Henry Bolingbroke severely constrain him. Bolingbroke is but a minuscule part of the Erasmian scope of Falstaff's performance. The very de-emphasis of Henry IV's role which is so evident in these plays suggests the author straining to get past the finally irresolvable problem of the weak king into subjects of greater depth and even importance. Falstaff steals the show more than simply through his satirical thrusts at king and court. Kings will be what they are. Men must concentrate on themselves, regardless of deficiencies in the kingly image.

What gives *1 Henry IV* life as a play and hope for mankind (though not for the state) is the vitality of its two leading figures, both of whom must finally be sacrificed for political purposes, as the Bastard had to sacrifice his own youthful innocence and exuberance for political purposes. Both Falstaff and Hotspur are creatures of appetite. Both are on intimate terms with the palefaced moon and are thereby at odds with all versions of order, discipline, and constraint. Hotspur's chivalry allows him as much freedom as Falstaff's mockery. They are probably the only true life forces in all these plays, but as such they are also quite anarchic. The question that seems implied in *1 Henry IV*, and is perhaps the one on Hal's mind, is whether the life-constraining forces of government must give way to or resist the anarchic impulses represented by Hotspur and Falstaff. And the answer is paradoxical. If life is anarchic, then it must lead to its own destruction—as Hotspur and Falstaff most certainly do. Living life to its fullest must shortly bring an end to living life. Government, then, is life-destroying even as it performs its imperative function of preserving life. Man is doomed either by his own life-forces or by that outside constraining force which is government. Government wins out in the plays, of course, but at the expense of the only genuinely life-giving figures in them. And as for government, its only efficient and effective shape, as the Bastard realized, is the Machiavellian—the way chosen by Hal and employed by him a good deal more successfully than by his father. The history plays thus represent a triumph of the Machiavellian spirit over the human. Just as Hotspur and Falstaff had to be destroyed, the weak king had to be destroyed. Small wonder Shakespeare turned to tragedy, for only in a play like *King Lear* could the relationship of the human and the kingly once again be given its due.

As the Bastard came to realize that a new kingly image was needed in *King John,* Hal comes to realize that a new kingly image is needed in *2 Henry IV*. The king had to be as Machiavellian as Bolingbroke, but he also must be untainted by the stain of usurpation and be possessed of a charisma Bolingbroke only sporadically attained. Hal's taking the crown from his sleeping father's head is more ambiguous than Hal admits. He may be innocent of wishing his father's death and he is certainly cognizant of the many burdens represented by the crown, but what prompts him to take it is the same long-suppressed energy which bursts forth colorfully in the language of the play's conclusion. And it is a Machiavellian energy. Hal has discovered how to be a successful king. The vitality and exuberance associated with the apolitical Hotspur and Falstaff must be put to use in service to the state, no longer spontaneous but the raw materials of a carefully conceived image. Hal's triumph is that, like the Bastard, he employs vitality and exuberance as essential ingredients in the vigorous new language of the Machiavel.

Henry V is hardly a complete acceptance of the Machiavellian spirit. It only seeks to make the spirit palatable, and Shakespeare makes it palatable with a sound rather than a rationale—a sound which fills the world of *Henry V* as the richness and volatility of Hotspur and Falstaff filled the world of *1 Henry IV*.

HENRY V

Two points should be clear enough about *Henry V*. First, despite the objections of some critics (once more on the increase), Henry is intended to be a successful, admirable, and heroic figure; second, Henry is as consummate a Machiavel as any king represented in these plays. And whereas James Winny in *The Player King* feels these two facts suggest basic contradictions in his character, I feel they are intended to be in harmony with each other, despite occasional dissonances. The play articulates through its art the feelings of a society attempting to come to terms with a political outlook it had only recently considered diabolical and degenerate. What was in *Richard III* an image of horror and malignancy bent on power by any means possible has become an image of practical politics cast in a beautiful, heroic mold. As in *Henry VI*, the best Machiavel among many triumphs in *Henry V*. The differences are largely those of appearance and ambiance. Henry V sheds blood with a less ready will than Richard III, but that in itself would not be enough to transform the national devil into the national saint. What is accomplished is the work of an entire production team: from playwright to actor, costumer, and whoever might have been the equivalent of makeup man and scene designer. The transformation is a monumental job of theatrical and political image-making.

It may no longer be necessary to underscore Henry's Machiavellian qualities. Bolingbroke's last instruction to his son was to "busy giddy minds with foreign wars" and one of our earliest impressions in *Henry V* is of giddy minds busied with a foreign war. The most unsympathetically giddy by Elizabethan standards are the clergy—here seen as sluggish, half-effective Machiavels troubling the kingdom in their attempts to gain or maintain massive wealth and power. The first indication that Henry has far out-Machiavelled them is in Canterbury's fragmentary response to Ely's inquiry whether the king is sympathetic to their cause:

> He seems indifferent,
> Or rather swaying more upon our part
> Than cherishing the exhibiters against us.
> [I.1.72–74]

What we learn, of course, is not that Henry is "inclined" to the clerical cause so much as that he is keeping both sides uncertain and thus loyal to him.

Henry's Machiavellianism is more apparent the minute he appears. *Henry V* I.2 bears an unexpected resemblance to *Richard III* III.7. In both, a practiced Machiavel, with thinly disguised reluctance, is zealously "persuaded" at great length to take an action of tremendous importance which it is perfectly apparent he has meant to take from the start: Henry to invade France and Richard to assume the throne. Canterbury's Salic law supports Henry's action chiefly from the point of view that nothing so verbose and boring could possibly be devious. In fact, of course, his case is the most blatant example of political trumpery in the history plays. And Machiavellian planning is further revealed in the carefully rehearsed, precisely spaced urgings of Ely, Exeter, and Westmoreland. The invasion is Henry's own strategy to unify and strengthen the country, but he has successfully given it the aura of a national movement. The Dauphin, hoping to surprise and frighten Henry with his unexpected insult and challenge, is himself surprised by the care, swiftness, and thoroughness of Henry's response and preparation.

A simple recitation of Henry's actions before and during battle suggests as determined a leader as any of the conquerors in Elizabethan drama. His discovery of the traitors at Southampton is built around a seemingly arbitrary cat and mouse ritual, and their execution is merciless and uncompromising. One wonders about the fate of Worcester, Northumberland, and Hotspur had this king and not his father been presiding in Act I of *1 Henry IV*. In France, his threats before Harfleur seem frightening in their intensity and in the detail of their images of rapine, murder, and destruction. Of lesser magnitude, perhaps, but equally ruthless seems Henry's easy approval of Bardolph's hanging for petty thievery and his order that the English soldiers kill their prisoners. Machiavelli's lion was never more leonine than this.

On the deceitful side once more is Henry's never-failing invocation of God as motivator and ultimate beneficiary of his actions. This is a ticklish point, of course, in any discussion of a work written in the sixteenth century, but the issue is made clear by the placement of Henry's invocations of the deity. Machiavelli is quite explicit about the ruler using God and the church wherever possible to strengthen his position. Henry does this handsomely early in his challenge to France and freely, of course, preceding and following battle—to assure all present that he is fulfilling his role of "Christian King." Yet the God who fights for England and deserves credit for the victory is notably absent from those passages in which Henry speaks of God in more personal terms. The God he invokes for Michael Williams in IV.1 cares little for England. He is concerned only with punishing sinners unlucky enough to find themselves in the army. And in his soliliquy on ceremony, where some sort of religious invocation might be expected, there is no mention of God. Following Gloucester's interruption of this soliloquy, Henry prays to a "God of battles" who seems more personal than the English patron of his public invocations, and he ends by appealing to the "Lord" to forget Bolingbroke's crime— just for the day at hand. This, if any, is the God Henry believes in. The one appealed to at court and before battle is the official state God, to be employed by the good Machiavel as he sees fit to assure unity, strength, and victory.

Is this, then, the marvel of all monarchs, national and international model for all future leaders? In short, yes. He is a Machiavel conceived in the happiest terms Shakespeare knows, and as such would undoubtedly have prompted the Florentine to make a large and honorable place for him in his study of effective political leadership. Machiavelli would have been far readier to accept Henry as his ideological offspring than Richard of Gloucester. And for the English play-going public he represents the state of their own thoughts and assumptions about leadership, whether these assumptions were acknowledged as Machiavellian or not. The real villain was the weak king, the monarch whose inescapably human qualities provoked constant vacillation and uncertainty in his subjects. That vacillation, as we have seen, gave shape to what is almost a new dramatic genre in the 1590s—so great was its impact in that period. *Henry V*, which smothers the weak king image in a brilliant, magnificent cloak, has little shape of its own. There is no shift in sympathy toward the king—only an occasional glimpse beneath the surface. Making our emotional reaction to him consistent is Henry's triumph. He shows us an audience ready to turn away from dramatic articulation of their political doubts and uncertainties. They want a strong kingly image—and that could only be achieved by Machiavellian means. Like societies before and after, they show themselves, through this play, willing to sacrifice the small measure of freedom they possess in exchange for a sense of stability in the state and the illusion of personal security.

Shakespeare's problem in *Henry V* was how to make it all seem right. Creating the divinely *ordered* state was not his purpose. In *Henry V* the ordered state is as laughable a prospect as is the archbishop of Canterbury, its sponsor in his description of the honey-bees (I.2.187–204). Canterbury's honeybees are the type of Tudor propagandistic pabulum which was undoubtedly familiar enough to the audience but hardly the serious ideal of any experienced or even realistic monarch. The semblance of order achieved through outward appearances is acceptable, but not the rigid, utterly dehumanized set of roles and functions set forth in the archbishop's speech. The "right" in the play is the aura which surrounds all the king's statements and actions, and has little to do with any kind of system or order. And that aura is largely the result of a language which, as the essence of Henry's Machiavellianism, effectively suppresses the shift in appeal to our sympathies which has come to characterize monarchy in these plays. Henry's achievement is the impression of continuous success he manages to convey.

To repeat, then, Henry's technique is not sprung on us by surprise. Those who were listening heard it from the Bastard in *King John* obscuring the utter horror of that serpent monarch and helping elicit sympathy at his death. And they heard it again in *2 Henry IV*, in the entrancing sounds of Hal's opening as king. Shakespeare, in the opening scene of *Henry V*, prepares us for Henry's method of asserting his will. It is described by, of all people, Canterbury, who only partially understands that it is indeed a method and not a miracle. Henry, we are told, has developed the ability to render any subject whatever inspiring, beautiful, and impressive:

> List his discourse of war, and you shall hear
> A fearful battle rendered you in music.
> Turn him to any cause of policy,
> The Gordian knot of it he will unloose,
> Familiar as his garter—that, when he speaks,
> The air, a chartered libertine, is still,
> And the mute wonder lurketh in men's ears,
> To steal his sweet and honeyed sentences.
>
> [I.1.43–50]

Canterbury further understands that all this is a tribute to Henry's mastery of the practical and his willingness to use theory and ideology in any way that will enhance his power: "So that the art and practic part of life/Must be the mistress to this theoric" (I.1.51–52). But Canterbury cannot comprehend that Henry learned that pragmatism in Eastcheap, and that his "hours filled up by riots, banquets, sports" were a laboratory far more effective than anything that court or battlefield might provide. Ely adds that "the prince obscured his contemplation/Under the veil of wildness" without taking into account that wildness itself in the presence of a Falstaff could be a form of intense contemplation.

The "music" which Canterbury accurately identifies as the end of all subjects which have passed through Henry's verbal machine has been described in various ways. To some it is simply the "majestic verse" of *Henry V*. To others it is "an astounding inflation of style." Rose Zimbardo sees it as the superimposing of language and imagery which "might have come straight from a Renaissance book of rhetoric" to create a formal, highly polished surface which suitably stands for flawless monarchy.[2] She is correct in seeing it as something laid on to achieve a particular effect rather than the spontaneous outgrowth of plot and character, but the majesty is only seemingly flawless. Language is used in this play to sweep the dust under the rug. Shakespeare's "perfect" king has created the illusion of perfection. But that is as much as

2. Rose Zimbardo, "The Formalism of *Henry V*," *Shakespeare Encomium* (New York: The City University of New York, 1964), pp. 16–24. Quote is from p. 19.

one should expect of monarchy, it seems implied. Order is no more than the semblance of order, and the perfect king is that king who makes the greatest number of people believe he is the perfect king.

Even though the word *music* perhaps does not tell the whole story, Canterbury is right to use it. The overall impression is unquestionably musical. This is because we have had the brilliant visual effects and rich connotations in other history plays, but they are here set in prolonged, controlled rolling periods which can have the effect of a hypnotic. To speak of metrical ease with a preponderance of accented syllables is accurate but not enough. Henry interrupts his majestic iambic progressions with the same homely familiarity that is suggested by his frequent homespun phrases and allusions. The spellbinding effect throughout has the ring and ease of the familiar. As Henry's "gayness" and his "gilt" are so "besmirch'd" by the long march to Calais that he and his men have become "but warriors for the working-day," the gayness and the gilt of his language is regularly specked with rhythm and images which evoke (though they never actually equate) the shop and tavern. And this, more than anything, is Henry's peculiar stamp. He has made good use of having "plodded like a man for working days" at the Boar's Head.

Henry's "music," of course, has more than a single sound. It can be martial, jocular, vindictive, threatening, and—as we are surprised to discover in the last act—even amorous. Yet it is always unmistakably Henry. The prose he shrewdly employs in the last act to simulate the wooing soldier has the same broad-gauged, free-flowing, familiar effect as his patriotic exhortations. He always mingles that inimitable quality of good-willed determination with that fierce control which Traversi finds central to the entire conception of the play.[3] But there is no conflict between Henry's emotions and his rhetoric. Monumental passions are part of Henry's self-created image, just as are the stock rhetorical devices identified by Miss Zimbardo, which constrain those passions. Both are ultimately Machiavellian instruments:

3. D. A. Traversi, *Shakespeare from Richard II to Henry V* (Palo Alto, Calif.: Stanford University Press, 1957), pp. 108–65.

for many a thousand widows
Shall this his mock mock out of their dear husbands;
Mock mothers from their sons, mock castles down;
[I.2.284–86]

Without the passion, I doubt whether Henry could have brought
it all off, but he uses his own strong feelings as he uses everyone
and everything else to achieve his coolly conceived objectives.

But Henry does not work alone. Shakespeare provides him with
a powerful ally who is called the Chorus but is in fact perhaps the
first special-effects man in dramatic history. The Chorus sets the
tone at the start and helps maintain it through his overtures to
each act. In a sense, he is the Bastard's successor in that he creates
the proper tone and ambiance for the regal illusion, though the
Chorus has a far better equipped king to work with. In employing the Chorus, Shakespeare uses an old extra-dramatic convention to look down the centuries, by means of words alone, to our
own wide-screen, stereophonic era:

O for a Muse of fire, that would ascend
The brightest heaven of invention,
A kingdom for a stage, princes to act
And monarchs to behold the swelling scene!
Then should the warlike Harry, like himself,
Assume the port of Mars; and at his heels,
Leashed in like hounds, should famine, sword, and fire
Crouch for employment. . . .
[I.Prol.1–8]

The brilliance of his fire-images that open the first two acts serves
at once to blind us to the hard political realities of the plays we
have been looking at: "Now all the youth of England are on fire,/
And silken dalliance in the wardrobe lies" (II.Prol.1–2).

Similarly, the opening of Act III envisioning the majestic fleet
setting sail creates the same miraculous illusion that another
Machiavel, the bewitching queen of Egypt, creates from her royal
barge, as described by Enobarbus. The first three acts all open
upon brilliant images of fire and majesty. The prologues abound
in phrases like "brightest heaven," "vasty fields," "silken streamer,"
and "winged thoughts," and with such images is suppressed all

thought about the deceit and force underlying the action at hand. The prologue to Act I appeals to our imaginations to compensate for the limitations of the stage, but the stage had held such vast spectacle before without the need of such excuse. Shakespeare's larger purpose through the Chorus (and Henry) is to achieve that semblance of political stability which has been absent from all the other plays considered here. For once, the human qualities which must inevitably provoke the vacillations in our sympathy toward the king disappear. Colors, sounds, rhythms, and images create the conditions whereby he may be made to seem a god: "For 'tis your thoughts that now must deck our kings" (I. Prol. 28).

The only real trouble with Sir Laurence Olivier's film spectacular of the 1940s was that it was made some thirty years too soon. Much though his Henry has been attacked for being too praise-worthy, Sir Laurence was aware, I think, both of Henry's Machiavellian tendencies and of his willingness to subordinate his human qualities for the sake of his image. Olivier should, however, have been willing to include the Harfleur speech and other instances of the brutal, merciless aspects of that image.

Henry's rhetorical mastery is illustrated in just about all the play's best-known episodes, including those which have earned him both scorn and praise. To some his treatment of the traitors in II.2 is devious and sudden, cat-and-mouse tactics at their worst. To others, it is a superbly effective example of justice appropriately rendered. In fact, it is both. The three lords are guilty; no one doubts that. What Henry must prevent is the bifurcation of our feelings which accompanies so many previous conflicts between crown and rebel. Thus the piercing, all-encompassing nature of his accusation:

> Show men dutiful?
> Why, so didst thou. Seem they grave and learned?
> Why, so didst thou. Come they of noble family?
> Why, so didst thou. Seem they religious?
> Why, so didst thou. Or are they spare in diet,
> Free from gross passion or of mirth or anger,
> Constant in spirit, not swerving with the blood,
> Garnished and decked in modest complement,

Not working with the eye without the ear,
And but in purged judgment trusting neither?
Such and so finely bolted didst thou seem.
[II.2.127–37]

Any potential division in our sympathies is overwhelmed by Henry's verbal onslaught. He so completely smothers issues here that whatever rationale might exist for the rebels' behavior is overlooked. We are ready to accept their guilt without a hearing. And the brainwashed effect of the victims' responses is necessary if the image of the weak king is to be destroyed. We must not be allowed to sympathize with them for a moment lest that sympathy begin to create doubts about the king.

In the battle scenes, of course, Henry's new fustian is used to create illusions suitable to the image of the conqueror. The speech that is hard for defenders of Henry to swallow and is always the focal point of those on the attack is the speech before Harfleur. Its precise images of bloodshed, rapine, and suffering are so vivid as to prompt Winny, in *The Player King*, to see in their author the motives of a genuine pacifist who uses Henry to show how a basically sincere and sensitive youth can be victimized by a brutal social system. But the Harfleur speech is of a piece with the Machiavellian whole and with the linguistic artifice that we have been considering that whole. It is pointless even to wonder whether Henry would carry out his threats at Harfleur. It never crosses his mind or anyone else's that the citizens would resist his challenge. Rather, we hear the lion roaring his loudest. The vivid details exist for the benefit of the citizens, who are as impressed by Henry's gifted imagination as we. Miss Zimbardo feels that the speech's "horrible subject matter is rendered as still as statuary by stylistic formality."[4] It seems that it is rendered theatrical rather than "still" by our knowledge that this monarch's skills are more those of the scene-designer than the butcher. He creates tangible, visible details for his listener but always with an eye for effect—never really considering the matter of sincerity at all. The evidence of his success as king is that his effects are achieved. Were they not, then Henry would have failed as king, whether

4. "The Formalism of *Henry V*," p. 20.

through compassion he failed to carry out his threats or savagely he did carry them out. It would make little difference either way. On the one hand he would be considered a fraud, on the other a brute. He considers himself neither. Since later he for once confesses to genuine anger at the report of the massacre of the boys, it is safe to assume that in the Harfleur speech he is not angry. And if he is not angry, then he is play-acting, confident that the objectives of this bit of theatre will be accomplished. He has created an image for himself which if he keeps intact will assure his success. The real test for Henry is his ability to keep up the illusion.

Henry is naturally at his best before Agincourt. His brilliant military innovation was well-known to the audience. What Shakespeare concentrates on is his skill in verbally employing the outmanned, sorry condition of his troops to enhance the heroic effect he seeks to maintain. Another knight in a similar situation in *1 Henry IV* also fancied how greatly his personal honor might be enhanced by a victory against great odds. The failure of Northumberland to appear in his son's support before the Battle of Shrewsbury inspires Hotspur to consider the greater chivalric honor to be achieved if he fought anyway. Henry uses similar logic:

> God's peace! I would not lose so great an honor
> As one man more, methinks, would share from me
> For the best hope I have. Oh, do not wish one more!
> [IV.3.31–33]

But whereas Hotspur's response emanates from the center of his chivalric soul, Henry's emanates from the center of his Machiavellian brain. He is using the old Hotspurian sense of honor to inspire his soldiers, to win from them the admiration which will insure their loyalty and the energy and determination to fight their hardest. Here, as in the "Once more into the breach" exhortation, his images are vivid, immediate, and artificial. They give the unreal a living, familiar flavor. The image of the cowardly soldier shamefully sailing back to England or of homespun old age recounting the glories of this day have about as much relationship to the realities of the situation as Henry's enraged tiger of the earlier speech. Men must be drugged or hypnotized to face the prospect of death, and Henry's images help supply the sopo-rific. As before Harfleur there was little thought that Henry's threats might be carried out, here there is little thought that he might be defeated. That thought is left to the French, who reveal their folly in part by being so confident of his defeat.

Henry knows, and the audience knows, that his military in-novations should win him the day, but even were he to lose, then all would be lost anyway. Honor in defeat would be meaningless. A Hotspur might be genuinely after honor; but a Henry is after victory only, and without it all the honor in the world would be useless to him. Hence his "theme of honor," the gift of Hotspur, is so much window-dressing. He uses it, as he uses Falstaff's pragmatism, his father's commanding presence, the Chief Justice's insistence on order and discipline—in short, all the attitudes that have been part of his past—to achieve the single objective of creating the appearance of monarchic superiority which will pro-duce victory in battle and the semblance of order in the state.

There are breaks in Henry's armor, though, and I believe they are intentional. First, whether they admit as much or not, the comic characters know him for what he is. Falstaff's heart has been "fracted and corroborate," and if Shakespeare in fact wished to omit the hurt associated with this fact, he could have omitted Falstaff's death entirely. It is present to reinforce the theme that to avoid being the weak king, Henry had to muffle his human qualities. He has to let Falstaff die as later he lets Bardolph die. To the residents of Eastcheap, he is not an admirable man; but they, like the rest, view him as an admirable king, so the final effect is the same. His new comic associate Fluellen knows none of this, so Henry can establish with the Welshman something vaguely resembling the relationship he had with his erstwhile companions. But Henry tricking Fluellen into challenging Wil-liams to fight is a paltry image. It is about on a level with the Hal of the Francis episode in *1 Henry IV*. Were it at all the standard action of the play, we would quickly have the image of another weak king. Henry has reserved this byplay for a moment of relaxation following victory, and thus it proves no threat to his image of flawless majesty—any more than do the silent and not-so-silent accusations of Bardolph and the Hostess. It serves only as a reminder that beneath the most impressive monarch resides a man.

But more important is Shakespeare's unexpected treatment of Act IV, scene 1: "A little touch of Harry in the night." The Chorus opening the act actually prepares us for another illustration of flawless monarchy. There are many Alfredian legends of the good king who goes among his people disguised to learn the conditions of life in his realm and to discover signs of incipient rebellion. And that legend may even include challenges which the king finds himself hard pressed to answer. But one imagines the stage-managing Chorus complaining behind the scenes about Henry's failure to carry out his interview with the troops according to plan. "A little touch of Harry in the night" comes too close to a little touch of the weak king in the daylight for comfort. Whether it be the necessity that Henry use prose among commoners or something awfully penetrating about Michael Williams' remarks, Henry is unable to respond in the inspiring manner or with the brave tones that have been his wont. Actually, Henry's logic is not so bad. He is perfectly justified to ask whether a son's miscarrying on a father's errand means that the father is at fault, or whether the servant injured on his master's business actually throws guilt upon the master. But the overall effect upon the soldiers is to make them question whether any commitment to the cause is really worthwhile, which is quite the opposite of Henry's objective. Henry, who throughout considers the king a great vessel of responsibility, says that men finally owe their answers directly to God without the king to serve as intermediary. Thus, here, when he is really at his most logical, he is at his least effective. He confesses that kings are men, and that the conception of the king as all-protecting, imperturbable, and flawless is an illusion. This is not what he went into the camp to bring about, but Michael Williams has caught him up where neither English rebel or French opponent can.

In his soliloquy ending IV.1, Henry restates what Michael Williams has revealed, this time in the language we are more accustomed to. He acknowledges that he has in fact led his subjects to believe that they may lay all their sins, souls, and spiritual debts upon a king who is in reality only a man with the same weaknesses as other men, who must, if he is to be successful, create through an agency called *ceremony* the illusion that he is something other than a man. He acknowledges that all the external attributes of monarchy are parts of this illusion, and if he has been most successful in maintaining it, it is no less illusory for that. Henry has some awareness of the moral irony involved in this situation—but that irony in no way affects his view of political necessity, which is Machiavellian throughout. This is his least Machiavellian moment, and it is thus his least political moment. But it is also spoken to no one but himself, and the soldiers do not know who joined them in the night. That Henry is still the weak king is for his private ruminations only.

Henry is grossly mimicked in the play by Ancient Pistol. While I do not think this mimicry is intended as genuine satire, it is not altogether without purpose. Pistol is a mouther, one who attempts to obfuscate his lazy, vice-ridden, essentially ignorant human condition by a volley of words, phrases, and purple passages, many of them drawn from the speeches of conqueror heroes in the older Elizabethan drama—notably, of course, Marlowe. The figures who, figuratively, reside at the top and bottom of the play—the conquering monarch and the boasting buffoon—function in parallel fashion. Henry, of course, is never forced to eat the leek by a blunt Welshman. But then Henry is to die after a reign of a mere nine years, and no observer of the play could be forgetful of what followed. The flawless image can be kept up just so long. Behind all the glory and the heroism in *Henry V* lies the same awareness Richard II expresses most deftly in terms which fit Henry best of all:

> for within the hollow crown
> That rounds the mortal temples of a king
> Keeps Death his Court, and there the antic sits,
> Scoffing his state and grinning at his pomp,
> Allowing him a breath, a little scene,
> To monarchize, be feared, and kill with looks,
> Infusing him with self and vain conceit,
> As if this flesh which walls about our life
> Were brass impregnable, and humored thus

> Comes at the last and with a little pin
> Bores through his castle wall, and farewell King!
> [*Richard II* III.2.160–70]

Death ultimately renders all kings weak, and Henry's rhetoric finally must be revealed as the same artifice as Pistol's. But for the brief moment of his reign, he bids us take comfort and pleasure in the illusion of harmony and order he creates with language. We laugh at Pistol and are awed by Henry for essentially the same approach to life.

The surprising thing about *Henry V*, especially in light of the divorce of Henry's magnificent speeches from political realities as they were well known to the audience, is that the play is really quite free of irony. The horror at the fact that men of affairs should profess to be Christians yet survive by devious and brutal means has been intentionally and forcefully suppressed in this play (though it occasionally shows through). Shakespeare seems firmly committed here to the view that in political life Henry V is a necessity. In this play more than any other he is thus paying tribute to his reigning monarch, whose techniques were Henry's if her precise image could not be. Act V is nothing so much as a *pax Britannica*. Burgundy's detailed longing for peace articulates the longing of audience, actor, monarch, and court for not only peace but that elusive *order* as well. But it is a dream. The best that could be hoped for was the peace imposed by the successful Machiavel and the illusion of order that might accompany that peace. Burgundy's wish is a pipe dream, one that Henry is happy to foster for the likelihood that he can achieve his objective without further bloodshed. But France, not peace, is Henry's chief goal, and his cavalier treatment of the French king suggests his readiness to renew hostilities should that appear necessary. The only peace available is that which lies beneath Henry's wit, which bears the face of the lion temporarily smiling and satisfied but quite ready to devour again in due course:

> But in loving me you should love the friend of France; for I love France so well that I will not part with a village of it, I will have it all mine.
>
> [V.2.180–83]

For a long time, critics have either been charmed by Henry's courtship of Kate or have felt with Samuel Johnson that it is vulgarly out of keeping with the rest of the play. Rarely has it been observed that what we are witnessing is political marriage pure and simple, carried out by a consummate politician. Henry might be quite taken with fair Katharine of France, but we really have no way of knowing, because the subject of his actual feelings is not raised in these final scenes. Vestiges of our nineteenth-century, sentimental selves make us perhaps easier prey to Henry's strategy in his courtship even than the audience of his own time. That courtship is as much a part of the Machiavellian Henry as anything else in the play. As he had done before, Henry borrows the sound of his old adversary in wooing Kate. He becomes for the nonce the bluff soldier, the Hotspur of old; he is the more effective lover for rejecting the traditional image of the courtly versifier. The appeal of this image lies in its being masculine, honest, articulate, and unaffected—qualities which by the late 1590s might appeal to audience and lady alike more than the worn-out, mockable conceits and rimes of the Petrarchan lover. But the role is as much a stratagem as his patriotic exhortations of the previous act. And that Kate is a match for him is illustrated not so much in this scene as in the scene two acts earlier, well before the English have won their victory in France, in which she requests and receives her English lesson. This princess knows well the meaning of political alliance through marriage, and like Henry she appears to enjoy the role she is playing.

The fifth act closes *Henry V* on a successful note. He has France, a queen, and unity. His mastery has been complete; he has maintained the royal image through the chief challenge of his reign. Nothing now can destroy it—nothing, that is, but the "antic" death, who will bore through Henry's castle wall in a shockingly brief time. No royal reign in drama could give more satisfaction to its audience than that of Henry V, but beneath the satisfaction was knowledge that even Henry the master of political illusion must soon be revealed for the weak king he is by that most human of disabilities—mortality.

The play, then, is a plea to men with the desire for improvement in political life to accept the perhaps ugly realities of that life. What emerges from all these plays is the idea that the real destroyer of harmony in a hierarchical system such as monarchy is the king himself, a necessarily human figure locked into a role which demanded superhuman control at all times. Looking toward the future, the nation could only have the discomforting assurance that a true example of the weak king was waiting in Edinburgh for his summons and that the very fortunate reign of a monarch who had made herself the master of royal illusion, perhaps beyond any monarch before her, was soon to come to an end. To the sixteenth century, monarchy in and of itself was doomed to failure —and Shakespeare gives us the first intimations of this realization in art. The monarch was by nature an anarchic being plunging headlong into one catastrophe after another. Nothing could save the kingdom from strife and bloodshed because nothing could save the king from his own divided nature. Only adherence to the method of *The Prince* could save him, and that but temporarily. What was a decade before the most horrible of realities to Shakespeare had become the grim necessity of which Sanders speaks in *The Dramatist and the Received Idea.*

Politics never is absent from a Shakespearean play, but it will be in later plays reduced to a single segment of life. Its central importance is finally subordinated in *Henry V* with the submerging of the weak king and the acknowledgment that successful monarchy is as much involved with effect and artifice as Shakespeare's theatre itself.

VI "To Govern Better"

Pessimistic as they seem finally to be about the capacity of leaders to govern humanely, the history plays are not without hope. The various versions of the Richard II–Edward II figure make the king unable to subordinate his natural laziness and desire for sensuous pleasures to his intelligence, sensitivity, and capacity to be benevolent. But the compassion for that figure in his demise is not solely audience guilt at deposing a legitimate if incompetent heavenly deputy. It is also sadness at the waste of potentially creative leadership. Shakespeare's Richard and Marlowe's Edward are gifted individuals, if what they say in their respective deposition scenes is any indication. And even John, who tests the degree to which an audience can be antagonized and still remain loyal to the prohibition against deposing a monarch, is represented as tormented—and a small part of his torment is over his failure to rule better. The stuff of alert, thoughtful, compassionate leadership is not altogether missing from these men. If the coming of the image-makers Bolingbroke, the Bastard, and Hal is a "tragic necessity," Richard's recognition that he "wasted time" suggests that the tragedy lies not in his nature but in the waste of his powers.

But the reign of the wanton king does fail, and the image-makers seem the only real alternative, politically. The Bastard, Bolingbroke, and Henry V all agree that to rule successfully, one must be an attractive Machiavel. One must learn to temporize and coerce with subtlety, originality, alertness, and intelligence. No kingdom of heaven on earth might thereby result—men might persist indefinitely in being bestial—but the semblance of order would be achieved and an illusion of existence as something beyond what men knew in the cave created, though only the illusion. So it has been with subsequent image-makers. Men are getting by (so far), but wars involving ever-increasing slaughter must periodically be fought, many to preserve a leader's or a nation's image; and despite astonishing technological progress, too many human beings in the world are still condemned to eternal hunger and privation because too few leaders have made the effort necessary to improve their lot. For most leaders, maintaining the semblance of order has been enough. The spirit of the history plays, expanded by Western man's experience since, appears to hold little promise for man's ability to govern or to be governed as his being the most highly developed intelligence among living creatures would lead one to expect.

Except that there is also Henry VI. In the Henry IV–Henry V trilogy, Shakespeare's judgment of the Machiavellianism of Bolingbroke and Hal is left unresolved, but his earlier judgment of the Machiavellianism among the nobility in *Henry VI* is quite clear. That Machiavellianism is thoroughly animal, both in its cunning and its brutality. Against it, the one king who is neither lazy nor the prisoner of his appetites is utterly powerless. Dedicated to governing to the best of his inevitably limited abilities, this gentle, peace-loving king—wise in Part 3 as well as deeply humane—can never assert his leadership but by the consent and even commitment of his people. And Henry can only govern with his weaknesses and eccentricities, which are many, in full view. His leadership in Shakespeare's plays indicates little about what he might do if his subordinates were to follow him instead of devouring him, but neither do we know what the newly compassionate Lear might do had he his reign to live over. ("Take physic, pomp, and feel what wretches feel. . . .") The point is that issues and proposed solutions are less important than the true compassion of leaders, then and now. Henry VI believes his nobles are like himself—humble, earnest, flawed, and searching. They, however, not only refuse to see themselves in these terms but also refuse to recognize the value of his humanity. They insist upon a government which masks the humanity of the leader while ignoring the humanity of his subjects.

What *Henry VI* suggests to us today is that if a consciousness prevailed in which men acknowledged the human in both the governors and the governed, we all might be freer to make disinterested decisions. It should be obvious that fear of the loss of power, or of failure to increase power, plays a large part in the decisions and actions of both elected and the electorate today. To keep power, many in positions of responsibility have learned to manipulate the responses of masses of people by creating external images of themselves suited to what they feel their constituents seek, by appealing to the fears and prejudices of those constituents, and by subtle coercion of those whose support they cannot get otherwise. And the result is frequently superficial concern on the part of those officials for their real responsibilities and exclusive self-interest on the part of the constituents. The political commonplaces of our time and country concern the whole question of political expediency: the manipulation of groups and individuals, the packaging and marketing of candidates for high office, the committing of atrocities in the name of freedom or order. These commonplaces seem clearly the outgrowth of the broad acceptance of Machiavellian attitudes we see acted out in the history plays nearly four hundred years ago, and from these commonplaces stems our sense of seemingly endless decline in political morality and political stability.

What many seek today is a new but simple political consciousness in which a leader's natural weaknesses—his fear of humiliation (especially the humiliation of losing power), his myriad struggles with flesh and spirit, his capacity to suffer physical and psychological breakdown, his tendency to make simple errors—these weaknesses might be openly acknowledged by all as part of the human condition, and yet not eclipse the strengths by which leaders should be evaluated. Such straightforward acknowledgment would naturally have to coupled with the corollary belief that most human weaknesses can be remedied or at least countered. A public which insisted on leaders honest with themselves and others might bring men and women into political life more capable of finding solutions to the massive social and environmental problems we face. And leaders completely open about personal fears, prejudices, and predilections could cut through the artifice which surrounds much of what passes today for negotiation, national and international. Such leaders would spend less talent in creating external images of themselves or in the arts of subtle coercion; and recognizing their own humanity, they might also have more true compassion (like that of Henry VI). They might be more genuinely dedicated to feeding hungry mouths and minds, to seeing justice made available to all men. But certainly the era of the Machiavel must pass before this kind of political consciousness can exist, and there is still some question today whether that era is ready to pass.

The only possible conclusion to these chapters is that the plays considered have deep and immediate significance in our own time. For a recent president of the United States (whom I greatly admired and still admire) to suggest he looked upon Shakespeare's Henry V as a hero and example is to say that the Machiavellian compromise made by Christian nations and their governors in the late sixteenth century is still very much with us. The best of our political leaders still believe that all or the most genuinely human characteristics in a man's public image must be obscured if he is to have any hope of achieving his objectives—worthy as those objectives may be.

The sixteenth century came to accept the Machiavel as the inevitable alternative to the weak king. But another inevitability has persisently disturbed political life since: that the Machiavel, in maintaining his image and authority, must harm others and must sacrifice most of his objectives because of the means he employs to achieve them. The young today seem unable to go easily through the Bastard's transformation, despite (or because of) centuries of example. After four hundred years we are just beginning again to confront the problems Shakespeare bitterly confronted in *Henry VI*. It is possible that the Machiavel, even well-intentioned, cannot survive today any more than could the weak king in the last decade of the sixteenth century. Men may now be ready to accept their leaders in human terms in order that they might be governed better. But the change is really not up to the governors. It is up to the governed.

Bibliographical Remarks

Rather than include extended footnotes and a traditional bibliography, I shall in the paragraphs that follow briefly discuss the works used most frequently in writing this book.

CHAPTER I—Of Strong Kings and Weak

As is the case with almost any interpretive study, this work is in part a reaction against one set of critics of our time in favor of another, more recent, set, with whom I generally identify. The overwhelming influence of E. M. W. Tillyard's *Shakespeare's History Plays* (New York: Macmillan, 1946) and Lily Bess Campbell's *Shakespeare's Histories: Mirrors of Elizabethan Policy* (San Marino, California: The Huntington Library, 1947) resulted in a spate of scholarly works over a period of fifteen to twenty years which view these plays in light of the workings of Divine Providence as interpreted by Elizabethan political doctrine and Church of England Homilies of the period: in effect, as propagandistic works dedicated to supporting and perpetuating the regime in power and the established church. In addition to the numerous book-length studies, articles, doctoral dissertations, and master's theses which were undertaken to refine and expand Tillyard's ideas, most allusions to the history plays in works on other Shakespearean subjects have usually taken for granted the truth of Tillyard's theory. The best-known books in this tradition—certainly the ones I have worked with most closely—are Irving Ribner's *The English History Play in the Age of Shakespeare*, revised edition (New York: Barnes and Noble, 1965); and Max Meredith Reese's *The Cease of Majesty* (New York: St. Martin's Press, 1961).

To many of these works I am of course deeply indebted. Tillyard establishes the value of studying these plays as a group unified by a single theme; Ribner extends Tillyard's ideas to plays outside the Shakespearean canon; and Reese sensitively analyzes the plays scene by scene within the Tillyardian frame. More directly dependent on Elizabethan history and politics than the others, Campbell comes closest to seeing the weakness of the king as central to these plays. She suggests that the kings represented hardly provide testimony to England's past greatness. Had she gone a step farther, Miss Campbell might have reached the conclusion that the plays could also be questioning rather than mirroring Elizabethan political policy. Wilbur Sanders, discussed below, considers the limitations of Miss Campbell's approach at some length in *The Dramatist and the Received Idea* (Cambridge: At the University Press, 1968), pp. 143–57.

The anti-Tillyardian perspective started slowly in the early 1960s but has accelerated at an extraordinary rate in more recent years. My own article, "The Weak King Play of the Early 1590s," *Renaissance Drama,* n.s. II (1969), 71–80, is of course the basis of this study, but it has been modified in theme a good deal. Two works which have greatly influenced that modification are David Bevington's *Tudor Drama and Politics* (Cambridge, Mass.: Harvard University Press, 1969) and Wilbur Sanders' book mentioned above. Both consider the dramatist an intelligent, well-informed professional intent upon bringing the important philosophical and/or political attitudes of his day to bear upon living controversies and dilemmas with which his audience would be familiar. The playwright thus articulates dilemmas in dramatic terms, though he is himself neither philosopher nor teacher. In discussing the history plays, Sanders is clearly convinced that with regard to Tudor political propaganda, doubt and uncertainty rather than blind conformity is their motivating force. Bevington, on the other hand, sees them as a somewhat uncertain effort to uphold the *status quo.* But Bevington also suggests the existence of a "pattern of transferred sympathies" (p. 218) in several of the plays which indicates shifting audience attitudes toward the dramatic situation they see developing. Bevington aided my thinking a great deal in seeing this pattern as an aspect of "straightforward" rather than unusual or complex dramatic construction in the period. Others have seen transferral of audience sympathies in individual plays, but few have seen the pattern running through so wide a variety of plays as Bevington touches.

I should also mention Henry Ansgar Kelly's *Divine Providence in the England of Shakespeare's Histories* (Cambridge, Mass.: Harvard University Press, 1970) at this point because Kelly makes clear the abundant ways the much-discussed "Tudor myth" could be interpreted by a sixteenth-century English audience. In popular treatments of the Wars of the Roses, the particular chronicle being used by a poet or a dramatist usually indicated the side being favored by Divine Providence. Kelly concludes that Shakespeare's history plays, which follow several different chronicles, embody no consistent view of the workings of Divine Providence, certainly not one carried over from play to play.

In developing my ideas on the nature of Machiavellianism in Shakespeare's England and its influence on the plays, I have made use of a wide variety of works. Among these are historical studies: Felix Raab, *The English Face of Machiavelli* (Toronto: University of Toronto Press, 1964); W. G. Zeeveld, *Foundations of Tudor Policy* (Cambridge, Mass.: Harvard University Press, 1948); Christopher Morris, *Political Thought in England: Tyndale to Hooker* (London: Oxford University Press, 1953); George L. Mosse, *The Struggle for Sovereignty in England* (East Lansing, Mich.:

Michigan State University Press, 1950); and Wallace McCaffrey, *The Shaping of the Elizabethan Regime* (Princeton, N.J.: Princeton University Press, 1968). I have also gone back through a number of primary works cited in these studies: among them, manuscript translations of *The Prince*—see *Machiavelli's Prince: An Elizabethan Translation* edited by Hardin Craig (Chapel Hill, N.C.: University of North Carolina Press, 1944); Wolfe's pirated editions printed in Italian; and especially the many passing comments of Gabriel Harvey. See Harvey's *Works*, edited by A. B. Grosart, 3 vols. (1884–85); and T. H. Jameson, "The Machiavellianism of Gabriel Harvey," *PMLA*, LVI (1941), 645–56. And I have of course been strongly influenced by Edward Meyer's *Machiavelli and the Elizabethan Drama*, *Litterarhistorische Forschungen*, No. 1 (Weimar: Emil Farber, 1897) and Mario Praz's *Machiavelli and the Elizabethan Drama* (London: H. Milford, 1928) and by those literary interpreters who, explicitly, have considered Machiavellianism an influence on the drama of the age going beyond that which results in the stage Machiavel. These include Sanders, *The Dramatist and the Received Idea*, especially pp. 57–101; J. B. Steane, *Marlowe* (Cambridge: At the University Press, 1970); Una M. Ellis-Fermor, "Shakespeare's Political Plays," *The Frontiers of Drama* (London: Methuen, 1964), pp. 34–55; H. B. Charlton, *Shakespeare, Politics, and Politicians* (London: The English Association, 1929); and the most recent interpreters of the history plays discussed in ensuing paragraphs.

Four books on the history plays have appeared recently. Robert Ornstein's *A Kingdom for a Stage* (Cambridge, Mass.: Harvard University Press, 1972) opens with an excellent introductory chapter on the probable relationship between audience ambivalence toward Tudor authority and the nature of the plays. Having begun his work in 1961, Ornstein may well have been one of the first to see the limitations of Tillyard's approach, though his book did not appear for eleven years, and his interpretations of individual plays in later chapters, though sensitive, lack the focus he establishes at the start. Ornstein's notes indicate great familiarity with the chronicles and other primary sources of the sixteenth century but perhaps not enough with recent criticism of the history plays. John C. Bromley's *The Shakespearean Kings* (Boulder, Colo.: Colorado Associated University Press, 1971), a book rooted in considerably less scholarship than Ornstein's, sees Henry V as an image of a successful, new Machiavellianism whose influence is still very much felt today. Bromley's identification of Hal with certain living public figures in America, whom he detests, blinds him to the attractions Shakespeare obviously implanted in his hero of Agincourt. And Bromley's genuine admiration for Shakespeare's image of Richard of Gloucester, whose energy and wit are more to his taste than Henry V's political skills, ignores much that is in *Richard III*, especially the whole question of conscience which Sanders discusses so well.

Less directly related to my work are David Riggs's *Shakespeare's Heroi-*

cal Histories: Henry VI and its Literary Tradition (Cambridge, Mass.: Harvard University Press, 1971) and Robert B. Pierce's *Shakespeare's History Plays: The Family and the State* (Columbus, Ohio: Ohio State University Press, 1971). Probably the most focused of any of these works, Riggs's book studies the shift in the image of the hero from the Talbot-like figure descended from the epics, whose talents are part of his heritage, to the Richard III–Tamburlaine style conqueror, who depends on his own rather than inherited prowess. Riggs's assessment of Bolingbroke and Hal as attempting to recreate through their attractive Machiavellianism the older type of heroism is mystifying, but Riggs does, I think, correctly identify "the Bolingbrokes" for what they are. Pierce, who as he says follows Tillyard, stresses the importance of family relationships as symbols of ideal relationships in the political sphere. Disruptions in the state parallel disruptions in the family; Richard III, who dismisses kinship altogether, is thus farthest from the political ideal.

These four books all continue the custom of seeing Henry VI as weak and ineffectual, and all four either ignore *King John* or condemn it as a work of art. Ornstein is particularly severe in his condemnation of the play.

CHAPTER II—The Wanton King

The first critic to compare the anonymous *Woodstock*, Marlowe's *Edward II*, and Shakespeare's *Richard II* in detail—and the first to suggest the possibility of a rebellious theme in the anonymous play—is A. P. Rossiter in the Preface to his edition of *Woodstock*. His discussion is clear and sensitive in suggesting that plain Thomas articulates growing audience dissatisfaction with the political *status quo* and in observing the anonymous author's adept use of farce in touching on abuses which were undoubtedly current in Elizabethan England. Only in dealing with King Richard himself does Rossiter overstate his case and thus miss the point that there is a shift in appeal to our sympathies late in the play. Failing to think about the guilt the audience must have felt when a penitent king appears, Rossiter does not emphasize sufficiently the counter pull of orthodox feeling underlying the play. He also fails to see that precisely the same elements which produce strong inclinations toward rebellion in *Woodstock* are also present in the Marlowe and Shakespeare plays.

In considering rebellious impulses in the plays in this chapter and the next, I also seem at times to be inviting straight topical interpretation of a kind whereby events and characters in the plays may be identified with specific happenings and people in late sixteenth century England. There may, of course, be allusions to particular persons in these plays. Bevington, however, and very wisely I think, in *Tudor Drama and Politics*, a work which must set the guidelines for topical interpretation of Elizabethan drama in the future, is wary of referring to specific individuals. He finds politics "germane to a remarkable percentage of Tudor plays, but in terms of ideas and platforms rather than personalities" (p. 25). That statement has been my own guide in considering the relationship of these plays to the political life and conditions of the 1590s.

Classes of men, if not individual personalities, certainly may be observed underlying some of the characterizations in these plays, and a new class of politicians late in Elizabeth's reign seems directly related to the image of Tresilian in *Woodstock*. This new class is discussed by J. E. Neale in "The Elizabethan Political Scene," *Essays in Elizabethan History* (London: Jonathan Cape, 1958), pp. 59–84. A "new moral climate" in the last decade of Elizabeth's reign, says Neale (p. 79), was clearly pointing the way to that of James. Power was being "transferred to the new generation at a pace dangerous to the digestive capacity of the system." And the rapidly rising costs of political patronage, Neale observes, was making personal wealth more important than birth in achieving political position. Such considerations may well underlie not only the character of Tresilian, but the whole struggle in the anonymous play between an older, responsible nobility and a youthful band of ne'er-do-wells led by a lowborn manipulator. The activities of the "new men" of the 1590s may prompt what we see in *Woodstock* concerning the Blank Charters, the atrocities at Dunstable, and the "farming" of England.

Turning to Marlowe's *Edward II*, my ideas have been chiefly influenced by Clifford Leech, "Marlowe's 'Edward II': Power and Suffering," *The Critical Quarterly*, I (Autumn 1959), 181–96; J. B. Steane, *Marlowe*; Harry Levin, *The Overreacher*, pp. 81–105; Eugene M. Waith, "Edward II: The Shadow of Action," *Tulane Drama Review*, VIII (1964), 59–76—in addition, of course, to Briggs and Sanders, who are discussed in Chapter II. Douglas Cole's *Suffering and Evil in the Plays of Christopher Marlowe* (Princeton, N.J.: Princeton University Press, 1962), pp. 161–87, contains an excellent discussion of the deposition scene in *Edward II* which stops just short of observing its similarity to the deposition scene in *Richard II*. In discussing Edward's homosexuality, which few interpreters question today, I reject the notion first introduced by William Empson that the final scene is Edward's cruelly ironic punishment for that weakness. Empson makes the suggestion in a review of Kocher's *Christopher Marlowe* in *The Nation*, CLXIII (1946), 444–45, and it has recently been reemphasized by Sanders (pp. 124–25, 140–41).

In regard to Shakespeare's *Richard II*, I refer to few specific critical analyses which have influenced me, obviously because there are far too many to do justice to them here. A few which are important and by less well-known scholars are alluded to in the text and footnotes, and I acknowledge my debt to Ernst Kantorowicz in the first chapter. My thoughts concerning the play have been most recently affected by Sanders (pp. 143–57) and by John R.

Elliott, "History and Tragedy in *Richard II*," *Studies in English Literature*, VIII (1968), 253–71.

CHAPTER III—The Meek King

Most criticism of *Henry VI*, whether Tillyard-oriented or not, does not look upon Henry himself as anything more than a cipher—a shy, even retarded, coward unwilling to assert his God-given leadership in time of need. In Jan Kott's *Shakespeare Our Contemporary* (New York: Doubleday Anchor Books, 1966), pp. 3–56, he is merely the silent victim of the piracy of others, and his image has remained essentially the same among critics, like Brockbank, "The Frame of Disorder," who bear him no animosity. But most recent critics are less kind to Henry. Sprinkled throughout the comments of Ribner and Reese are statements suggesting that he is at best a well-meaning incompetent, and in H. M. Richmond's *Shakespeare's Political Plays* (New York: Random House, 1967), pp. 19–74, he appears an effete intellectual whose dependency on learning and manners and whose fear of violent emotion constitute a crime against his own state. Such views are also held in the extreme by Bromley and to a lesser extent by Ornstein. Goddard, in *The Meaning of Shakespeare* on the other hand, takes a view seminal to mine, as does Mattie Swayne in a not-very-scholarly but quite sensitive and energetic article "Shakespeare's Henry VI as a Pacifist," *College English*, III (1941), 143–49.

My discussion of Duke Humphrey has been influenced by a wide variety of works, chief among them Samuel Pratt, "Shakespeare and Humphrey Duke of Gloucester," *SQ*, XVI (1965), 201–16; James K. McConica, *English Humanists and Reformation Politics* (Oxford: Oxford University Press, 1965); W. G. Zeeveld, *Foundations of Tudor Policy*; and Felix Raab, *The English Face of Machiavelli*. The anonymous play *Sir Thomas More*, discussed in the text, may be found in *The Shakespeare Apocrypha*, edited by C. F. Tucker Brooke (London: Oxford University Press, 1908), pp. 383–420.

This discussion of works which have influenced my approach to the art of *Henry VI* could not be complete without mention of Hereward Price, "Mirror-Scenes in Shakespeare," *Joseph Quincy Adams Memorial Studies* (Washington, D.C.: Folger Shakespeare Library, 1948), pp. 101–14. Price foreshadows all those, including me, who see a "frame of disorder" as the carefully conceived principle of construction in these plays.

CHAPTER IV—John

Although a good deal has been written about the relationship between *The Troublesome Reign* and Shakespeare's *King John*, much remains unclear or uncertain—even the question of which play was written first. Despite the arguments of E. A. J. Honigmann in The New Arden Edition (Cambridge, Mass.: Harvard University Press, 1969) that *King John* precedes *The Troublesome Reign,* I remain faithful to the more widely accepted view that Shakespeare's play follows the anonymous work and is heavily influenced by it in content, though less so in language. As my discussion indicates, the development of the role of the Bastard in Shakespeare suggests a date for *John* of some time between *Richard III* and *Richard II,* probably 1595 or 1596.

But of greater importance to me is the question of the relative competence of the kings in the two plays. John R. Elliott, "Shakespeare and the Double Image of King John," *Shakespeare Studies,* I (1965), 64–84, finds the John in *The Troublesome Reign* based on Protestant oriented chronicles and therefore morally superior to Shakespeare's king who, rooted in a variety of chronicles, is presented in morally complex terms. John Elson, "Studies in the King John Plays," *Joseph Quincy Adams Memorial Studies* (Washington, D.C.: Folger Shakespeare Library, 1948), pp. 183–97, also identifies John in *The Troublesome Reign* with the Protestant martyrs of Foxe's *Book of Martyrs,* but Elson assumes that Shakespeare's king closely follows his model in *The Troublesome Reign.* Others compare the two kingly images without coming to such fixed conclusions as Elliott—viz., Reese, Ribner, Honigmann, J. D. Wilson, and Ornstein—so, too, does Virgil Whitaker in *Shakespeare's Use of Learning* (San Marino, Calif.: The Huntington Library, 1953), pp. 123–43.

As indicated in my discussion, the work which has influenced me most in my approach to the Bastard in Shakespeare's play is John Danby's *Shakespeare's Doctrine of Nature.* But other recent studies have also had their effect, particularly Adrien Bonjour's "'The Road to Swinstead Abbey'"; James C. Calderwood's "Commodity and Honor in *King John," University of Toronto Quarterly,* XXIX (1960), 341–56; William Matchett's "Richard's Divided Heritage in *King John";* and Bonjour's response to Honigmann's attack on him, "Bastinado for the Bastard?" *English Studies,* XLV (1964), Supplement, 169–76.

A most perceptive recent note on the play which alone recognizes its shifting appeal to audience sympathies is J. R. Price's "*King John* and the Problematic Art," *Shakespeare Quarterly,* XXI (1970), 25–28.

Special mention should be made concerning the remarks identifying the Citizen of Angiers as Hubert de Burgh. This view, enunciated in J. D. Wilson's Preface to *King John* (Cambridge: At the University Press, 1954), pp. xlv–xlvii, and in Honigmann's Preface, pp. xxxiv–vii, is possibly the most important single result of the textual study of the play in this century. Our whole view of the scene involving Angiers as a pawn in the battle between John and Philip is affected by it and thus, finally, our outlook on the play's basic dilemma concerning loyalty to an unlawful monarch.

CHAPTER V—New Thoughts To Deck Our Kings

Two of the most recent interpretations of *Henry V*—John Bromley's and C. H. Hobday's "Imagery and Irony in *Henry V*," *Shakespeare Survey*, XXI (1968), 107–14—follow a long tradition of Hal-haters, notably among literary figures: Hazlitt, Swinburne, Masefield, Yeats, and Mark Van Doren, to name a few. I find myself closer to the views of those who can admire Henry while not ignoring his Machiavellian craftsmanship. Ornstein is one who does this, but the best all-round affirmative view of Henry V as the attractive Machiavel is Una Ellis-Fermor's "Shakespeare's Political Plays," *The Frontiers of Drama*. A similar though more questioning view of Hal is by Honor Matthews, *Character and Symbol in Shakespeare's Plays* (Cambridge: At the University Press, 1962), pp. 51–62. An excellent treatment of the problem is Dain Trafton's unpublished dissertation, "Ideology and Politics in the Second Tetralogy" (University of California, 1968), pp. 141–77. Trafton perceives that Shakespeare does not condemn Henry V for his Machiavellianism but presents him as the best image one can hope for in political man. Like Sanders, I find somewhat more regret in Shakespeare at this state of affairs, though not so much regret as is found by Honor Matthews and certainly not so much as is found by the Hal-haters.

Index